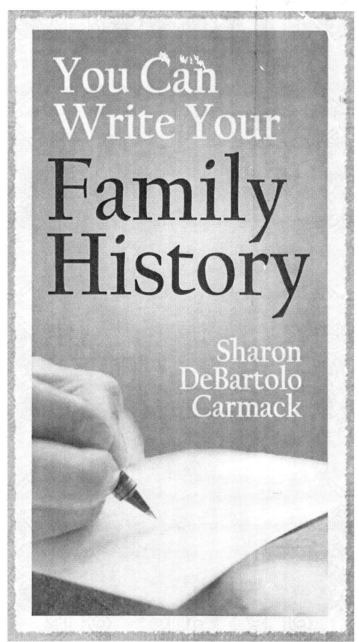

You Can Write Your Family History

Sharon DeBartolo Carmack

Genealogical Publishing Company

Originally published by Betterway Books, Cincinnati, 2003
Reprinted 2008 by Genealogical Publishing Company
3600 Clipper Mill Road, Suite 260
Baltimore, MD 21211-1953
www.genealogical.com
Library of Congress Catalogue Card Number 2007938194
ISBN 978-0-8063-1783-0
Made in the United States of America

Other Books by Sharon DeBartolo Carmack

GENEALOGICAL GUIDEBOOKS
Your Guide to Cemetery Research
A Genealogist's Guide to Discovering Your Immigrant and Ethnic Ancestors
Organizing Your Family History Search
A Genealogist's Guide to Discovering Your Female Ancestors
The Genealogy Sourcebook
*Italian-American Family History: A Guide to Researching and
    Writing About Your Heritage*
Finding Your Ellis Island Ancestors
Carmack's Guide to Copyright & Contracts

FAMILY HISTORY NARRATIVES/COMPILED GENEALOGIES
*Italians in Transition: The Vallarelli Family of Terlizzi, Italy, and Westchester County,
    New York and The DeBartolo Family of Terlizzi, Italy, New York, and San Francisco,
    California*
*A Sense of Duty: The Life and Times of Jay Roscoe Rhoads and his wife,
    Mary Grace Rudolph*
*My Wild Irish Rose: The Life of Rose (Norris) (O'Connor) Fitzhugh and her mother
    Delia (Gordon) Norris*
*David and Charlotte Hawes (Buckner) Stuart of King George County, Virginia,
    Including Three Generations of Their Descendants*
American Lives and Lines, co-authored with Roger D. Joslyn
*The Ebetino and Vallarelli Family History: Italian Immigrants to Westchester County,
    New York*

PUBLISHED ABSTRACTS
Communities at Rest: An Inventory and Field Study of Five Eastern Colorado Cemeteries

Critical Acclaim for Author
Sharon DeBartolo Carmack
and You Can Write Your Family History

"Step by step Sharon Carmack shows how to turn names and dates into real human beings for a family history. Anyone who has ever had thoughts about writing a family history will want to have this book to refer to again and again."

—HENRY B. HOFF, CG, FASG

EDITOR, *THE NEW ENGLAND HISTORICAL AND GENEALOGICAL REGISTER*

"Carmack's imaginative approach and appealing examples excite and challenge readers to write their own family histories."

—EMILY ANNE CROOM

AUTHOR OF *UNPUZZLING YOUR PAST*

"Engaging and informative, *You Can Write a Family History* shows family historians how to 'add life and history' to the genealogical facts they've gathered. Carmack shares the elements of the writer's craft—plot, character, and description—and illustrates how they can be used in preparing a family history for publication.

—ANN HEGE HUGES, PRESIDENT, GATEWAY PRESS, INC.

"Almost all genealogists want to share the fruits of their research with the rest of the family, but fear that their relatives won't be interested in a standard genealogy. Sharon Carmack shows us how to create a family history that is much more than basic genealogy, a book that will be read and enjoyed for generations to come.

—HARRY MACY, FASG

EDITOR, *THE NEW YORK GENEALOGICAL AND BIOGRAPHICAL RECORD*

About the Author

 Sharon DeBartolo Carmack is a Certified Genealogist, editor, and author of numerous scholarly and popular books and articles. Along with teaching nonfiction writing through WritersOnlineWorkshops.com, Sharon offers writing, mentoring, and editing services for nonfiction books, with an emphasis on memoirs, family histories, life stories/biographies, and annotated letters and diaries. She can be reached through her Web site: www.SharonCarmack.com.

For Becky,
Whose light was extinguished far too soon.

⊙⊷⊙⊷⊙

"There is something that draws people to the past,
A delicate thread of spirit and soul
that binds us with our past.
This is the essence of our ancestors
that does not die when they do.
It is a persistent part of their life's force
that waits quietly for someone to listen."
—REBECCA "BECKY" (SIMONS) SHY
(1957–2002)

Acknowledgments

From the time I could read, I knew I wanted to be a writer. There was something magical about putting words on a page for thousands of people to read. So it probably comes as no surprise that English was my favorite subject throughout my schooling. I was the nerd in high school who took English courses as electives instead of something "fun" like band, art, wood shop, or auto mechanics. One of my English teachers wrote in my high school yearbook, "My dear Sharon, Anyone who would take 3 English courses [in one year] can't be all bad." I never understood why my classmates didn't think English was fun. Maybe it was because I had been blessed with exceptional English teachers. In junior high, it was Larry Spigelmyer. Despite what I thought was harsh criticism of my class essays, when he hand-picked the small school newspaper staff, I was among them. He must have seen talent in me that I didn't. In high school, there were several teachers who influenced me (remember, I took English classes as electives, so I had more English teachers than most students): Mrs. Allaire, Mrs. Harney, Mrs. Hansen, Mrs. Lane, and Mrs. Fitzpatrick. (I'm sorry I never got to know your first names, and that darn yearbook didn't include your first names either!) And there were more in college: in particular, Penny Jackman, Pat Kirk, and Pam Banikowski.

When it came to writing family history narrative, I had two major influences: Katherine Scott Sturdevant and Lawrence Gouldrup. In 1989, I took an American history course from Kathy, and for the term paper, I asked if I could write about my Italian immigrant ancestors who came through Ellis Island. She agreed, but said I had to put my ancestors into historical context for the paper. She explained that I had to research what the immigrant experience was like and weave that in with my ancestors' stories. Later, we both thought I must have been exceptionally bright or had a natural talent for the type of writing she was explaining, because with that little instruction, I quickly caught on to what she said and got an A on the paper. As much as I hate to dispel the myth about my intelligence, talent, and ability to learn things quickly, I later remembered that before I had taken that history class, I had been exposed to the concept of writing family narrative when I read Lawrence Gouldrup's *Writing the Family Narrative*.

I learned even more about writing family history narrative when I began team-teaching family history writing courses with Kathy Sturdevant nearly thirteen years ago—not only from Kathy, but from our many students. Those who read Kathy's *Bringing Your Family History to Life Through Social History* as well as this book will see some of the same concepts and approaches to social history research and family history narrative writing. Teaching together for so many years became like a marriage: our ideas, thoughts, and even similar ways of expression have become so intertwined that it's nearly impossible to separate our work. To avoid too much overlapping, I've included only those concepts from Kathy's social history book that are necessary for the reader to understand and use this book; thus, I'll often refer you to Kathy's book for more information. Although each of our books can stand alone, the two contain essentially the entire curriculum that we taught together. (We invite other instructors to use these complementary texts in their genealogy writing courses.) Also blended into this book are ideas I gleaned from authors of general writing instruction manuals: Jon Franklin, William Noble, William Brohaugh, and David Fryxell, to name a few.

Part of learning how to write family history narrative is reading other authors who have done it successfully and, as I've encouraged students to do, emulating those whose writing styles you like best. So my appreciation goes to the many family history writers who have given me models to emulate.

Where would a writer be without editors and readers? A hearty thank you to Katherine Scott Sturdevant and Brad Crawford who served as content editors, and Roger D. Joslyn, Anita Lustenberger, and Suzanne McVetty who read drafts. Some readers see the trees, others see the forest. Brad Crawford and Suzanne McVetty always see the forest, for which I'm most grateful. Two special acknowledgments are due: to Anita Lustenberger, who is always on the lookout for things I can use in my books. She found a wonderful tell-all family history, from which I used some excerpts in chapter five. And to Roger D. Joslyn, my "best bud in genealogy" and co-defendant, for helping me become established as a professional family history writer, and for giving his permission to use material from the project we'll never forget.

Finally, heartfelt appreciation goes to my readers for being so supportive. I am grateful that you have taken time to read my books, and especially that some of you have taken time out of your busy lives to write me. I try to respond to each e-mail and letter, although it may take me several weeks. But I want you to know your words mean a lot. Thank you!

Table of Contents
At a Glance

Foreword

Nothing is as easy or as hard as it seems at first. If we plunge into a project expecting ease, we're sure to find difficulties. Such things always take longer than expected, of course—unless we've been hesitating because we thought the project was going to take forever. If we procrastinate beginning a task because it seems overwhelming, we may be surprised to find that it wasn't so time-consuming after all. Anticipation and anxiety can rule our lives, and dread can waste our precious time. But research and writing projects need not fall prey to this aspect of human nature. This perspective may help us control our tendencies: We need not under- or overestimate our projects; we just need to complete them.

You want to "do" your family history. What does that mean, really? For most of us it means accumulating information about our families. Starting with sources at home and at hand, such as family documents, heirlooms, and remembered stories, we move on to the Internet and its storehouse of names and connections, some exactly right and some fantastical. We go to genealogical libraries, society meetings, and conferences. We buy books to find out what to do next, and how to go about doing it. Meanwhile, the more we hear or read advice from experts, the more we may think that we've been doing our family histories not to the experts' standards. We vow to reform, or even start over.

At this stage, we could call our efforts to accumulate family history information "research." It seemed more casual than that in the beginning, but now it's a serious effort: following expert advice, evaluating sources for their reliability, and keeping track of those sources for future footnotes. Footnotes in what? Footnotes are for books, right? So, are you going to write your own book?

When you started, you probably looked at other genealogists' published work with awe and thought, *I'll never achieve that*. But some day, some moment, you will want to achieve that. You will want to *write* your family history. If you haven't accepted that idea yet, then examine what you do now with the information you accumulate. Don't you copy it onto many forms, file it in many boxes or drawers, paste it into many scrapbooks, film it onto many videotapes, or cart it around from library to archives as though it is your special burden, a veritable albatross or ball and chain? Worst or best of all, don't you talk about it? Perhaps you just share it with your family. They listen to your latest-find stories; you make sure they do. They may roll their eyes and humor you about your hobby ("obsession," they call it) but because they love you, you have a captive audience.

Have you ever told someone else about your family history discoveries and seen their eyes glaze over? They hold still for a while, nodding and humming polite encouragement until they can find an excuse to escape. Darn. You let it spill out. You told it one too many times to the librarian, archivist, teacher, or professional genealogist who's heard it many times before. On the other hand, you can tell the stories to fellow researchers; they identify with you, care, and will listen. Confess, though. We listen to each other partly because we can hardly wait to plunge into telling our own family stories. Our conversations can become dueling genealogies.

Writing your family history is a tonic for many of these frustrations. I know better than to call it a cure. Cures remove ailments permanently, but family history is a disease for which there is no remedy. We finish one portion of our family history, but still accumulate more material, drag it around, and talk too much about it. Writing, however, is a tonic that alleviates the worst symptoms, and gives us much relief. Imagine how good it will feel to unburden yourself by finally completing a written family history!

When you write your family history, you achieve something complete. When you see it in print—whether the people binding it are your family, your neighborhood copy center, the vanity press that you paid, or a "real" commercial publisher—it looks wonderful! Sure there will be mistakes, and you will discover information later that makes you want to revise it. But that completed project is the remedy for so much. It is a finished product, duplicated, that you can distribute to family, friends, and colleagues. No longer are you the person who "always says she's going to write." You have written. Best of all, I hope you have recorded stories, not just the names and dates, to be part of the movement of folks helping to bring history alive.

Sharon Carmack has been a primary leader of that movement, writing books and articles, and giving motivational speeches for more than a decade. More than anyone else in her field, she strives to reach *you*. She has mastered the sources, methods, and high standards of professional genealogy and genealogical publishing, but she avoids the highbrow tendencies that some professionals have. She writes to you because she's been you. She wants to help you earn the rewards of writing family history, and so makes the information as accessible and appealing as she can. Go ahead. Take this good-tasting tonic for writer's block. You can produce a quality family history for the benefit of all.

—Katherine Scott Sturdevant, Author of *Bringing Your Family History to Life through Social History* and *Organizing and Preserving Your Heirloom Documents*

A Labor of Love?

A book is the only immortality.—RUFUS CHOATE

You know you should do it. The relatives are nagging you to do it. You've probably attended a class or workshop on how to do it. You may have even bought or read other books telling you that you should do it and how you should do it. Write the family history? Sure. Sounds like a good idea. Maybe you've started, but for some reason, your enthusiasm to keep going wanes. You keep getting writer's block, or you can't figure out how you're going to cover all those generations in one book and make it interesting. Or you may be thinking, "I don't even know where to begin, because, heck, I'm no writer!"

Being a "writer" is really a frame of mind. Sure, some of it has to do with talent or learned skills, but if you think you're not a writer, then you won't be one. I believe practically everyone has the potential to write a family history. Some people are destined to be great writers; the rest of us will be so-so. But that's okay. I'm not a great writer. But, like you, I can put words together to form a decent sentence, and a couple of sentences make a paragraph, and a couple of paragraphs make a chapter, and a couple of chapters make a book. See, it's not so scary once you break it down.

Most family historians agree that research is the fun part. For some, just entering their data into a computer software program is a sufficient and effective way to leave their genealogy for their descendants. But to actu-

Quotes

Many of the writer's quotes in this book came from The Written Word—Quote a Day, <www.topica.com/lists/TheWrittenWordEZine>, a daily source of inspiration for writers, editors, and publishers.

ally sit down and write a family history is—okay, I admit it—scary. And hard. And overwhelming at times. Besides, you're just sure your family will be enthralled with all those names, dates, and places you've gathered, right? Unfortunately, I doubt it. If you don't believe me, show your charts to a non-genealogist. Then time how long it takes before they politely smile and hand the chart back to you. Now put a narrative account of a family history in their hands, and I'm certain you'll get a different reaction.

By narrative, I don't mean magically converting your genealogy data in a computer software program to what the software calls "narrative reports." I mean creatively writing your family history as a *story*. It should be one that grabs the readers' attention from the opening paragraph; one that has a beginning, a middle, and an end; one that has suspense, humor, and maybe even some romance; one with real characters that readers love and hate; but, one that is completely nonfiction, with every fact supported by what you've found in your research. A family history your family can't put down. A page turner. Yep. That's the kind of family history narrative I'm talking about. And you *can* write one just like that.

There's no magic formula. To become a competent writer, you write until you start to sound like you, and then you keep on writing. Finish things you start. Get better.—NEIL GAIMAN

ONE STEP AT A TIME

Important

You will make the whole process of writing your family history easier and give yourself a better night's sleep if you **think through the family history you want to write before you begin writing, then tackle it one step at a time.** Since you're holding this book in your hands, you are obviously motivated to make it work this time. To make it really happen. And this time you can do it. I'll be right by your side the whole way, showing you exactly what you need to do to make that dry, sterile data on your family group sheet or in your computer evolve into an interesting, readable, and compelling family history narrative. Whether you want to write about recent generations or generations in the distant past, this book will help you and introduce you to examples from a variety of time periods to show you how it's done.

I'd like you to think of the chapters in this book as "steps." Although nineteen steps may seem like a lot, I've tried to break it down into easily manageable steps. I suggest you read this book all the way through first—or skim through the steps—so you know what's ahead of you. Then go back and use it like a workbook. Take each step, one by one, apply the suggestions and techniques, then move on to the next. Throughout the book, so you can see how to take information from charts and gradually transform it into a narrative essay, you'll find examples from the history of one family in particular. (Appendix A has the complete narrative of that family.) I'll also use other families from different time periods, parts of the country, and ethnic backgrounds as mini-examples of how you can turn facts about any family into a narrative.

One thing you need to understand from the start, though, is that it's not going to happen overnight. Plan at least nine months to a year—working at it part time—to write your family history. Don't let Aunt Annabelle convince you that you can have it all written and published in time for the family reunion in June when it's February already. It ain't gonna happen. And that nine months to a year is just for the writing and background research; I'm assuming you have already completed as much genealogical research as you're able (see STEP 3). Then tack onto that another nine months to a year for production aspects, such as preparing the camera-ready copy, proofreading, indexing, and having it copied and bound. Whew! This *is* a lot of work, and no wonder it's called a "labor of love." In fact, you can think of the labor in two ways: the nine months of writing you'll put into it, followed by the labor of giving birth to your

3

first family history book. So consider me your writing midwife, and we'll get through this delivery together just fine.

Just remember that as the author of the family history, you can make your baby—I mean, your final product—as elaborate or as simple as you like. You can write a fifty-page family history and have it duplicated and bound at your local quick-copy shop, or you can draft a four-hundred page, illustrated epic family history that you'll take to a printer. Regardless of how big or small your family history book turns out to be, there are certain aspects to producing a family history you can't escape:

1. It has to be your best work. If you were making a quilt or building a dollhouse for a favorite grandchild, you wouldn't do it haphazardly and think: *Well, I'm just doing it for the family,* would you? Heavens no! You'd want it to be your best work because (a) you take pride in what you do, (b) you want your family to show off your project with pride, and (c) you want your work to last for generations. The same is true for writing your family history.

2. So, if number one is true, then you need to
   a. cite all your sources of information.
   b. edit and proofread.
   c. include an index.

No matter what. These aspects aren't optional; they are required.

Patricia Law Hatcher, in her excellent guide, *Producing a Quality Family History*, gives eight characteristics of a quality family history, which I recommend you review. **Here are my ten characteristics of a quality family history narrative.**

A quality family history narrative

Notes

1. is based on thorough and sound research from a variety of sources within and outside the field of genealogy, such as historical documents, social history, local history, oral history, women's history, ethnic history, and family legends.

2. is creative or dramatic nonfiction, ever mindful of the boundaries between truth and fiction.
3. tells a nonfiction story about ancestors' lives.
4. is well organized in thought and presentation.
5. documents all of its factual information, both genealogical and historical.
6. reports information accurately, making it explicitly clear when the author is speculating.
7. includes details about family artifacts, papers (letters, diaries), and photographs.
8. includes illustrations, such as photographs, maps, and appropriate charts.
9. includes genealogy summaries that use one of the standard, accepted numbering systems and formats.
10. includes a name, place, and subject index.

Let's Get Started!

It's time to get started. Don't be nervous. I've midwifed several first-time authors, and I haven't lost one yet. And they've given birth to some beautiful family histories. You *can* make this family history happen. You have the enthusiasm, the motivation, and now the know-how and guidance to write your family history—not to mention all those well-researched pedigree charts and family group sheets waiting in your files or binders. So what are we waiting for? Let's get going!

What Type of Family History Will You Write?

Writing a book is not as complicated as it seems; it's just a series of stories.
— DAVID MCCULLOUGH (AS QUOTED IN LEE
GUTKIND'S *THE ART OF CREATIVE NONFICTION*)

I f you like to read fiction, I'll bet there is a particular type (or types) of fiction you prefer reading: science fiction, romance, historical, detective, mystery, westerns. These are what literary scholars call *genres*, and each has elements that you've come to expect. The romance always has a happy ending with the hero whisking the heroine off into the sunset. A historical novel immerses you in a time period and place of the past. A good mystery novel keeps you guessing who the murderer is until the last page. These elements that you've come to expect when you pick up a particular genre hold true for family histories, as well. To the casual observer one family history may look the same as the next, but there are actually different genres, or types, of family histories, too.

About 20 years ago, I met Stephen King at a book signing in New York. Just starting out, I asked him what advice he could offer on becoming a writer. Mr. King replied, "Read everything you can on the genre that interests you. Then write—every day. Don't worry about spelling and grammar, you can take care of that later—just write. Wade into the stream and go with the flow."—WERNER F. MEYER

Step By Step

The first step in this process of writing your family history is to think about the type of book you want to write. While I advocate writing nonfiction family history narrative (number four in the chart on page 9), there are six other genres of genealogical writing I've identified as common in the field of genealogy. This is not to say you must write family history as a narrative. You can choose from among any of these genres or devise one of your own. Along with the descriptions of each, I've given you a few examples (complete information is in the bibliography), and some books you may want to read for further reference. Remember that there are many other examples and reference books listed in the bibliography, beginning on page 208.

WRITING FICTION VS. NONFICTION

Many people choose to write genealogical fiction simply because they don't know how to write their family history as creative, narrative nonfiction, making it interesting to read. While there is nothing wrong with turning your genealogy into fiction, do it because you are choosing to, not because you haven't learned yet how to write nonfiction creatively. My colleague, Kathy Sturdevant, and I often have wondered if this is the reason Alex Haley chose to tell *Roots* as fiction. Maybe he didn't realize that he could write his family history factually and creatively so that it read like a novel, but without fictionalizing. Maybe, like many family history writers, he didn't know how to write nonfiction narrative for generations where few records exist to document their lives. If you choose to write genealogy fiction and then self-publish it, make certain you inform your readers in the introduction that this is a work of fiction based on fact. The use of dialogue and attributing thoughts, feelings, and emotions to your long-gone ancestors is usually a dead-give-away that you're writing fiction. A big disadvantage of writing your family history as fiction is that your descendants won't be able to tell what really happened and what didn't.

THE SEVEN GENRES OF GENEALOGICAL AND FAMILY HISTORY WRITING

Genre	Description	Examples	For further reference
1 Reference Genealogies	A "bare bones" genealogy. It covers mostly the facts about ancestors: names, dates, and places. This type of genealogy is not meant to be read; it is a reference book. There is little, if any, biographical material. The reader looks up an ancestor, gets the information, then moves on. Many genealogists simply print out their computer data and publish it. A good genealogy in this genre is fully documented and uses a standard numbering system, such as the *Register* or *NGSQ* system. The majority are self-published.	Reference genealogies abound and were more commonly published in the late nineteenth-century up until about the 1980s.	Hatcher, *Producing a Quality Family History* Hoff, *Genealogical Writing in the 21st Century* Both give guidance on numbering systems, book design, style, and formatting your family history for camera-ready copy.
2 Genealogical Narratives	This takes the typical "bare bones" genealogy one step further. Under this category are genealogies that include biographical material, case studies, discussion of research analysis and methods of research, with the main focus being the research and analysis. This genre is typically written in an academic style (using a lot of passive voice—see STEP 9), incorporates full documentation, a standard numbering system, and seems to aim for an audience of other researchers, rather than family members. The majority are self-published or published by scholarly genealogical presses.	Simons, *The Langhornes of Langhorne Park* Dorman, *Twenty Families of Color in Massachusetts* You can also find "mini" examples of genealogical narratives in scholarly journal articles in the *National Genealogical Society Quarterly*, *The American Genealogist*, and *New England Historical and Genealogical Register*, to name a few.	Hatcher, *Producing a Quality Family History* Hoff, *Genealogical Writing in the 21st Century*

THE SEVEN GENRES OF GENEALOGICAL AND FAMILY HISTORY WRITING continued

Genre	Description	Examples	For further reference
3 Life Story Writing (Historical Biographies of Ordinary People)	Biographies, personal memoirs (about your life or your immediate family based on your memories), and autobiographies. The self-published ones in this category usually contain a lot of biographical or autobiographical material and family stories, but the information, unfortunately, is generally undocumented and relies on little outside research beyond the author's memory. Typically, pedigree charts and family group sheets are included. A well-done, commercially publishable life story or biography has characters and plots that appeal to a wide audience. These writers use the same creative nonfiction writing techniques covered in this book.	McCourt, *Angela's Ashes* Navas, *Murdered by His Wife*, (contains documentation) Bundles, *On Her Own Ground* (contains documentation)	Barrington, *Writing the Memoir* Hauser, *You Can Write a Memoir*
4 Family History Narratives	Narrative family histories are fully documented and tell the story of a family. One might call this creative, dramatic, or literary nonfiction writing. Written in third person (using *he, she*—as opposed to *I*), the focus is on people and the setting; the story has a plot and reads like a novel. Woven in with the facts about the family gleaned from genealogical research are family lore and social, oral, ethnic, and women's history. A combination of this genre and genealogical narrative makes an ideal book: the first part of the book is the family history narrative; the second part contains the genealogical family summaries. Depending on the quality of the narrative and its audience appeal, these can be commercially published, published by a scholarly genealogy press, or self-published.	Judd, *The Hatch and Brood of Time* McFarland, *A Scattered People* Carmack, *My Wild Irish Rose and Italians in Transition*	Sturdevant, *Bringing Your Family History to Life through Social History* Goes into more depth on historical context research and social history themes.

THE SEVEN GENRES OF GENEALOGICAL AND FAMILY HISTORY WRITING continued

	Genre	Description	Examples	For further reference
5	Family History Memoir	Unlike a personal memoir that focuses on the author and his or her immediate family, a family history memoir tells a nonfiction story centered around the author's search for his or her ancestors. Writers of this genre also use creative nonfiction devices as in family history narratives. Family history memoir is typically told as a first-person account (using *I*), and the narrator (author) shows growth as a person as a result of the family history search. The better ones in this genre are documented, although some commercially published ones may not include the documentation. Depending on the quality of the writing and the audience appeal, this genre has the best chance of being commercially published.	Logue, *Halfway Home* Ball, *Slaves in the Family* Paolicelli, *Dances with Luigi* Connelly, *Forgetting Ireland*	Polking, *Writing Family Histories and Memoirs*
6	Edited Letters and Diaries	This genre is for those who have a substantial or notable collection of an ancestor's letters, diaries, or other memorabilia. The author becomes an editor of an ancestor's papers, transcribing and publishing the documents. The editor adds annotation to unexplained or seemingly mysterious references in the documents and historical perspective. The editor weaves together family documents to tell the story of people's lives.	Blakey, Lainhart, and Stephens, *Rose Cottage Chronicles* Ulrich, *A Midwife's Tale* Carmack, *A Sense of Duty*	Sturdevant, *Organizing and Preserving Your Heirloom Documents* This guide not only shows you how to organize and preserve documents to keep them from harm's way, but it goes into great detail on how to annotate, augment, and arrange documents for publication.
7	Fictional Family Sagas Based on Truth	Because it is fiction, this type of writing is not documented, but some historical or genealogical fiction writers add an author's note, which includes the sources they consulted.	Haley, *Roots* Tademy, *Cane River*	Martin, *Writing Historical Fiction* Hemley, *Turning Life Into Fiction* Woolley, *How to Write and Sell Historical Fiction*

While I will be encouraging you to apply techniques fiction writers use to make your narrative more lively and readable, let me stress here and now that **I'm an advocate of writing creative, *nonfiction* family histories.** I will explain this in more detail in STEP 9. Assuming you have chosen to write a nonfiction family history or life story, then it must be completely nonfiction; you can't cross over into fictionalizing. If you do so without letting readers know that you are writing fiction, they will question and doubt the nonfiction parts of your work. And believe me, readers can tell when you are fictionalizing. If you include dialogue inappropriately or attribute feelings, emotions, and thoughts to your ancestors inappropriately, these are red flags that you're writing fiction. Then your readers won't know whether to believe your nonfiction parts.

Important

DECIDING UPON A GENRE

If you aren't sure in which genre you want to write your family history, read and review some of the samples given with each genre's description. Pick one that suits your research, your talents, and your time constraints.

If you've decided upon writing a nonfiction life story, a family history narrative, or a family history memoir, then you've come to the right place. This book focuses on these three genres. But choosing a genre for the family history that you would like to write is only the first step.

ADDITIONAL READING

Read, read, read. Read everything—trash, classics, good and bad, and see how they do it. Just like a carpenter who works as an apprentice and studies the most. Read! You'll absorb it. Then write. If it is good, you'll find out. If it's not, throw it out the window.
—WILLIAM FAULKNER

The guides I recommended in the table are specific to a genre, so I encourage you also to explore some books on creative nonfiction writing and writing in general. The bibliography lists several books on how to write creative nonfiction. My personal favorite is Jon Franklin's *Writing for Story: Craft Secrets of Dramatic Nonfiction*, but the others also will give you solid writing tips and techniques. Another must-read is David A. Fryxell's *Structure & Flow*. Unfortunately, it's out of print, but you should be able to find a copy through a library, or a used one online or at a used bookstore. Although it's geared for nonfiction-article writers, you can apply the same structure techniques to your family history chapters.

Although your goal may be to write nonfiction narrative, also read some fictional family sagas. You'll find examples of these in the bibliography, too. The reason I recommend you read fictional family sagas is to study the author's writing techniques. I often get ideas on how to craft a nonfiction family narrative from reading historical novels. You will, too, once you start reading with that eye.

As you're mulling over which genre to choose, let's start thinking about the next step: the scope of your family history book.

Defining the Scope of Your Project

There is no one right way. Each of us finds a way that works for him. But there is a wrong way. The wrong way is to finish your writing day with no more words on paper than when you began. Writers write.

—ROBERT B. PARKER

Continuing the fiction analogy from STEP 1, when you find a genre of novel you like to read, you probably choose books within that genre based on their scope: the time period, place, and topics covered. For example, I like to read romances, but if a book is set in a country I'm not particularly interested in, I won't read it. I like to read historical novels, too, but if it's about a time period or event in history that doesn't excite me, it stays on the shelf. I also like to read mysteries, but if a story includes a lot of graphic violence, I won't bother with it.

Just as a novelist must determine the scope of his or her book within a chosen genre, you, too, must decide not only which type of family history you want to write, but also define the scope of the book. In other words, what will you include and what will you leave for another book? Will it cover one branch of your family or will it be an "all my ancestors" book, that is, covering all lines on your pedigree chart and maybe your spouse's chart, too? Having written both types, I think it is far easier and more efficient to write several smaller family histories or monographs, than one huge volume. Writing a small family history isn't nearly as overwhelming and is more attainable; but if the

Great American Family History is your goal, then see page 18 for ways to structure it.

WHO WILL BE YOUR AUDIENCE?

For More Info

For more on writing family history monographs, see Patricia Law Hatcher's article, "Do We Share the Blame?" *Association of Professional Genealogists Quarterly* 15 (December 2000): 146-150.

Reminder

Most genealogists immediately think that their relatives and descendants (children, grandchildren, and so on) will be their only audience, so they write their books with just family in mind. But consider this: I am sure that in the course of your own research you've used other genealogists' published family histories. So besides your family, your fellow researchers will be part of your audience, especially if you donate a copy of your family history to a library. Other types of researchers who may use your book as a springboard or part of their own research are social historians. Social historians study the lives of everyday, ordinary people in society, and I've read many works by social historians who reference published family histories as part of their sources.

Realizing now that other researchers—genealogists and historians—might read and use your family history, will that change the way you write your book? If you are writing solely for family members, your inclination may be to omit footnotes or endnotes, thinking that your family won't care where you got your information. Maybe they won't; but maybe one of them is a budding genealogist and will. When I wrote *The Ebetino and Vallarelli Family History* in 1990, few, if any, of my relatives were interested in doing family history research themselves—or they didn't have the time for it. Eleven years later, after one of my Ebetino cousins retired, he was bitten by the genealogy bug just as the rest of us were, and he's following up on leads that I didn't have the time or the access to records to pursue in 1990. Sooner or later, even if your book is distributed only among family, some other researcher is going to find your work, and that person will want to pick up where you left off or take one of the branches further.

Methods for documentation (citing sources) and determining what you need to document will be discussed in STEP 15, but for now, make it a habit. Citing sources is not an option when writing a nonfiction family history. Without source citations, other researchers will use your efforts as clues only.

THE BOOK'S SCOPE

As the author, you need to set some parameters for your family history. I recently wrote a history of the Vallarelli and DeBartolo families in Italy and America, called *Italians in Transition*. The original narrative was going to cover just the Vallarelli family. For the DeBartolo family who married into the Vallarelli family, I was only going to compile a genealogy and include extra biographical information about them in an appendix. Three-quarters of the way into the project, that plan didn't feel right to me because I realized that I had enough information on the DeBartolos to give them equal attention in the narrative. I decided to weave their stories into the chapters on life in Italy and give the DeBartolo immigrants their own chapter.

What have we learned from this example? It's okay to keep redefining the scope of your book as you get into it. If you feel overwhelmed and think this book will never get finished, narrow your focus. Or, if you find that you have more information on an allied family than you thought, bring them into the forefront.

Here are four common "formulas" for narrative family history. In STEP 4, I'll go into more depth on the structure and flow of the narrative.

1. Single Line of Descent

For this type of project, you begin with the earliest known ancestor for a particular surname. Let's say your surname is Gibson, and you have the Gibson line traced back to colonial America. Joseph Gibson is the earliest ancestor you've identified. Your narrative would begin with him and come forward following just your line of descent. Each chapter would cover one ancestor or generation, as shown below:

Chapter One   Joseph Gibson [your fourth great-grandfather]

Chapter Two	Isaac Gibson [your third great-grandfather]
Chapter Three	William Gibson [your second great-grandfather]
Chapter Four	Samuel Gibson [your great-grandfather]
Chapter Five	Henry William Gibson [your maternal grandfather]
Chapter Six	Fern (Gibson) Hamilton [your mother]
Chapter Seven	Jean Hamilton [you]

This single line doesn't have to be male-bound. You can do a similar single line of descent with what genealogists call the "umbilical line": that is, your mother, your mother's mother, your mother's mother's mother, and so on. The surnames, of course, will change with each chapter. Here's an example (maiden names are in parentheses):

Chapter One	Margaret (Griffin) Johnson (third great-grandmother)
Chapter Two	Polly (Johnson) Becksdale (second great-grandmother)
Chapter Three	Mildred (Becksdale) Cusack (great-grandmother)
Chapter Four	Mary (Cusack) Martin (grandmother)
Chapter Five	Karen (Martin) Clark (mother)
Chapter Six	Gabrielle Clark (daughter)

2. All the Descendants of . . .

Another way to structure your narrative is to cover all the descendants of one couple, setting up your chapters like this:

Chapter One (or Generation One)
    David and Charlotte Hawes (Buckner) Stuart
Chapter Two (or Generation Two)
[all of David and Charlotte's children]
    William Gibbons and Sarah Foote (Ashton) Stuart
    Mary Fitzhugh (Stuart) and James Madison Fitzhugh

Lucy Fitzhugh (Stuart) and Jacob Shough
Chapter Three (or Generation Three)
[all of David and Charlotte's grandchildren]
Martha T. (Stuart) and John Corey
Catlett Conway and Ellen Somerville (Conway)
Fitzhugh
John Stuart and Susan Blackwell (Pannill) Fitzhugh
and so on . . .

3. The Big Four (or Eight or Sixteen)

The Big Four would be your four grandparents, the Big Eight your eight great-grandparents, the Big Sixteen, your sixteen great-grandparents. This book will probably work best for you if you divide your book into sections.

Section One	Grandpa Jones (your paternal grandfather)
Section Two	Grandma Collins (Grandpa Jones's wife—her maiden name—and your paternal grandmother)
Section Three	Grandpa Lewis (your maternal grandfather)
Section Four	Grandma Turner (Grandpa Lewis's wife—her maiden name—and your maternal grandmother)

Then within each section you would handle the narrative by either beginning with Grandpa Jones's life and working backward through his ancestry, or starting with the earliest known Jones ancestor and coming forward to Grandpa. The latter is much easier to write. There are good reasons history is written from past to present.

4. All My Ancestors

This approach is the granddaddy of family histories, or, as I like to call it, the Great American Family History. Most genealogists would handle this type of tome by including a section for each surname they've been able to trace, arranging them by chapters in alphabetical order. Within each surname section, begin with the earliest known ancestor and come forward in time. To keep it manageable, focus on only the ancestors in each line, not the siblings of your ancestors (the collaterals)—although they could be included as part of the narrative with their parents. (For more on structuring this type of narrative, see STEP 4.) Here's an example of how the chapters in an "all my ancestors" narrative might look:

Part I: Paternal Ancestors
1. Bloomfield Family
2. Davis Family
3. Hamilton Family
4. Wallace Family
5. and so on . . .

Part II: Maternal Ancestors
1. Dailey Family
2. Doyle Family
3. Hunt Family
4. Lewis Family
5. and so on . . .

Within each chapter the family would have subchapters for each family group, like this:
1. Maxwell Family
   a. William Maxwell (bpt. 1651–1701) (the immigrant)
   b. Henry Maxwell (ca. 1686–1758)
   c. Henry Maxwell (1723–1783)
   d. Henry Maxwell (1750–1777)
   e. Henry Maxwell (1773–1830)
   f. James Maxwell (1809–1845)
   g. Michael Maxwell (1831–1908)
   h. William Maxwell (1870–1926)
   i. Thomas Maxwell (1903–1955)
   j. Loraine Maxwell (see Jackson family)

Carry the ancestral families forward chronologically until you reach the female who marries into another surname, then direct the reader to that family surname.

Other Formulas

As you start reviewing and reading other family histories, you'll find different formulas that other authors have used in their books. If none of the ones presented in this chapter strikes your fancy, create your own formula.

Numbering Systems

It's best to use a numbering system that has been established and is used by a majority of researchers, rather than inventing your own. The two most widely accepted numbering systems are the *National Genealogical Society Quarterly* System (*NGSQ* System) and the New England Historic Genealogical Society's *Register* System. See STEP 17 for examples and more information.

BREAKING IT DOWN

Technique

Once you have decided on the scope of your family history, you will need to break it down into manageable chunks for research and writing purposes. Even though you may be covering several generations in one book, tackle each family group one at a time so that it won't feel so overwhelming, and so you can easily manage and organize your background research. If you are working with family group sheets, put the ones you'll be covering in your book in a separate binder. If you have stored your data electronically using a genealogical software program, print out the pertinent family group sheets. Put the group sheets in the order in which you are likely to cover them in the book: that is, chronologically from past to present, with the earliest generation first and succeeding generations coming forward in time. Presumably, you have been citing your sources for each piece of information on your family group sheets, so make sure you include your documentation in the binder with the sheets. Now that the information for your chosen families is isolated in a separate binder, in the next step we'll see whether you are ready to write—or if there are some loose ends in the genealogical records that you still need to tie up.

How Much Genealogical Research is Enough?

The goal is not the unimaginative listing of the facts from the family group sheet or the pedigree chart but the sensitive rendering of a human being's story told with control and focus.

—LAWRENCE P. GOULDRUP, *WRITING THE FAMILY NARRATIVE*

In *My Wild Irish Rose*, a family history narrative I published in 2001 about the lives of my grandmother and great-grandmother, I stated that Delia (Gordon) Norris's origins in Ireland were unknown. That book had been out about six months when, with some help from my friends, I finally broke through the brick wall and identified the place of origin in Ireland. Did I publish that book too soon? Shouldn't I have done more research until I found the place in Ireland? No. I had been searching for *years* to find Delia's origins in Ireland, and nothing on the horizon indicated that an answer could be found any time in the near future; otherwise I would have put off publishing until I found it. At the time the book went to press, I was certain I would have to search for several more years— if not the rest of my life—to uncover her origins. Sure, I could have waited, hoping there would be another lead, another breakthrough; but then the book would have never been written and published. In some respects, writing and publishing your family history is a way to guarantee that you'll break through any brick walls you may have—for it's a cruel, ironic, Murphy's law of genealogy that as soon as you publish, new information becomes available to you. But it won't become available to you *until* you publish.

For many genealogists, putting on the research brakes is the hardest part of writing a family history. How do you know when you're ready to stop researching and begin writing? Frankly, there is always going to be another record to check, and as you begin writing, that's when you really see any holes in your research. In fact, you might consider the first draft of your narrative as a way to find out if you're ready to publish.

Here are two gauges to determine if you're ready to turn off the microfilm reader and begin writing.

Notes

1. Have you searched every possible record for the family, including records that the individual family members may have generated? Below are the typical, obvious sources (see STEP 6 for how these records can provide the facts and insights you need to make your family history compelling).

For More Info

If you aren't familiar with these records, try Emily Anne Croom's *Unpuzzling Your Past*, 4th edition (Cincinnati: Betterway Books, 2001), and *The Genealogist's Companion and Sourcebook*, 2d edition (Cincinnati: Betterway Books, 2003) for in-depth coverage of records. In STEP 6, you'll find guides specific to record groups as well.

- cemetery and funeral-home records
- church records
- city directories
- family histories and genealogies (what's already been written about the family)
- family sources (such as Bibles, letters, diaries) and oral history
- immigration records (naturalizations, passenger lists)
- land and tax records
- military service records, pensions, bounty land warrants
- newspaper articles, obituaries, and death notices
- nonpopulation censuses (agricultural, manufacturing, mortality)
- population censuses (federal, state, slave, Indian—for every census year your family may have been recorded on them)

- probate and court records (wills, administrations, inventories)
- vital records (births, marriages, deaths)

If you haven't searched for *all* of these records for each family or family member you want to write about, you are not ready to write. That's not to say that you have to find all of these records for each family member. If you're dealing with a family that has been in America for generations, they might not have immigration records. If the family lived in a rural community, they won't be listed in a city directory. But certainly, you need to have checked for every possible record your family of interest might have generated. There are many other types of sources, of course, such as school records, business and employment records, coroner's records—the list is endless, and you should look for all that apply to your family. It's exhaustive research, in more ways than one.

2. Have you turned your family group charts into "family summaries" to get the full picture? This is a crucial step toward pulling your data together into a family history narrative, so when you believe you are ready to write, don't bypass this step. A family summary should include

    a. all genealogical facts you've gathered in research (births, marriages, deaths, etc.).

    b. your analysis of records and research, plus any biographical data.

    c. clearly identified speculations about why something happened, who someone's parents were, and so forth.

Figure 3-1 on page 24 is a standard family group sheet for the Charles Henry Fearn family. Notice that there is room to squeeze only so much information onto these forms. That's one reason I'd like you to take that information and type it up as a family summary as shown in Figure 3-2 on page 25. In this summary, include every

FAMILY GROUP SHEET	
Husband: Charles Henry Fearn	
Born: 26 Mar. 1852[1]	Place: Groveport, Ohio[1]
Married: 26 Mar. 1878[2]	Place: Columbus, Ohio[2]
Died: 15 Mar. 1916[1]	Place: Grant Hospital, Columbus, Ohio[1]
Buried: 17 Mar. 1916[3]	Place: Greenlawn Cemetery, Columbus, Ohio[3]
Parents: George William Fearn and Anna May Snyder	
Other Spouses: none	
Wife: Martha Jane "Mattie" Bainter	
Born: 8 Jan. 1851[4]	Place: Muskingum Co., Ohio[4]
Died: 23 Mar. 1928[4]	Place: South Bend, Indiana[4]
Buried: 26 Mar. 1928[5]	Place: Greenlawn Cemetery, Columbus, Ohio[5]
Parents: Arza Brunson Bainter and Elvira Tamar McCashland	
Other Spouses: none	

Children:[6]

Name	Birth Date & Place	Death Date & Place	Marriage Date, Place & Spouse
1. Charles Elliott Fearn	18 Jun. 1879 Columbus, Ohio		
2. Warren Foss Fearn	30 Sept. 1881	21 Jul. 1882 Little Rock, Ark.	
3. Otto Evelyn "Jimmie" Fearn	17 Sept. 1883 Ft. Grant, Ariz. Territory		
4. Guy Victor Fearn	23 Sept. 1885 Ft. Lowell, Ariz. Territory[7]		

[1] Ohio death certificate of Charles H. Fearn, Columbus, Ohio, 1916, #431, copy in pension file of Charles H. Fearn, #186125, National Archives; death notices of Charles H. Fearn, *The Columbus Evening Dispatch*, 16 March 1916, p. 2, col. 5, and p. 11, col. 5.

[2] Franklin Co., Ohio, Marriages, 14:337.

[3] Record of Family Lots, Greenlawn Cemetery, Columbus, Ohio, FHL 1402482.

[4] Indiana death certificate of Mrs. Mattie B. Fearn, 1928, #340, showing she was born 6 Jan. 1851; obituary of Mrs. Mattie B. Fearn, *The South Bend* (Indiana) *Tribune*, 23 March 1928, Sec. 1, p. 6, showing she was born in Zanesville, 6 Jan. 1851; obituaries of Mrs. Mattie B. Fearn, newspaper clippings in possession of the client.

[5] Record of Family Lots, Greenlawn Cemetery, Columbus, Ohio, FHL film 1402482.

[6] Pension file of Charles H. Fearn, #186125, National Archives; 1900 Census, Ohio, Franklin Co., Columbus, Ward 18, Pct. D, ED 126, p. 11, #236-246, National Archives micropublication T623, roll 1270; 1910 Census, Ohio, Franklin Co., Columbus City, Ward 11, ED 168, p. 8, #202–204, National Archives micropublication T624, roll 1183.

[7] Ohio death certificate of Guy Victor "Fern," 1940, #4095, indicates he was born in Kansas, 23 Sept. 1886.

Figure 3-1
Family Group Sheet for the Charles Henry Fearn Family. This is probably how you have your family information recorded. This is a good format to use while doing your genealogical research.

Family Summary of
Charles Henry and Martha Jane (Bainter) Fearn

CHARLES HENRY[3] FEARN (*George William*[2], *John*[1]) was born in Groveport, Ohio, 26 March 1852, and died of organic heart disease in Grant Hospital in Columbus, Ohio, 15 March 1916, aged 63 years, 11 months, and 18 days.[1] He was buried at Greenlawn Cemetery in Columbus.[2]

On 26 March 1878, Rev. J.C. Jackson married Charles to MARTHA JANE "MATTIE" BAINTER in Columbus.[3] Mattie was born in Muskingum County, Ohio, 8 January 1851, and died of mitral insufficiency at the home of her son Charles at 821 Diamond Avenue in South Bend, Indiana, 23 March 1928, aged 77 years, 2 months, and 17 days. She was buried at Greenlawn Cemetery in Columbus.[4] Martha was the daughter of Arza Brunson and Elvira Tamar (McCashland) Bainter.[5]

Charles served in the regular Army as a hospital steward. He enlisted in the United States Army in 1874. He was first stationed at the Columbus Arsenal, then Little Rock Arsenal, then Fort Grant, Arizona (1882–85), and finally at Fort Lowell, Arizona (1885–86).[6] After his military service, Charles worked as a druggist in Columbus, Ohio.[1]

Mattie was a member of the King Avenue Methodist Episcopal Church in Columbus. She was also a member of the Loraine Chapter, Order of the Eastern Star.[8]

Children:[9]

i	Charles Elliott[4] Fearn, b. 18 June 1879 in Columbus.
ii	Warren Foss Fearn, b. 30 Sept. 1881; d. in Little Rock, Ark., 21 July 1882, aged 10m 21d; buried in Little Rock National Cemetery.[10]
iii	Otto Evelyn "Jimmie" Fearn, b. 17 Sept. 1883 at Fort Grant, Arizona Territory.
iv	Guy Victor Fearn, b. 23 Sept. 1885 at Fort Lowell, Arizona Territory.[11]

---

[1] Ohio death certificate of Charles H. Fearn, Columbus, Ohio, 1916, #431, copy in pension file of Charles H. Fearn, #186125, National Archives; death notices of Charles H. Fearn, *The Columbus Evening Dispatch*, 16 March 1916, p. 2, col. 5, and p. 11, col. 5.

[2] Record of Family Lots, Greenlawn Cemetery, Columbus, Ohio, FHL 1402482.

[3] Franklin Co., Ohio, Marriages, 14:337.

[4] Record of Family Lots, Greenlawn Cemetery, Columbus, Ohio, FHL 1402482.

[5] Indiana death certificate of Mrs. Mattie B. Fearn, 1928, #340, showing she was born 6 Jan. 1851; obituary of Mrs. Mattie B. Fearn, *The South Bend* (Indiana) *Tribune*, 23 March 1928, Sec. 1, p. 6, showing she was born in Zanesville 6 Jan. 1851; obituaries of Mrs. Mattie B. Fearn, newspaper clippings in possession of the client; record of Family Lots, Greenlawn Cemetery, Columbus, Ohio, FHL 1402482, showing she was born in Adams Co., Ohio.

[6] Pension file of Charles H. Fearn, #186125, National Archives.

[7] 1900 federal census, Ohio, Franklin Co., Columbus, Ward 18, Pct. D, National Archives (NARA) Microfilm T623, roll 1270, ED 126, p. 11, #236–246. Stationery letterhead of Fearn Drug Company, Manufacturing Druggists, P.O. Box 999, Columbus, Ohio. The letterhead has pre-printed "190_" for the year to be filled in.

[8] Obituary of Mrs. Mattie B. Fearn, *The South Bend* (Indiana) *Tribune*, 23 March 1928, Sec. 1, p. 6.

[9] Pension file of Charles H. Fearn, #186125, National Archives; 1900 Census, Ohio, Franklin Co., Columbus, Ward 18, Pct. D, ED 126, p. 11, #236–246, NARA T623, roll 1270; 1910 Census, Ohio, Franklin Co., Columbus City, Ward 11, ED 168, p. 8, #202–204, NARA T624, roll 1183.

[10] Clipping of newspaper death notice of Warren Foss Fearn, "younger son of Chas. H. and Mattie B. Fearn," in possession of the client.

[11] Ohio death certificate of Guy Victor "Fern," 1940, #4095, indicates he was born in Kansas, 23 Sept. 1886.

Figure 3-2
Family Summary of the Charles Henry and Martha Jane (Bainter) Fearn Family. Convert the data on your family group sheet into a genealogical narrative or family summary. This will help you get into the mindset of writing data in complete sentences. It also allows you to record information that won't conveniently fit on a family group form.

tidbit of information about the family that you know or can document. Notice that on the form in Figure 3-1 there is no room to write cause of death and the age at death. In the summary, you'll be able to include that information. I also wasn't able to include any information on the family group sheet about Charles's military career, but in the summary, I could.

Quotes

New technology can help get a writer's words in front of more readers' eyeballs, but it can't make them care about what you've written. That's a much harder job— one that the coolest computer in the world can't help you with.—JEFF GOODELL

I realize that if you're using a genealogy computer software program, you probably can make this "narrative report" happen by clicking on an icon, which will convert the data into narrative form so you can copy it into your word processing program. Once you have copied it, you'll be working with the narrative in the word processing program only. This copy of your family summary will become the working text that you'll use to see plots, isolate themes, and guide your background research. If the genealogy software program did not allow you to include everything you've gathered on the family, now is the time to add details, speculation, and analysis to this family summary. Doing so will help you spot any holes and identify additional areas you may want to research. For now, reformat the information for only one family group.

I don't want you to lose sight of why you are moving data from charts or genealogy software into your word processor. Creating and using family summaries will help you:

1. get into the mindset of writer by editing and constructing sentences and paragraphs.

Technique

2. reevaluate what you've gathered. Do you really have a good source for that birth date, other than family knowledge? Are your sources complete citations?

3. see any holes in your research that you need to

fill. As you reformat the information from charts or a genealogy software program, you may discover that you hadn't gotten around to checking for a probate, or for the family in the 1850 census as you had intended, or in another source you may have unintentionally neglected. Or, there may be new resources, such as the 1930 census that was released in April 2002, that weren't available when you last did research on that family.

Referring only to information stored on family group sheets or in the data files of your genealogy software program limits your ability to see the whole picture, to analyze, make connections, and speculate. Forms—even most computerized versions—have limitations and typically allow you to record only basic facts and meager notes. For this reason, some genealogists don't use forms; they write out information in a narrative style from the get-go. The narrative format allows you to include more details, such as complete military service or immigration information.

As you write your family summary, go back through all the files and records you've gathered for the families you plan to write about and make sure you've included everything. It's amazing how you will discover new things with a fresh pair of eyes. Once you have reviewed your files and compiled all of your research, analysis, and speculations for one family group into a family summary, review it for any additional genealogical research you still need to do.

Besides seeing holes in your research, you may find topics you want to explore in more detail as you transform sterile facts into narrative. Use your word processor's highlight feature or change the color of the text to mark sections for further study. For example, if you discover that one of your ancestors suffered from tuberculosis and you'd like to learn more about the disease, highlight *tuberculosis* as a reminder that you want to research that topic. Highlighting features may also be used to mark places for insertions. For example, if I have a photograph that I plan to include with the text, I'll put a note between paragraphs (such as *Insert photo of Aunt Mabel holding baby Jennifer near here*), then change the font color to pink. If I have a page cross-reference or a question about something, I use boldface for an easily searchable string of characters (See page **xx** for Higgins genealogy summary, or Samuel died in 1842—is that correct??) If I need to check a source, or I didn't get a complete source citation, I will highlight that source in yellow or some other color.

I know what I've asked you to do in this step is a huge task, one that doesn't sound like much fun, but it will pay off when you begin to write. Even though I believe that—no matter how organized and prepared you are to write this book—inevitably you will uncover something new before the ink is dry, all this preparation will help to reduce the odds of that happening to you. In the next step, we'll consider another element of your family history that you should be thinking about as you organize and prepare what you have already gathered: the story's plot.

Determining the Plot and Structure

To write history is to tell a story about the past.
—RICHARD MARIUS, *A SHORT GUIDE TO WRITING ABOUT HISTORY*

I f you read a lot of fiction or watch a lot of movies, you have probably realized that there are only so many basic story plots. Ronald B. Tobias identified twenty of them in his writing guidebook, *20 Master Plots*. As he explains, a *story* is a chronicle of events, whereas the *plot* is a "chain of cause-and-effect relationships that constantly create a pattern of unified action and behavior. Plot involves the reader in the game of 'Why?' " The plot reveals conflicts and resolutions for the characters. We keep reading because it's clear there is a conflict, and we want to see how the plot unfolds and how the characters will resolve their problems. I'm sure you've heard the saying, "The plot thickens." It thickens as twists and turns are added to the story.

In the case of your family history, the characters are your ancestors. What problems did your ancestors have to resolve? Who or what stood in the way of an ancestor's success? **Look for family and personal struggles.** Think about the four basic conflicts: man against man, man against nature, man against society, and man against himself. Which of those four conflicts underlies the plot in your family history? Then, how will you reveal the plot to your reader? Here are some common family history plots:

Tip

Immigration. Just about everyone has an immigration plot in their family history. Indeed, many published genealogies begin with the immigrant ancestor, then come forward in time. Instead of just recording the facts about an ancestor's immigration to America, think about the obstacles or problems that might have arisen that your ancestor had to resolve. I can guarantee that your fourth great-grandfather from Ireland didn't wake up one morning and say to his wife, "Bridget, pack your bags. We're going to America this afternoon." Their decision to leave homeland and relatives may have been an agonizing one. If your own family lore doesn't reveal the problems encountered or the solutions devised by your immigrant ancestors, then consider the experiences of other immigrants who came from the same country or area at around the same time period. Remember, we're not going to fictionalize; we're going to research what might have happened and speculate on the possibilities.

Pioneer saga. Just as most American families have stories with the immigration plot, many of us have one about migration. Rare are the families who came to America and settled in one spot for generations. Moving to the wilderness and westward migration are common plots in family histories. What did that entail? What was it like along the trail? How did the family build their house? Clear the land? As in many immigration stories, the women may not have been keen on the idea of leaving their mothers and family behind. Many didn't want to go. How did they cope? What was it like to raise a family on the frontier? There's a lot to explore in this plot.

Rags to riches, or in my family's case, riches to rags. Your ancestors may have been dirt poor, but with each new generation the family prospered. Or, maybe your ancestors were like my colonial Virginia people, who had acres upon acres of land, then lost it in the Civil War or from dividing it among generations of heirs. Again, people don't wake up one morning and decide to be rich (or poor). Circumstances, events, or people helped them make their decisions or got in their way. What happened in your family history?

Rising out of slavery. This, of course, is a common plot for African-American writers, and it's been so widely researched and written about that you should have ideas already about the obstacles your ancestors faced. Do the records you've uncovered reveal anything specific or out-of-the-ordinary for your family? Will you have to deal with issues of miscegenation (mixed-race marriages or relationships)? How did your ancestors overcome the biggest obstacle of humankind?

War and military survival. Family historians seem comfortable in writing about the war or military service experience for their male ancestors. But what were the problems the soldier's wife and family had to deal with while he was serving his country? Look at the whole picture, not just half the story. Remember that most men spent more time during a war either in camp or sick than they did in battle, and you can describe those typical experiences. If your ancestor was taken as a prisoner of war, you'll have even more obstacles to write about.

City dweller to country dweller, or vice versa. If you have ancestors who left a city in the East or South to settle on the western frontier, they had quite a few adjustments to make. Think about what it must have been like to leave the neighborhood dry goods store far behind, to have to live off the land. We know from letters and diaries that most women had no choice in the move to the desolate areas where their husbands wanted to settle. How did they cope with their new environment? What challenges did they face in the course of everyday survival? The Fearn family narrative that I used as an example in STEP 3 is going to have this overarching plot. They will go from city dwellers in Columbus, Ohio, to desert frontier dwellers in Arizona Territory.

Consider these aspects of your ancestors' lives in terms of what conflicts and resolutions you might address:

- human contact
- work

31

- language
- living quarters
- geography
- climate
- food

"The stories that you tell about your past shape your future."—ERIC RANSDELL

OUTLINING THE PLOT

Pulitzer Prize-winning author Jon Franklin, in *Writing for Story*, suggests outlining conflicts and resolutions. Here is his plot-outlining technique applied to a family history plot.

Complication (or, conflict): Famine strikes the O'Connor Family in Ireland.
Development:
1. John O'Connor hangs on as long as he can.
2. He realizes there is no hope in sight and begins thinking of emigrating to America.
3. John sells what few possessions the family has and books passage to America.
Resolution: John and family emigrate.

Now, let's apply this plot-outlining technique to the Fearn family story:

Complication (or, conflict): Charles Fearn gets military orders to move to Arizona.
Development:
1. Charles and Mattie encounter terrain and climate different from their home in Ohio.
2. Mattie must adapt to a military camp dwelling.
3. Charles becomes a "jack of all trades" in the remote military post.
Resolution: The family adjusts to new living quarters and the demands of the desert.

Outlining in this manner helps you to see the plot in your family history and to think through the narrative before you begin writing. Give it a try.

If you are covering several generations in your family history narrative, you may have one major plot with subplots (or themes) throughout. For example, in McFarland's *A Scattered People*, the main plot woven throughout the narrative is the migration story of families moving west over the course of two centuries. But each ancestor's story has subplots (or themes) covering individual struggles, successes, and defeats.

Don't worry about whether your plot is original; the important thing is to make sure you have one. What makes your family history different from another one with the same plot is the characters, events, and how you isolate and develop themes.

STRUCTURE AND FLOW

It's probably safe to say that all writers outline the plot structure of their stories in some manner before they begin writing, but you don't have to use the *I. A. i. a.*-type outline you were taught in English class. Believe me, as soon as I got away from those English teachers, I never made another outline like that. In fact, rarely, if ever, do I make an outline. Not on paper, anyway; I do it in my head. After I've done all the research I'm going to do on a family, I spend days mulling over how I'm going to structure and organize the narrative. There are many possible scenarios, so I run them all through my mind to see which one feels best.

With a large project like a book, I mentally outline the structure of the actual story, but I also make a skeletal outline on paper, usually in the form of chapters with a brief description of what each chapter will contain. So you see, every writer does what works for her. In fact, most writers spend quite a bit of time thinking about how they want to structure a piece before they even put fingers to keyboard.

Consider several different structures based on your material, then decide which structure will help you achieve the

Tip

goal of your book most effectively. For example, one of my clients, whose children were in grade school when he commissioned the project, wanted his book to be enjoyable and informative for his children when they got older. With that in mind, I decided that if I began the narrative with the earliest ancestor, the children might have trouble connecting themselves to someone from the 1800s, even though they happened to share a surname. I thought it would be better to begin with someone they could relate to, preferably someone they already knew about. I considered a flashback/flash forward structure (see page 38), but that can be confusing to a young reader unless it is skillfully done. Instead, I decided the best way to structure this narrative was to begin with oral history interviews with the client's immediate family: aunts, uncles, the client himself—people the kids knew personally. This first chapter wouldn't tell the whole story of these peoples lives, however; I needed to include some "cliffhangers" to keep the kids reading. So chapter one would stop at some dramatic high point with a transition to chapter two, which would then flash back to the earliest ancestor. In subsequent chapters, the story would be told pretty much in chronological order, with the final chapter circling back to the client and his siblings. This way, the children would be able to see how one generation led to the next, and how the past generations affect their own. That was how I first *imagined* I would write it. When I actually began writing, things could have changed, and a different structure may have come to me that would work better.

If it's easier for you to outline on paper (or computer), then go for it. Here's an outline method that worked well for author John McPhee (as told in David Fryxell's *Structure & Flow*), which might work well for you, too. McPhee used index cards, with one card per major topic. So let's say we've got these topics we want to cover in the narrative of Hugh and Mary McGuire, who lived in Ireland in the 1840s:

- houses in rural Ireland
- Mary's daily chores around the house

- Hugh's farming chores
- livestock (cow, chickens, sheep, pig)
- childbearing
- seasonal festivals and saints' days
- climate and geography
- responsibilities to the landlord
- religion
- national atmosphere in the pre-famine years that would have affected the McGuires

If you're using note cards or loose-leaf paper, use one card or sheet per topic, then start playing writer's solitaire like McPhee did and contemplate the different possible orders. Or, if you're doing it on computer, you can cut and paste to rearrange your notes.

Look at the topics above. There's nothing wrong with the order they're in now: but would housing in rural Ireland be the most interesting, dramatic, or controversial aspect of the McGuires' lives to grab the reader's attention from the start? **Reader-grabbing appeal should be foremost in your mind, dictating where you will begin the narrative (more on this in STEP 9).** It might be better to start with responsibilities to the landlord, or with the national atmosphere of Ireland in the pre-famine years that would have affected the McGuires.

Important

It doesn't matter whether you outline the structure on paper or in your mind. Just remember that outlines can and often will change. You can modify your structural outline at any time, or even abandon it completely and create another one. Now let's look at five possible structures.

1. Chronological and Altered Chronological Order

Typically, when writers write about history, they write from the past to the present in chronological order. But when it comes to writing biography or family history, that cradle-to-grave approach—writing about the events as they actually happened—can lend itself to a dry, old-fashioned, history-textbook feel and read.

Consider altering the chronology slightly by writing your narrative as a fiction writer or nonfiction-magazine writer would. Start on a dramatic high point (which could be any time in your ancestor's life—even a scene at someone's deathbed), then after you've grabbed the reader's interest in the lead, go back and tell the story chronologically up to the point where you began. In *Structure & Flow,* David A. Fryxell reminds us that "reader-grabbing appeal is the main factor" in choosing where to start the story. "Without changing the facts or being unfaithful to *what really happened*," writes Fryxell, "the nonfiction writer—by choices in what to include and what to leave out, by ordering the unfolding of events—can and must do more than merely write 'First *this* happened, then *that.*'" He offers an example of diagramming the sequences of events in this way: "D (the dramatic lead in the middle of things), A (the chronological start of the story), B, C, back to D, E, F, and so on." Or, to slightly modify Fryxell's nonfiction-article formula to family history writing, here's how it would flow:

1. Grabber lead: the dramatic opening based on a conflict, controversy, or interesting part of your ancestor's life (see STEP 9).

2. Hook: the transition that begins to set the stage for the rest of the narrative; it should answer the reader's question: *Why should I keep reading?* or *Why should I care?*

3. Background: any information the reader needs to know before we get into the chronology.

4. Chronological beginning of the story: this could be the birth of the ancestor; or, if you don't have enough material for a discussion of the ancestor's childhood, then begin with the ancestor as an adult or when the ancestor marries.

5. Continuation of the chronology up to and through the dramatic lead.

6. Completion of the chronology.

7. Dramatically satisfying ending (or circle back to the lead).

This is perhaps the easiest method for writing family history narrative, and the structure I used in the Charles Fearn narrative in Appendix A.

As you write, you may find other appropriate places for true flashbacks. Writers use flashbacks to interrupt the narrative if it's necessary to add explanation to a story or answer pending questions. For example, in *The Great Shame*, Thomas Keneally begins the story by describing Hugh Larkin's crime and why he was banished from Ireland to Australia. But now Keneally needs to tell the reader about Hugh's upbringing, so he uses a flashback. Keneally moves us back in time by starting a new paragraph and using language that suggests a clear transition: "During Hugh's childhood people had believed . . . ." He also switches from the past tense of the previous paragraph to the past-perfect tense ("had believed"). When you read family history narratives, become conscious of how each writer moves the characters (and the reader) through time. Flashbacks can be useful, but beware of using too many. If there are more than one or two, the reader may get confused about the true sequence of events, and your narrative will read as if it had no logical structure.

2. Reverse Chronological Order

In one family history I wrote, I structured the narrative from the present to the past. It began with the client's parents, then each succeeding chapter moved back another generation, ending with the client's colonial ancestors. That was extremely difficult to do, because the events of each chapter somehow had to link to the events of the next. This means that if you cover someone's life span in one chapter, you can't just kill him off at the end; you must propel him back in time and connect him somehow to his parents' lives (which will be the focus of your next chapter). It took every ounce of creativity I had to figure out how to do that, so this is not a structure I would recommend for beginning writers. See Appendix B for an example of leaping backward in time with each generation.

3. Parallel to Convergent

A good analogy of a parallel structure would be any television drama series, such as *The Practice*, *ER*, *Law & Order*, or *Six Feet Under*. In these shows, there are two or more story lines per episode that run parallel to one another, with scenes that alternate between the story lines, but sometimes never converge. Similarly, your family history has ancestral lines that run parallel, but they eventually converge when an ancestral couple marries. To add suspense and more drama to your narrative, you can construct your narrative with a parallel to convergent structure. Figure 6-1 on page 59 shows how the chapters would be structured. Notice how the generations run parallel to each other within a chapter, until a couple meets and the lines converge.

4. Flashback/Flash Forward or Flash Forward/Flashback

Another technique is to use a flashback/flash forward or flash forward/flashback structure. In this type of narrative, you alternate chapters about the past with chapters about the present until the periods merge in the final chapters. Edward Ball does this in both of his family history memoirs, *Slaves in the Family* and *The Sweet Hell Inside*. The first chapter begins in the present, telling the reader how Ball got interested in the family history and what it meant to him. In the second chapter, he propels the reader back to the most distant past of his story. The third chapter returns to the present, detailing more of his search. The fourth chapter picks up in the past where we left off in the second chapter. The chapters alternate in time until the past and present converge.

5. Journey

Kem Luther used this structure in *Cottonwood Roots*. The book describes not only the spiritual journey to discover his ancestors, but also his physical journey to the places where his ancestors lived and died. This literary family history memoir is written in first person, as you would expect a memoir to be, and also in present tense to give the reader the illusion that you are traveling along with Luther on his journey. On the long drives between stops, he has time to ruminate on his ancestors' lives. It's a relaxing, yet exciting journey, and the reader feels the same mix of contentment and excitement the author does. His chapters are broken down by counties he visits, like this:

Custer County	*Warren County*
Broken Bow	Remembrance
Mason City	A Warren Record
Solomon Butcher	City of Water
	The Probability of Actuality
Saline County	Colleges
Dynasty	
Saline	
Roll of the Dice	
Trees	
Cousins	

and so on . . .

COMBINING STRUCTURES
(Kids! Don't Try This at Home!)

When Certified Genealogist Roger D. Joslyn asked me to write a narrative family history for a client he was working for, it was to be an all-my-ancestors, back-to-the-immigrant-ancestor project for the client's paternal and maternal lines. Roger and I discussed the structure the narrative would take, and at first we thought the best way to handle it was as I've described for this type of book on page 18: one section or chapter for each surname, with the surname sections arranged in alphabetical order. But as I got into the project, I wasn't happy with the way things were turning out. It made the families feel disconnected rather than linked. I wanted to show how all of these families came together, so I developed the Carmack Formula for Structuring an All-My-

Ancestors Book, using a combination of several different structures.

The overall structure was parallel to convergent, but the couple that I needed to merge were the client's parents, who had no common ancestry. This meant I had eleven generations on the dad's side and twelve generations on the mom's side to cover before they would meet, marry, and unite the ancestry of the client! I toyed with dividing the book into two parts. Part one would begin with the dad's earliest known ancestor and be written chronologically to the present where dad is born and meets mom. Part two would do the same with mom's ancestry, then part three would be when mom and dad meet, marry, and the lines converge. I felt, however, that readers would have a problem with the shift in time periods. They would begin reading a narrative about the colonial period, come forward to the twentieth century, do another mental time-travel back to colonial America when they began part two, and then have to come forward in time again. To me, that interrupted the reader's flow—although it certainly would have been the easiest way to write the story. But, no. I wanted it to be more creative and to have more continuity.

Instead, I wrote the dad's part in reverse chronological order, starting with dad in chapter one, then as I brought him to the brink of death, I did a line break and shifted to a memory he had recorded about his childhood and parents, creating a transition backward to his parents' lives. Each chapter pushed the ancestry back another generation, reaching the earliest known ancestors in colonial America. Then, while the reader's mindset was still in the colonies, I began part two—the mom's ancestry—and told it in chronological order from the earliest known maternal colonial ancestors forward to mom. Part three then merged the histories, with mom and dad meeting and getting married. Whew!

But wait—there's more. Within each chapter, different sections discussed different family lines as they lived parallel to one another in time. For each family section,

I used the altered chronological structure: that is, I began with a grabber lead, then transitioned to the beginning of that family's story and told it chronologically. To a degree, each section could have been a stand-alone essay; but I kept them tied together by emphasizing a common thread, or by comparing and contrasting one family or generation with another.

Below is the chapter outline based on *American Lives and Lines* by Roger D. Joslyn and Sharon DeBartolo Carmack (the client's parents' names have been changed).

THE BOOK FEATURES TWENTY-FIVE FAMILY SURNAMES AND IS DIVIDED INTO TWO VOLUMES

Volume One: Narrative
(Parallel to convergent structure)

PART I: Philip McCann's Ancestors (client's father), writing from his parents backward to colonial times (reverse chronology)

PART II: Ethel Hunt's Ancestors (client's mother), writing from colonial times forward to her parents (chronological), but each essay within a chapter written in altered chronological structure

PART III: Philip and Ethel (chronological, beginning with their meeting)

PART IV: Philip and Ethel's children and grandchildren (chronological)

- The main characters are Philip McCann and Ethel Hunt (the client's parents)—transitions will describe them in relation to their ancestors, as shown in this paragraph:

> Philip's great-grandfathers—William McCann, George Goss, Alfred Martin, and Joel Townsend—made a difference in Fulton County. Along with his great-grandmothers—Louisa McCann, Elizabeth Goss, Hannah Martin, and Vesta Townsend—they raised large families, survived personal losses from illness and war, and taught their children good,

Christian values. They had what was known as the "American pioneer spirit," which they inherited from their parents, Philip's second great-grandparents, who helped settle the wilderness of Ohio and Kentucky.

- A generation of ancestors is discussed in each chapter; each family within that chapter is discussed separately in a section that begins with a new subhead and is told in an altered chronological order (parallel construction).
- Mini drop-line charts with dates are placed before each subhead to give readers a visual guide.

Volume Two: Family Summaries

Surname sections are arranged alphabetically, with genealogies presented in chronological order from past to present.

Narrative Chapter Outline Example

PART I, Chapter 5: "A Place Among Nations" (chapter opens with Thomas and Sarah McQueen)
Family sections:

- "Remember the Ladies"—Abraham and Sarah Collins
- "We Are Peaceable"—Davis and Elizabeth Allen
- Post-War Expansion of the Nation—Nehemiah and Margaret Park and Bailey Williams
- Casting a Vote for Basil—Jacob Goss
- Kids, Kids, and More Kids—William and Elizabeth Love

Here's how I described the structure in the book's introduction

The book, *American Lives and Lines*, is divided into two sections in two volumes. The first section (Volume One)—the *Lives*—is a narrative treatment in seventeen chapters. These chapters tell the story of the ancestors of the client's father and mother, Philip and Ethel (Hunt) McCann, their family, and descendants. The family summaries are in the second section (Volume Two)—the *Lines*—with documented treatments of the ancestors of Tom and Ethel, including all children and, in most cases, the grandchildren of these ancestors.

Structure of the Narrative

The narrative section of *American Lives and Lines* is unique and is meant to be read as a story from start to finish. Those who attempt to isolate one line of interest, reading only those narratives, may become frustrated, since a connective thread and story line is woven throughout.

Part I covers the ancestors of Philip McCann; Part II deals with the ancestors of Ethel Hunt; Part III covers Philip and Ethel's lives and concludes with biographical sketches of their children and grandchildren. What makes this narrative unique is that it does not begin in the past with Philip's earliest American ancestor and come forward in time; on the contrary, it starts with Philip's parents, Tom and Iva McCann, with each succeeding chapter in Part I taking the reader backward in time to Philip's earliest known colonial ancestors. Part II, which begins Ethel's ancestry, however, reads in the more traditional past-to-present chronology. It starts by continuing the overall narrative in colonial America and brings the story forward in time to when Ethel and Philip meet and marry (Part III).

Philip and Ethel are the main characters in this family history narrative. As such, the ancestors under discussion are identified by their relationship to these individuals. A generation of ancestors is discussed within each chapter; thus, chapter one in Part I covers Philip's parents, chapter two his grandparents, chapter three his great-grandparents, chapter four his second great-grandparents, and so forth. Ethel's part works in reverse, with chapter

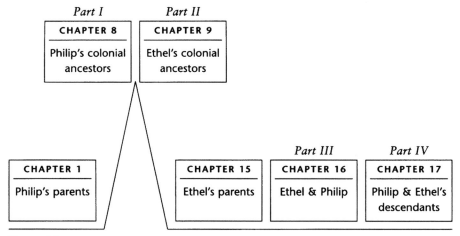

Figure 4-1
Carmack Formula for writing a multi-generation family history.

nine dealing with her sixth through ninth great-grandparents, chapter ten her fourth and fifth great-grandparents, chapter eleven her third great-grandparents, and so forth.

With a huge cast of characters in an all-my-ancestors treatment such as this, drop-line charts appear in each chapter subsection to give the reader a visual guide. Each of these charts brings the ancestral line under discussion down to Philip or Ethel. For each ancestor, we show dates of birth and death when known or approximated. . . .

As you can imagine, this was an extremely complex family history to write, but if you're up to the challenge, by all means, give it a try. I'm not sure I'd ever tackle such a project again. Unfortunately, this family history was privately distributed—out of respect for the living descendants and their privacy—so no copies are presently available in libraries for you to read. However, the appendixes include a couple of narrative essays about deceased generations, so you can see how they are structured.

Regardless of which structure you use, all your ma-

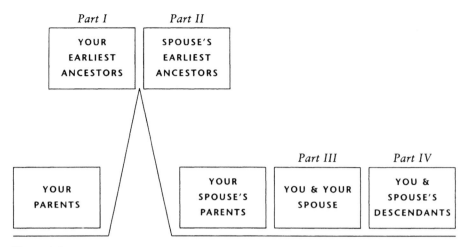

Figure 4-2
Variation of the Carmack Formula, focusing on your ancestry and your spouse's in one book.

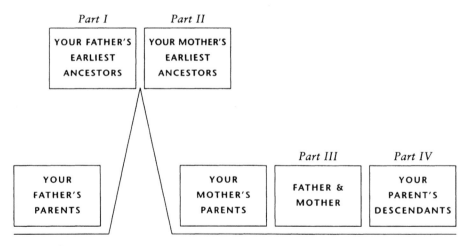

Figure 4-3
Variation of the Carmack Formula, focusing on your paternal and maternal ancestry.

terial needs to flow into one cohesive narrative, weaving common threads together throughout the story. Mull over the options and imagine your family history narrative as it might be written using each of these different structures. You'll know which one feels right to you.

Isolating Themes in Your Family History

The author is re-creating a moment in time, presenting an experience for us to feel and think about rather than merely feeding us information or even ideas.
—CHARLEY KEMPTHORNE, *FOR ALL TIME*

W hen I think of the word *themes*, two things come to mind: English term papers and amusement parks. Since the former seems to have a negative connotation for a lot of people, myself included, let's think of family history themes in terms of an amusement park. When I was a teen, I worked at an amusement park in Rye, Westchester County, New York, called Playland. That park didn't have a theme at the time. Without a theme, what have you got? Roller coasters, merry-go-rounds, Ferris wheels, train rides, and those typical rides that spin, lift, toss, and drop you at hundreds of miles per hour and make you sick. (I'm already feeling dizzy.) Sure, each ride had a cutesy, enticing, fun, and exciting name like the "Dragon Coaster"; but lacking a theme, Playland was just another run-of-the-mill amusement park. Now think of amusement parks like Disneyland, Epcot Center, Sea World, and Universal Studios. Each has a theme, hence the name *theme parks*. They pretty much have the same or similar rides as Playland, but they are more entertaining and interesting because their themes can make us feel like we're in a movie, visiting a foreign country, or exploring the ocean.

Now consider family history. If you strip your family history of themes, what have you got? Names, dates, and places—just like the typical, ordinary, rides in Playland. But give it some themes—such as Frontier Life, or Traveling in Steerage to America, or the Depression—and now you have Disneyland.

Assuming you have done the tedious task of taking all of the information from your family group sheets and compiling it into family summaries, and that you have added any additional information from your files and records that wouldn't fit on the family group sheet, now we can start looking at how we'll transform Playland into Disneyland. Pull out one of the generations that you plan to write about so that you can develop the subplots or themes. At this stage, it doesn't matter which family you choose. It can be the earliest generation, the most recent one, or one somewhere in the middle. What you'll be doing now is locating themes from which you will identify topics for your background research, and on which you will eventually write. These should be topics that will put flesh on the bones. Start by categorizing your ancestors into general groups, such as by occupation, by ethnic group, by life event, by locality, and so on. For example, if your ancestor was a farmer in Kansas in 1870, one of the themes you'll develop in the narrative is what it was like to be a Midwestern farmer in the mid- to late-1800s. If your ancestor was a dry goods merchant in Philadelphia in the 1830s, your theme will be life in the dry goods business. If your ancestor was a plantation mistress in South Carolina, then a logical topic to research is plantation life from the landowner's point of view.

Step By Step

THEMES IN THE FEARN FAMILY

Let's look at the Fearn family summary again on page 25. What events or experiences jump out at you that you might write about? Before you read the next couple of paragraphs to see what themes I identified, look at the summary and make some notes. Then come back to this page and see if you found the same items I did, or if you discovered others.

Perhaps Charles's military experience is the first theme

to jump out at you. Most genealogists feel comfortable writing about this topic because they know how to find compiled military service records and pension files, so that's a good place to start. That's one theme you might develop in your narrative. What are some of the others?

For More Info

If you haven't discovered how to obtain military records yet, see James Neagles's *U.S. Military Records* (Salt Lake City: Ancestry, Inc., 1994).

Martha accompanied her husband to his duty assignments and gave birth to her children at different military installations. What would that have been like? There's another theme to explore. Martha and Charles lost a child in infancy, so a possible theme there would be handling the loss and grief. Martha also belonged to the Methodist Episcopal Church, and she was a member of the Eastern Star. We might develop the theme of women's participation in such organizations. After his military service, Charles worked as a druggist. We can explore that trade and what the requirements were for working as a druggist in the early twentieth century.

Do you see other, underlying themes, especially ones that lend themselves to conflict and drama? What about the cultural and climatic adjustments necessitated by moving to the Arizona desert after having grown up in Ohio? Or the struggles of bearing and rearing children in a desert environment?

MAKING A THEMATIC CHRONOLOGY

A method to help you organize and sort out the themes within a family group is to make a list or chart similar to the one on page 49, placing events in chronological order, since that is likely how you'll be discussing them in your narrative.

Tip

In the theme column, raise why, how, and what questions, rather than just listing topics. As you research or write, more questions will come to you to add to this category. In essence, these questions are those you would ask your ancestors if they were still alive for you to conduct oral history interviews with. In STEP 7, you'll see how to go about researching the answers.

You'll want to make a chronology for each family group you'll be covering in your narrative. It will become

CHRONOLOGY CHART AND THEMES		
Date	Event	Theme(s)
1874	Charles enlisted in the Army as hospital steward	*Why* might he have enlisted? *What* type of work would Charles do as a hospital steward?
1878	Charles married Martha	*How* would her life change now that she's an Army wife? *How* will she cope with frequent moves?
1879	Martha gave birth to first child	*What* was childbirth like in the late nineteenth century?
1881	Martha gave birth to second child who died the follwng year	*What* caused infant mortality during this time period? *How* would Martha and her family have grieved?
1882	The family arrived in Arizona Territory	*How* did the family adjust to desert life?

your prompt for research topics to add flesh to the bones.

Uh-oh. Are you feeling overwhelmed again? If so, you may have too many generations or family groups you want to cover in one volume. Now's the time to refocus your picture. Will your book be more manageable if you include only three or four generations or family groups instead of six? Don't be afraid to crop this particular family photo. After all, unless you are driven by a client or a demanding relative, it's totally up to you how much you will treat in your book. Get the experience of one small book under your belt, then tackle a major volume.

For More Info

For more on historical theme topics, see Katherine Scott Sturdevant's "Elements of Social History," pages 16-19, and "Conceptual Frameworks," pages 198-200, in *Bringing Your Family History to Life Through Social History*; David Hackett Fischer's "Folkways," in *Albion's Seed: Four British Folkways in America*, pages 8-9; and Patricia Law Hatcher's "Context," in *Producing a Quality Family History*, pages 138-143.

There are no dull subjects. There are only dull writers.
—H.L. MENCKEN

FINDING THEMES IN "DULL" FAMILIES

We all have them: dull ancestors or families, people who apparently didn't do anything particularly noteworthy in their lifetimes. They were born, married, and died— and it would seem from your research that this is literally all they did. They didn't go to court. They didn't participate in any wars. They didn't die of unusual causes. They worked from sunup until sundown on the family farm.

Ah-ha! There's the theme: the work they did on the farm. What kind of farming did they do? If agricultural schedules don't exist to tell you, research what other farmers in the area were growing. Remember, your readers don't know what daily life was like on a farm in Nebraska in the 1800s. You need to tell them. Every family has something you can research and write about, even if it appears to be mundane. You make it come alive with your description of how people lived, worked, dressed, ate, traveled, and so forth.

Let's not forget the women in your family history narrative. The childbirth experience is one you can easily cover for each generation. Giving birth in the 1700s was much different from giving birth in the 1800s. In the 1700s, a woman likely gave birth squatting on a midwife's stool, which was a low chair with an open seat. A woman might kneel, sit on another woman's lap, or she may have stood up for the birth, supported by two friends. Women in the mid- to late-1800s gave birth lying on their backs. While we can't know for certain how any of our female ancestors gave birth, that is a theme that you can research and explore in your narrative. (See STEP 14 for techniques on speculation and inference.)

Notes

Give this some thought: Will you be leaving your women ancestors' lives incomplete and inaccurate if you ignore topics like menstruation, pregnancy, reproductive control, and menopause?

Possible Themes to Cover

On page 51 is a list of themes to be looking for in your ancestors' lives.

Keep in mind, that if you write about a man's military experience, you should also write about what mom and the kids were doing while dad was being a soldier. Likewise, if you write about mom's childbirth experience, consider what dad and the other kids might have been doing at the time. Even though I've segregated themes according to gender, always remember that experiences often meld. For just about every theme, there will be another side to the story. Don't become so focused on an event in one person's life that you forget to look at others who may have been affected by that event.

POSSIBLE THEMES TO COVER IN YOUR ANCESTORS' LIVES			
For Couples and Families	**For Men**	**For Women**	**For Children**

• Migration/Emigration/
  Immigration
• Geography and
  environment
• Land ownership
• Community and
  neighbors
• Ethnicity
• Marriage
• Family structure
• Living quarters
• Food and eating habits
• Clothing
	• Military
	  experience
	• Occupation
	  and work
	• Religious
	  and civic
	  involvement
	• Education
	• Leisure time
	  activities
		• Childbirth
		• Child rearing
		• Reproductive cycle
		• House and
		  domestic work
		• Work outside (or
		  inside) the home to
		  supplement
		  income
		• Religious and civic
		  involvement
		• Education
			• Education
			• Chores
			• Play

As mentioned earlier, also look for hidden themes: those that may add underlying conflict and drama to your narrative. For example, suppose that from one of the censuses you discover that the household contained a child who was a deaf-mute or had some other disability. Research disabilities in that era to explore how that family might have coped with their situation. Or maybe a person is labeled idiotic or insane. What did that mean during the time period in which he or she lived? How would that person have been treated, both medically and socially? In STEP 7, we'll look at how to find the answers to questions like these. For now, note the unusual as well as the usual.

Reminder

NATIONAL HISTORICAL THEMES

When first attempting to write their family history as narrative, many genealogists look for famous national events to weave into their story. There is nothing wrong with that, provided you show how the events relate to the family under discussion. Charles Fearn, for example, was born 26 March 1852. Some genealogists might search a historical timeline on the Internet to find out what was happening in our nation when Charles was born. They would learn that *Uncle Tom's Cabin* was published that year, so they tie the events together in an attempt to place Charles into a historical context. I confess: when I was a baby genealogist, I thought that's what putting ancestors into historical perspective meant; but I learned later that I had missed the boat. I didn't write the following paragraph; Kathy Sturdevant and I adapted it from an actual family history and exaggerated only slightly.

> Elizabeth Jordon was the youngest of five children born to Robert and Catherine Jordon. Elizabeth was born in Jacksonville, Florida, about 1893, the same year Hawaii was proclaimed a republic. Jacksonville was named for Andrew Jackson, who attacked the Spanish and Indians there eighty years before. In 1913, just one year after the *Titanic* sank, Elizabeth married George Anderson. World War I brought the birth of their first two children. In 1929, after the St. Valentine's Day Massacre, their last child was born. Within a few months, the stock market crashed. Elizabeth's first grandchild was born 6 May 1945, and two days later the Nazis surrendered. Elizabeth died in 1973 during the Watergate hearings.

Notice how the famous events have nothing to do with the Jordon family, yet the way the paragraph is written implies a cause-and-effect relationship: "In 1913, just one year after the *Titanic* sank, Elizabeth married George Anderson." Unless Elizabeth married George *because* the *Titanic* sank, there's no relevancy here, I'm afraid. And if "Elizabeth's first grandchild was born 6 May 1945, and two days later the Nazis surrendered," that must have been *some* baby to cause the Nazis to give up!

Kathy and I use this example in our lectures, dubbing this type of attempt at placing ancestors into historical perspective as "*Titanic* Syndrome." Now, if the author had written: "Elizabeth's first grandchild was born 6 May 1945, while her husband, George, was in Europe fighting the Nazis. She recalled her relief when two days later the Nazis surrendered," then the famous historical event has relevance to the family, and we can understand why the author included it. However, just throwing in an unrelated historical event feels awkward and inappropriate. So if you are including themes from a larger, national scope, make sure you connect these with the family you are writing about.

HANDLING SENSITIVE THEMES

Sooner or later you'll run into the family skeletons: themes that are sensitive to deal with in a family history narrative. In *My Wild Irish Rose*, I had to address suicide, domestic violence, depression, mental illness, premarital sex and pregnancy, and alcoholism. Sure, I could have left these unpleasant issues out, but then my narrative would not have been completely honest. People have faults and failings, but it's not our job to judge them. It's our job to portray our ancestors in as honest a light as we can. According to Linda Wagner-Martin in *Telling Women's Lives: The New Biography* (page 9),

Warning

> The biographer has the responsibility to determine what life events have been most important to the subject. Even if the subject does not reveal or write about an experience, the biographer has the authority to place that event within the narrative. The biographer's art is that of refashioning and revising the life narrative, bringing to it more background and, it is hoped, more insight than the subject may ever have had.

How you handle the sensitive issue is perhaps more important than the skeleton itself. I wouldn't recommend emulating this writer's tell-all family history:

> They had no children, but [Keith] had a by-sexual [*sic*] condition that two months in —, New York, could not cure him of his way of life.

> While in the service he got to drinking and was to
> the point where he was an alcoholic. . . . My par-
> ents['] hearts were broken to know they had a son
> who drank so.

Your family history narrative is not the appropriate fo-
rum for family or personal therapy, revenge, or to per-
petuate family squabbles.

Keep in mind that with changing mores and values,
what may have been a skeleton fifty years ago may not
be one now; or maybe something that wasn't a skeleton
then has become one. For example, my daughter, Laurie,
worked as a telemarketer one summer. This is our family's skeleton that I don't want perpetuated in a family
history someday. As a more serious example, throughout
history and up until the late nineteenth century, abortion
did not carry the stigma it does today. It was a fact of
life and a method for limiting family size when no other
reliable means existed. Today it carries a stigma; so how
will you address the issue in your family history if you
discover that a relative died from a botched abortion in
1844? Premarital sex today is not nearly the scandalous
activity it was, say, fifty years ago. How will you handle
the story of a woman who conceived out of wedlock
and then married her lover? Miscegenation (mixed-race
marriage) was not only a scandal but illegal in the South
and even some northern states. Today, it's commonplace.
One way to handle sensitive issues is to simply report
them, without any kind of judgment, as in this example.

> Twenty-one-year-old William Zesinger very likely
> met his bride, Rosalie Steinegger, at their common
> church: the German Reformed Salem Congregation
> in Philadelphia. She, too, had been raised in that
> city, the daughter of immigrants from Switzerland
> and Germany, just like William. He married Rosa-
> lie, a handsome young woman, in this same church
> on 24 March 1873. Although most of their court-
> ship no doubt took place at church social events

and in the company of family and friends, like other young lovers, William and Rosalie managed to arrange occasional, private meetings. As nineteen-year-old Rosalie walked down the aisle in her wedding gown, white gloves, and veil, she was three months pregnant. Rosalie gave birth on 30 September 1873 in their home on Julianna Street in Philadelphia. She and her husband named their son for William's father, Rudolph.

Another way is more subtle, letting readers draw their own conclusions

Janie's life was not an easy one. Her husband, Ralph, was an aggressive man, who expected special treatment. Sometimes Ralph's aggressiveness turned violent. "The way he came down the stairs," said Janie's niece Kathryn, "we knew something was coming. We'd leave the house. We had a large piece of property, but even sitting on the swing, we could hear Aunt Janie screaming for mercy and crying in pain. It seemed the more she cried, the more aggressive it made him. And he was a strong man. He was a motion picture operator. He had to move the heavy cameras, equipment, and film cans. He also worked out on a punching bag. I used to sit out there on the swing and hear her crying and screaming, and I'd think, 'For God's sake, why don't you take it out on the punching bag instead of her.' " Ralph never laid a hand on anyone else in the family, only his wife.

In the above paragraph, it wasn't necessary to say "Janie was a victim of domestic violence" or "Janie's husband beat her"; the scene makes it quite clear what was happening. "Showing" can have a much greater impact and evoke more reader sympathy than "telling." (More on this in STEPS 9 and 10.)

Of course, the decision to include sensitive issues will depend on your comfort level with the situation, as well as that of your relatives. Sometimes it helps to put the controversial topic into historical perspective (see STEP 14). We all recognize that slavery is unacceptable, but when you place slave-owning ancestors into their day and time, we have a better understanding of it. We don't need to make excuses for our ancestors, apologize for them, or justify what they did. We simply report on the facts of their lives, whether we agree with their decisions or not. After all, we aren't responsible for their actions any more than they would be responsible for how we turned out. As Kathy Sturdevant says in her book *Bringing Your Family History to Life Through Social History*, you should take "no pride, no shame, no credit, no blame" for your ancestors' lives and actions.

All right. With your "theme park" ideas ready to implement, now we'll turn to gathering the building materials to make the rides. Or, in family history lingo, we'll start researching the background material to make the themes come alive.

Revisiting Genealogical Sources

Few seem interested in understanding how the family narrator can use [genealogical] sources to develop an accurate and interesting family narrative.
—LAWRENCE P. GOULDRUP,
WRITING THE FAMILY NARRATIVE

hew! I bet you didn't realize how much preparation goes into writing your family history narrative. You're probably anxious to begin writing, but remember that research is part of the writing process, and there are still just a few more steps left to gather the background material that will transform the foreground (your ancestors' names, dates, and places) into a story—or to stretch our amusement theme park analogy just a bit further, a Playland into a Disneyland. In this step and the next, we're going to look at some different research approaches. First, you'll be revisiting the genealogical sources you used to gather specific information on your ancestors. Then, we'll broaden research even more to find that historical context mentioned in previous chapters.

In STEP 5, you made a thematic chronology. Keep this handy for this step, as well, but now let's make a checklist of the localities your ancestors lived in and during which time periods. Here's one example using the Charles Fearn family:

Step By Step

Localities and Time Periods
for the Charles Henry Fearn Family

Columbus, Ohio	1874–1878
Baton Rouge, Louisiana	1878–1879
Fort D.A. Russell, Wyoming	1880
Little Rock, Arkansas	1882
Fort Grant, Arizona	1882–1885
Fort Lowell, Arizona	1885–1886
Columbus, Ohio	1886–1916

If you are dealing with several generations and several family groups in your narrative, you may want to arrange your checklist of localities and time periods as in Figure 6-1 on page 59 first, then further detail the localities and time periods for each family group. Remember, there's no right or wrong way to make this checklist. Keep it simple so that it will be easy for you to follow and work with.

Armed with this checklist and your thematic chronology, you're ready to head back to the library and dig out the documents you've gathered on each family. Your first goal is to find out what was going on in the places where your ancestors lived during the time they lived there. One of the most helpful sources for this type of background data will be local and county histories.

LOCAL AND COUNTY HISTORIES

While many local and county histories have a negative reputation among genealogists for inaccurate genealogical data, these books are excellent resources for background details about the area in which your ancestors lived. Do keep in mind, however, that some local and county histories were a means to promote a community, so take inflated claims of "paradise" with a grain of salt. Of course, local and county histories will vary in the information they contain, but look for topics that will give you details to place your ancestors into the appropriate setting:

topography	transportation
geology	commercial industries and
aborigines	manufacturers

CHAPTER OUTLINE WITH LOCALITIES AND TIME PERIODS		
Generation 7—Fourth Great-Grandparents		
1. **Bainter** (Godfrey & Marg)	here by 1771	Germany; MD; Muskingum Co., OH
Sprague (Jas & Mary Spooner)	(1760–1840)	Smithfield, RI; Coal Run, OH; Hardwick, MA; Bedford Co., PA
Generation 6—Third Great-Grandparents		
2. **Bainter** (Geo & Lydia Sprague)	(1771–1849)	MD; Muskingum Co., OH
McCashland (Ben & Eliz. Wheatley)	here by 1797	Ireland; Winchester, VA; Wayne Co., IN
Hague (Jonah & Martha Whiteacre)	here by 1767	Faquier Co., VA; Muskingum Co., OH
Generation 5—Second Great-Grandparents		
3. **Bainter** (John & Katherine Bruner)	(1797–1832)	PA; Muskingum Co., OH
McCashland/Hague (John & Maria)	(1797–1862)	Fauquier Co., VA; Muskingum Co., OH
Fearn (John & Marg. Brooks)	imm. 1838	England; Franklin Co., OH
Generation 4—Great-Grandparents		
4. **Bainter/McCashland** (Arza & Elvira)	(1824–1906)	Muskingum Co., OH; Columbus, OH
Zesinger/Bauer (Johann & Catherine)	imm. by 1840	Switzerland/Germany; Philadelphia, PA
Steinegger (Hans & Veronica Vondrach)	imm. by 1840	Switzerland/Germany; Philadelphia, PA
Fearn (Geo & Anna Snyder)	(1820–1887)	England; Franklin Co., OH; Groveport, OH; VA
Generation 3—Grandparents		
5. **Fearn/Bainter** (Chas & Martha)	(1852–1928)	Groveport, Columbus, OH; Muskingum Co., OH, South Bend, IN
Zesinger/Steinegger (Wm & Rosalie)	(1852–1895)	Philadelphia, PA; Canton, OH; Newport, KY

Figure 6-1

For a multi-generation book, outline your chapters by the families you'll cover, where they lived, and during what time period. Creating an outline like this will help you focus your background research. This outline utilizes the parallel to convergent structure discussed on page 38.

settlement patterns	trade organizations
county seats	banks and bankers
founding of towns	post offices
early pioneer	cemeteries
reminiscences	the telegraph
War for Independence	inns, taverns, and hotels
peace and independence	religious denominations
War of 1812	the press
Civil War	libraries, societies, and
progress after the Civil	associations
War	literature and music
municipal government	amusements
education	bench and bar
fires and fire companies	medical services
monuments, parks, and	secret societies and orders
squares	manners and customs

When you revisit local and county histories, you are not looking for your ancestors' names—unless you haven't checked these sources already for specific details on your ancestors. **Your goal this time is to gather information on the places your ancestors lived.** What was the terrain like? What events occurred in the area while your ancestors lived there? What folk celebrations did people attend, such as county fairs or barn raisings? Is there information on an organization your ancestor belonged to? What impact did various wars have on the community while your ancestor was living there?

Research Tip

You're no longer looking for the *who, when,* and *where*: the names, dates and places specific to your ancestors. You're now looking for the *why, how,* and *what*: broader information that explains why things were the way they were, how something happened, what life was like. This is what will put flesh on the bones of your narrative.

Finding Local and County Histories

You'll find hundreds of local and county histories at the Family History Library in Salt Lake City, Utah. Check its catalog online at <www.familysearch.org>

under your locality of interest. Unfortunately, not all of these histories have been microfilmed so that you can rent and view them at your local Family History Center. You'll also find local and county histories in public and state libraries and archives for the desired locality; but again, these may not be available through interlibrary loan. Some Web sites may have digitized county histories where the copyright has expired, but the odds of finding the one you need may be slim to none. I'm afraid this is research you will need to do in person either at the Family History Library (if you have several localities to check) or onsite at the locality's repositories. If the county history is still in print, you may be able to purchase a copy, but be forewarned that these books can be quite costly ($30 to $100).

You might get some information about an area by writing to its Chamber of Commerce for brochures or booklets. Or try consulting travel and tourist agencies. For example, if you belong to AAA (American Automobile Association), you have access to its free state guides, which give overviews of towns and cities. This will be helpful, but it won't give you the kind of historical detail a local or county history would. Conversely, these booklets will give you mileage information, so if you need to give a point of reference for a small community in your narrative (*The rural community of Simla is forty-five miles east of Colorado Springs.*) these sources will be ideal.

Another possible source for local history will be town and county historians, county historical societies, and museum curators in the area. They may have booklets about the locality that you can purchase. In the case of the Fearn family, it turned out that the best source for background information on military outposts in Wyoming and Arizona Territory was the museum curators at these facilities. Between telephone interviews with the curators and brochures they sent me, I learned enough to describe these places in detail.

For More Info

For more on using the Family History Library, see Paula Stuart Warren and James W. Warren's *Your Guide to the Family History Library* (Cincinnati: Betterway Books, 2001).

Finding Local History for Foreign Localities

If you are writing about localities in foreign countries, use the same approaches. Remember, however, that unless you're dealing with an English-speaking country, the sources you uncover likely will be in that country's language. I had this problem while writing *Italians in Transition*, half of which took place in Terlizzi, Italy, in the region of Apulia. I began with American sources, such as general Italian histories and travel guidebooks. Then I went to regional Italian cookbooks, which gave splendid overviews of the people and food of Apulia. Unfortunately, Terlizzi was too small a community to be discussed in the American sources I found.

Nothing can compare, of course, with a trip to the locality to see the town firsthand, but if I want to portray the town during the 1800s, when my ancestors lived there, I need a local history. In Terlizzi, there were a couple of community histories at the local library, but, naturally, they were written in Italian, which I can't read. My only other option was to hire someone to translate the town's promotional brochures and to take notes for me—in English—from the histories of Terlizzi. If this is your only option as well, you need to make clear to the researcher the kind of information you are looking for: that is, details that will tell you about the people and daily life of that community.

Internet Source

For general statistical information about a country, visit the CIA's World Factbook site at <www.cia.gov/cia/publications/factbook/index.html>. It provides a map and general data about geography, people, government, economy, communications, transportation, military, and transnational issues.

GENEALOGICAL SOURCES FOR BACKGROUND

In STEP 3, I listed genealogical sources that you should have checked for specific information on your ancestors before you undertook the project of writing your family history. **Now let's revisit those sources for broader information that could provide additional details for your narrative.** Using that same list, I've annotated each source with some of the general information you might look for. (Remember, if you don't have experience using or finding these sources, consult Croom's *Unpuzzling Your Past* and her *Genealogist's Companion and Sourcebook*.)

Step By Step

Cemetery and funeral home records. In the cemetery, you'll want to take a broad look at your ancestors' final resting places. Besides noting who was buried in nearby graves (in case further research reveals a relationship), also note items like the artwork and symbols on your ancestors' headstones. Do these reveal any memberships in organizations popular in your ancestor's community? By the type of headstones, you can also tell if the community was well-off or economically depressed. Note the type of grave decorations, foliage, and landscaping. In your narrative, you may include photographs of ancestors' grave markers, but also describe the cemetery for your readers.

Some funeral home records give explicit information about funeral costs, as well as how the deceased was buried—right down to the type of casket and clothing the deceased was buried in. Use these details as well in your narrative.

Church records. Besides doing some background research on the church your ancestors attended (its founding, religious denomination, ministers, and so forth), look to see if any minutes still exist for members' activities. As they say, if you're looking for politics and gossip, look at churches and academia. Quaker meeting minutes in particular are often quite detailed, and many of these have been microfilmed or abstracted and published. Check the multivolume *Encyclopedia of American Quaker Genealogy* by William Wade Hinshaw (Baltimore: Genealogical Publishing Co., 1999). If you find in the church minutes that your ancestor was disciplined for some action, try to discover why this behavior was frowned upon, and what typical disciplinary actions took place (see STEP 7). Even if your ancestor is not named in any church minutes, what was going on in the church while your ancestor attended it?

City directories. Some city directories have what is called a reverse directory, criss-cross directory, or a householder's index. If available, this is the section you want to look for. It's arranged by street and house number, so for

For More Info

For more information on cemeteries and funeral home records, see Sharon DeBartolo Carmack's *Your Guide to Cemetery Research* (Cincinnati: Betterway Books, 2002).

the time periods between censuses, you can find out who your ancestor's neighbors were and get a sense of the neighborhood community. City directories will also tell you what businesses were in the area that your ancestor might have patronized. Gather addresses for the businesses, then, if there's a map in the city directory, see how close the businesses were to where your ancestor lived. By analyzing the contemporary map in the directory, you can also discover where your ancestor lived in relation to the main part of town, any rivers, lakes, train tracks, churches, cemeteries, fire departments, libraries, parks and playgrounds, schools, and banks. City directories might also contain information (perhaps brief histories) of the city, listings of organizations (sometimes with names of officers or members), population figures, voting and governmental information, and other minutiae to help round out your narrative.

Family histories and genealogies. Search library catalogs to determine what's already been written about the family. Recheck those published family histories and genealogies to see if these offer any details about daily life and community. You might also look for background material in the genealogies of other families who lived in the same locality as your ancestor. Check for published family histories of the neighbors you've identified on census records.

Family sources and oral history. Items such as family Bibles, letters, diaries, and oral history interviews will be a key part of your family history narrative. (The use of oral history will be discussed more fully in STEP 12.) Of course, letters and diaries can contain rich details to really bring your ancestors to life. Use quotes from them to reveal your ancestors' character (see STEP 10). If you have letters or diaries that could make a book in and of themselves, make sure you read and follow the advice in Katherine Scott Sturdevant's *Organizing and Preserving Your Heirloom Documents* (Cincinnati: Betterway Books, 2002). For ideas on using other home sources, specifically family photographs and artifacts, see Sturdevant's *Bringing Your*

Family History to Life Through Social History (Cincinnati: Betterway Books, 2000) and Maureen A. Taylor's *Uncovering Your Ancestry Through Family Photographs* (Cincinnati: Betterway Books, 2000).

Immigration records. If your ancestors became naturalized before 1906, records for those procedures may give you nothing more than the immigrant's name and country of origin. Post–1906 naturalization records, however, may contain a wealth of detail you can use to your advantage in your narrative, right down to a general physical description of your ancestor.

Passenger lists of the late nineteenth and early twentieth centuries will give you more specific information on your ancestors, but don't forget to look at the broader picture here as well. Estimate how many people were traveling on the ship by counting the number of people per page and multiplying it by the number of pages. Assuming there weren't hundreds upon hundreds of passengers, tally the number of males and females, adults and children, family groups and single passengers traveling with your ancestors. If you are dealing with passenger lists that identify the village of origin or birth, find out who else from your ancestor's village traveled on the same ship, even though those people might not have been traveling with your ancestor directly. In STEP 7, we'll look at how to find statistics on the ships themselves.

Land and tax records. You never know what land records will reveal about your ancestors that you can include in your narrative, but at the least they will give a legal description of the land your ancestor owned or lived on. If your ancestor owned land in a colony or state that used the metes and bounds land survey system, this description adds graphic detail about the topography and neighbors. Platting your ancestor's land to use as an illustration shows readers exactly how the land boundaries looked. Also take a look at land transactions that occurred within a few days of your ancestor's. You might discover something in those deeds that relates to your ancestor's land dealings.

For More Info

For more on immigration and naturalization, see Sharon DeBartolo Carmack's *A Genealogist's Guide to Discovering Your Immigrant and Ethnic Ancestors* (Cincinnati: Betterway Books, 2000), John Philip Colletta's *They Came in Ships* (Salt Lake City: Ancestry, Inc., 2002), and Loretto Dennis Szucs's *They Became Americans* (Salt Lake City: Ancestry, Inc., 1998).

For More Info

For more on land records and platting property lines, see Patricia Law Hatcher's *Locating Your Roots: Discover Your Ancestors Using Land Records* (Cincinnati: Betterway Books, 2003).

From tax records, you can learn not only about taxable property and personal items your ancestor owned, but also about the community as a whole. What were others in the vicinity taxed on? How does this compare or contrast with your ancestor? Was your ancestor wealthy, poor, or among the middle class?

Military service records, pensions, bounty land. Genealogists seem to have no trouble seeing the broader picture when it comes to military service. Once they determine the correct regiment from military service records, their natural instinct is to find regimental histories. Although these might not name your ancestor, they detail the battles and engagements in which the regiment was involved.

Pension records are often rich sources for a narrative, especially if a claim was initially denied, or the serviceman or his widow had to provide voluminous affidavits to support the claim. Look at the Fearn family narrative in Appendix A, pages 227-228. From affidavits about Charles's final days, I obtained quotes from his widow and friends about his condition and suffering. For another narrative, an affidavit from the Revolutionary War pension file of Thomas McQueen and his brother, Joshua, gave an explicit account of Tom's capture in Crawford's campaign and how he was treated as a prisoner. (See STEP 12 for how to use dialogue.)

For More Info

For more on military records, see James C. Neagles's *U.S. Military Records* (Salt Lake City: Ancestry, Inc., 1994).

When using bounty land information in your family history story, remember that your reader probably isn't familiar with how and why bounty land was granted, and that many soldiers never settled on the land. Explaining the bounty land system will add depth to your narrative.

Newspaper articles, obituaries, death notices. Obituaries and death notices can be transcribed verbatim for use in your narrative, or you can weave the details into the story. The information in the following paragraph came from an obituary

> In 1904, while Elvira Bainter was visiting her sister Mary Martin in Sheridan, Indiana, Elvira became

ill and was brought back to Columbus, Ohio. On Wednesday morning, 16 November, at 5:30, she died from a strangulated hernia at her home on 1058 Neil Avenue. Elvira was seventy-five. Elvira's body was placed on view for family and friends to pay their last respects on Thursday afternoon from 2 to 4 P.M.; funeral services were held the next morning at 10 A.M., conducted by the pastor of Elvira's church. The family opted for a private burial service.

You can do likewise with newspaper articles, either reprinting them verbatim or working the details into the narrative. But before you rewind the microfilm, what else was going on in the community as reported in the newspaper on the day your ancestor was mentioned? Remember to mention other events only if they relate to your ancestor's story.

Of course, newspapers in general are excellent sources for discovering what life was like in your ancestors' locality, giving you a glimpse into the intimate details of a community. Newspapers can

- show the cost of consumer goods.
- describe or picture fashions.
- reveal economic conditions through headlines and classified ads.
- show the public mood and political atmosphere in editorials.
- explain the educational and cultural setting.

Study all parts of a newspaper for the area in which your ancestors lived—even the cartoons, which are a great indicator of political atmosphere, pop culture, and important social issues of the day. Around the time of the Civil War, newspapers began publishing a women's section of the Sunday paper. From this section, you can learn about domestic life, fashion, etiquette, and products your ancestors may have purchased in department stores.

Non-population censuses. Even though agricultural,

manufacturing, and mortality schedules exist only for limited time periods and places, if your ancestors were enumerated on them, you'll have some great details to include in your narrative.

If your ancestor was listed on a mortality schedule, also note the causes of death for other people in your ancestor's community during the same time period. Was there an epidemic? If so, you may find more information on it in newspapers and local and county histories.

If your ancestor owned a business, manufacturing and industry schedules are important to your narrative. Even if your ancestor wasn't an owner, these schedules will give you a marvelous sense of the time period and what types of businesses and industries were in operation. No doubt your ancestor patronized some of these businesses. Once you learn the names and types of the businesses in your ancestor's area from manufacturing schedules (or city directories), you may be able to find some old account books that list your ancestor's purchases.

Many people have ancestors who were farmers, so agricultural schedules are extremely important. These documents give you a glimpse of your ancestor's farm life, right down to the numbers and kinds of produce and livestock. But don't stop with the details about your ancestor's farm. How does it compare or contrast with his neighbors'?

Population censuses. Check all federal, state, slave, and Indian schedules for all census years when your ancestors might be listed. I'm sure you've heard this before: always note who the neighbors were when you find your ancestors on a census. For the genealogist, you are noting them because they might later turn out to be relatives, or they might help you break down a brick-wall research problem. For the genealogist turned writer, you want to note more than the names of the people living around your ancestors. Obviously, each census gives slightly different information, but you want to get a feel for the neighborhood, noting things such as occupations and employment, personal and real property values, ethnic makeup, naturalization trends,

For More Info

For more information on censuses, see Kathleen W. Hinckley's *Your Guide to the Federal Census* (Cincinnati: Betterway Books, 2002).

family sizes and structures, ages of the heads of households and their children, people in the neighborhood with disabilities or physical handicaps, education and literacy, migration patterns, property ownership, rural or urban community, and military service.

DEFINING NEIGHBORHOODS

How did your ancestors define their neighborhood? Your rural ancestors' definition will be different from that of your urban ancestors. For those who lived in rural areas, a neighborhood might encompass households within a five-mile radius. For urban ancestors, it may encompass a block or two up and down the street, and maybe the families who lived behind their dwelling. It could also be an ethnic enclave, such as New York's Lower East Side or Little Italy, with a totally different ethnic community occupying the next block. Remember to explain to your readers the type of neighborhood your ancestors lived in.

Probate and court records. Look for wills, administrations, inventories, guardianships, and other court records that might include your ancestors. Here again, if you have ancestors who left wills or if an inventory of their possessions was taken after they died, you have some good material to add to your narrative. But, consider whether you'll merely reprint the record verbatim or work it into the story, like this:

Bailey Williams was a prosperous farmer of the early 1800s, owning three hundred acres of land in Henry County, Kentucky. When he made his will in 1817, he bequeathed and divided not only his land among his heirs, but also nine head of cattle, four horses, seventeen sheep, a wagon, numerous farm tools, and items of household furniture. With this property, Bailey provided a fairly comfortable life for his wife and family:

loom	bottles
reeds	crocks
dresser and ware	bowls

oven	candlesticks
pot and kettles	cupboard
bake oven	chest
barrels	smoothing irons
table and trays	hackle
chairs	beds, bed clothing, and
knives, forks, and	bedsteads
spoons	woman's saddle
teaspoons	rifle gun
tea ware	bureau
dishes	feather bed
tumblers	beehive

Some inventories might record in what room items were found, so that you can draw a more vivid picture:

The inventory of Mary Clark's personal belongings reveals a glimpse of her house and how she and her son lived. Their house consisted of three large rooms, a basement sitting room, and a cellar. The north bedroom was carpeted. In it were a bedstead and a feather bed. Two chairs—a steamer chair and a low chair—were also in the room, as were a bureau, washstand, lantern, and a trunk. Seven pictures adorned either the bureau or the walls, perhaps of family members. . . .

Civil and criminal court cases can liven your family history narrative more than any other document, so if you have these for your ancestors, utilize them to their fullest. They can also reveal much about your ancestors' characters (see STEP 10). Here is another record you will want to explore for other cases that may not involve your ancestors directly, but which may have had an impact on them. For example, if your ancestor served on a jury for a particular trial, you might want to research the court case to cover in your narrative.

Vital records. Traditionally, genealogists record the facts from births, marriages, and deaths, but family history writers need to look at them in a broader light. For example, if you're writing about an ancestor's marriage, and you also happen to have a photograph from the wedding, use the two in combination. Research who the witnesses were if you don't already know. What relation, if any, were they to the couple? If the couple was married in a church, give us some details about that church or religion. We already discussed in STEP 5 how you can relate the childbirth experience; what about the death experience? What did your ancestor die of? Was it a lingering disease like tuberculosis (consumption)? What would it have been like for your ancestor to die of that disease and for his family to provide care in the final stages of the disease?

As you can see, there's more than meets the genealogist's eye when you go back and revisit those genealogical sources with a *writer's* eye for details. As you are taking a second look at the genealogical sources, keep your thematic chronology handy to see if any of the documents will directly or indirectly answer the questions you raised about daily life, motivation, and behaviors. Now let's broaden the background research even more by consulting social histories.

For More Info

For more on death records and events related to death and burial, see Carmack's *Your Guide to Cemetery Research.*

Researching Social Histories

Part of our task is to work our way back into the past
mindset so that we think about experience as people in
different times thought of it.

  —RICHARD MARIUS, *A SHORT GUIDE TO WRITING*
    ABOUT HISTORY

I f you've ever taken a journalism course or worked on your school's newspaper, you'll remember the inverted-pyramid style of writing a news article. All the major facts—the who, what, when, where, why, and how—had to be crammed into that opening paragraph. The actual story, the more interesting part, came next, so that if editors had to cut copy to make it fit the page, they could cut from the bottom up and the reader would still have the facts. Thankfully, newspaper features have evolved so that the opening paragraph doesn't read like a police report. But it's the interesting part of the news article—why it happened, how it happened, what difference it made—that is similar to the background research you're doing for your family history narrative. In the newspaper feature, the eyewitness accounts and background information on the people or events make the story come to life. This type of information allows the reader to almost become an eyewitness to what happened, too. **For family history, background research serves the same purpose: it fills out the facts, breathes life into your ancestors, and turns the reader into an eyewitness of your family's life.**

Reminder

After you've been through the genealogical sources with a writer's eye, it's time to start answering those questions you raised on the thematic chronology you created in STEP 5. From some of the genealogical sources you revisited, you may have discovered answers, or at least possible answers, to some of your questions. If not, that's okay. We'll now research social histories, which examine the everyday lives of ordinary people in a past society. These sources will probably answer any remaining questions.

Maybe your ancestor didn't leave an account of his or her daily life, but someone who lived during the same time period in the same locality probably did. Social historians draw on these accounts (letters, diaries, family papers) and genealogical sources (probates, censuses, land records, and so on) to learn about the experiences of people in a given time and place. They look at a community or society as a whole; whereas we genealogists usually focus on individuals and specific families. From social histories, we can determine the typical experiences of people like our ancestors.

Finding Social History Books

You can find social histories that cover just about every topic you need to research and write about in your narrative. The bibliography contains a sampling of social histories to get you started, and thousands more are available. When you find a social history that covers your topic of interest, check that book's bibliography for additional sources.

Unfortunately, you may not find social histories in a genealogical library. You'll need to visit public, state, and academic libraries, as well as state archives—but don't limit your search to a genealogical section. Some of the best social history sources are in the children's department, because almost all history books written for children are accounts of daily life. Begin your search there, as these books usually give a bibliography of adult sources the author used in researching the children's book.

Start by checking online library catalogs and online bookstores. First, categorize your ancestors as discussed

For More Info

The best discussion on social history research in genealogy is Katherine Scott Sturdevant's *Bringing Your Family History to Life Through Social History.*

73

For More Info

If it's been a while since you've set foot in a college library—or you never have at all—you might want to read Sturdevant's chapter, " 'Here Come the Genies': Braving the College Library," in *Bringing Your Family History to Life Through Social History.*

in STEP 5. Then, in the computerized library catalog, type in the category of your ancestor, such as an ethnic group or an occupation, followed by: *social life and customs.* For example, if you want to know what life was like for your Boston Irish ancestors, type in: *Boston Irish social life and customs.* Let's use the Charles Fearn family for an example of how to categorize your ancestors. One of the Fearn family themes we can explore is nineteenth-century frontier life in the Arizona desert. To find books on that topic, I tried a variety of keywords in the catalog. In the Library of Congress online catalog <www.loc.gov>, under the "Basic Search," I did a keyword search, typing in: *frontier army life.* Sources are ranked by relevance to the keywords entered, but in this case there were more entries than I could reasonably examine, so I narrowed the search by adding the word *Arizona.* Now, two sources caught my eye: Martha Summerhayes' *Vanished Arizona: Reflections of the Army Life of a New England Woman* (Lincoln: University of Nebraska Press, 1978) and Oliver Knight's *Life and Manners in the Frontier Army* (Norman: University of Oklahoma Press, 1993). I'll check with my local library to see if they have these books, and, if not, I'll request them on interlibrary loan.

If you are a bibliophile and like to have your own copy of a book, look for social histories in used bookstores, both brick-and-mortar types and online. Some social histories go out of print rather quickly; others become instant classics and remain in print for a long time. But be creative when you are in a used bookstore. Look not only in the history section, but also in the sections for Americana, sociology, women's studies, black studies, folk studies, and local and regional histories.

FINDING SOCIAL HISTORY ARTICLES

Earlier I said that just about every topic you would need to research has been written about, but there may not be a full book on the subject. The topic you need may be covered in only one chapter of a book, or even in just a few paragraphs. Or, it may be the subject of an article in a magazine or academic journal.

To find print articles, you'll want to explore a reference guide called *America: History and Life*. Published since 1964, this bibliographic reference contains more than 450,000 entries of U.S. and Canadian history articles from more than two thousand journals. Each year, 16,000 new entries are added. You'll find this resource in most college and university libraries. Some will have it in book form; others might have the CD-ROM or the online version, both of which are easier and quicker to use than the book volumes, of course. The online version requires you to be a subscriber, which carries a hefty subscriber fee. Go to <http://sb2.abc-clio.com:81/> for more information and to sample the database.

The book version of *America: History and Life* contains four separate parts prior to 1989: Part A: Article Abstracts; Part B: Index to Book Reviews; Part C: Bibliography of Books, Articles, and Dissertations; and Part D: Annual Index. After 1989, a fifth volume was added for works in media such as film, videos, and microform, but the index is still the last volume in the series. This annual index is the one you'll use first. (The disadvantage to using the books is that you will need to check each year's indexes.) The annual index is arranged by topic, so, once again, you'll need to search it by categorizing your ancestors by ethnic group, occupation, economic class, locality, and so forth. Also search according to the themes you've identified for your family, such as Louisiana's yellow fever epidemic or female factory workers in Lowell, Massachusetts. Once you find a reference to an article that might be relevant to your research, you will see a rather cryptic reference such as: *8A:235*. This tells you to go to volume 8, Part A (Article Abstracts), entry number 235 (this is not a page number). Then read the abstract in Part A to see if the topic is indeed what you were looking for. If so, note the title, author, and publication information, then ask the reference librarian if that particular issue is in the university's collection. If not, ask if you can order it on interlibrary loan. At some universities, interlibrary loan service is available for students only, so you may need to go to your public library to request the article.

Finding Social History Information on the Web

For More Info

For social histories of various ethnic groups, consult Part II of Carmack's *A Genealogist's Guide to Discovering Your Immigrant and Ethnic Ancestors.*

You can find social history articles on the Web, too. Simply type the same keywords you would use for a library catalog into a search engine, such as Google.com. Be careful what you type, however. When I typed in: *frontier Arizona army life* or a variation, the search engine returned more than 12,000 hits. But by using Boolean search methods (including quotation marks, $+/-$ signs, and so on) I obtained a better result. When I typed: *"frontier army life"* + *Arizona*, the quotation marks isolated my search phrase so the search engine wouldn't look for every site with the words *frontier*, or *army*, or *life.* The plus sign limited the search to sites that included the word *Arizona*. This time I got only thirteen hits, a much more manageable search. Some of the links were to books I could purchase; others were to Web sites with relevant information. I'll also search for the forts where the Fearns were stationed. Be creative and play with the search engine, typing in different phrases and words for the topics you are researching.

For More Info

For more on using search engines in genealogy, see Rhonda R. McClure's *The Genealogist's Computer Companion* (Cincinnati: Betterway Books, 2001).

Evaluating Social Histories

As with any source you use for your family history, you need to evaluate the reliability of social histories, whether you find them in print form or on the Web. Read the author's credentials. If the author is affiliated with an academic institution or has higher degrees, then the work is likely to be accurate and reliable in its research findings. Keep in mind, however, that there are many good amateur historians as well. **The more you immerse yourself in the topic, the easier it will be for you to evaluate work by amateur historians.** If the work is published by an academic or university press, that speaks well for

Tip

the source. Read through the author's sources and bibliography. Like a good published genealogy, does it include a variety of published and original sources? If you find a social history article on the Web, who published it? Did you find it on a Web site that is affiliated with a university or college (one that has *.edu* as part of its Web address)?

Always try to get more than one writer's version of a story. This will not only broaden your knowledge, but different writers likely used different sources. One writer may build upon or augment the work of an earlier writer. You can usually determine the classic resource on a subject when all writers on a topic reference it. For example, when I was researching women and abortion in the nineteenth century, every book on the subject that I picked up quoted from or referenced James C. Mohr's *Abortion in America: The Origins and Evolution of National Policy, 1800–1900* (New York: Oxford University Press, 1978). I realized this was a respected source that I had to check for myself.

OTHER SOURCES OF BACKGROUND MATERIAL

While social histories will be the mainstay of your background research, there are several other resources you may want to explore.

Contemporary literature. Perhaps nothing will give you better insight into how your ancestors lived than books, magazines, and newspapers from your ancestors' day. In STEP 6, we looked at how newspapers provide clues and details about everyday life, but also consider reading books and magazines from the time period in which your ancestor lived. It isn't crucial to know whether your ancestors read these works; you just want to get a flavor of how people lived, worked, and played in those days. But, if you have an estate inventory that lists any books your ancestor owned, you might want to track down copies of these books to read yourself. It's like walking the land your ancestors owned; there's something cool about reading the same words your ancestors read. Books also reveal a piece of a person's personality. Was your ancestor a scholar who read classical works, such as Shakespeare, Greek and Roman mythology, or scientific treatises? Or did your ancestor enjoy spending time reading popular novels and magazines? Some of the books listed in your ancestor's inventory may be long out of print or considered rare books now, meaning you probably won't be able to obtain them through interlibrary loan. Or the work may be difficult to identify fully from just a title, but it's worth attempting to locate copies.

Cookbooks and food histories. If you are researching an ethnic group, cookbooks and food histories can provide you with cultural background information about both the old country and ethnic communities in America. Browse the cookbook section in your local new or used bookstore. Read introductions, prefaces, and other explanatory sections. You might be surprised at what you'll find that could be relevant to your family history narrative.

Historical biographies of famous individuals. Although biographies of famous individuals usually deal with the wealthy and elite of society rather than with ordinary people like our ancestors, if a famous individual originated from or lived in the same community and time period as your ancestors, the biographer may have used sources that would benefit your research. Read them also to see how biographers put their subjects into historical perspective. Some have even made the best-seller list; those may be particularly helpful for you to look at.

Historical fiction. If you love to read novels, historical fiction can give you insight into a time and place, as well as ideas on how to craft your family history narrative. Remember, when you write creative or dramatic nonfiction, you are using the techniques of a fiction writer. Some historical fiction writers have built reputations for a high degree of historical accuracy, such as James A.

Michener, John Jakes, Conrad Richter, Michael Shaara, and Jeffrey M. Shaara.

Memoirs, letters, and diaries. Remember, your focus now is to broaden your research beyond your own ancestors and to look for people *like* your ancestors who may have left surviving accounts of what their lives were like. Besides looking for published accounts, also search for manuscript collections. The most helpful source for family papers, memoirs, letters, and diaries will be the *National Union Catalog of Manuscript Collections*. NUCMC has been published annually since 1959 by the Library of Congress, which requests reports from repositories from all over the country about their manuscript holdings. Cataloged in NUCMC are descriptions of approximately 72,300 manuscript collections of personal, family, and corporate papers, located in more than 1,400 different repositories. You can find printed volumes for 1959 through 1993 in the reference section of university and metropolitan libraries. Volumes from 1986/87 to 1993 are searchable for free on the Web at <http://lcweb.l oc.gov/coll/nucmc/>.

A two-volume printed reference, *Index to Personal Names in the National Union Catalog of Manuscript Collections 1959–1984,* indexes all the personal and family names appearing in the descriptions of manuscript collections that were cataloged in the annual volumes for those dates, totaling about 200,000 names. This index isn't on the Web, but when you locate a copy in a repository, it is a quick and easy way to check for your family surnames, as well as for those of your ancestor's neighbors and associates. These people might have named your ancestor in a document, or they may have left papers that could give you a taste of life in your ancestor's day and community.

Museums. As mentioned in STEP 6, museums are excellent resources for local and social histories, and the curators can be helpful as well. Most museums have an adjoining library, or a gift shop with books and materials that may be beneficial to your writing project. (See STEP

16 for obtaining photographs from museums to illustrate your family history.) Of particular help for getting a feel for what life was like during your ancestor's day are the living museums (sometimes called folk parks), such as Colonial Williamsburg <www.history.org> and Plimoth Plantation <www.plimoth.org/Museum/museum.htm>. Museums like these are staffed with people who dress in period costume and take on the roles of people like our ancestors, interpreting history for visitors and explaining work and lifestyles.

Most museums now have Web sites with information about the museum and their research facilities, and items from their gift shop available for purchase. Some may offer electronic field trips or virtual tours. To discover museums of this type and others in your area of interest, consult state guides from AAA (American Automobile Association), as well as online search engines.

Remember that each museum has a different focus; you will find museums devoted to all sorts of topics. (I'll bet you didn't know that there's a National Museum of Funeral History <www.nmfh.org>.) At the Ellis Island Museum in New York City, you'll not only gain an appreciation of the immigrant experience, but you can do research at its library, which has more than 7,000 taped oral history interviews cataloged not only by the interviewee's name, but also by country of origin and subject matter. So even if your ancestors who came through Ellis Island left no oral or written account, you can listen to an interview of someone who very likely experienced the same thing as your ancestor or maybe even traveled on the same ship. You will have to go Ellis Island to listen to the interviews, however. On the Ellis Island Web site <www.ellisisland.org> you can find information on passenger ships as well, but you must first find your ancestor on the ship. Unfortunately, there is no way to key in the name of a ship to get information.

While we're on the subject of passenger ships—since that's a topic that will apply to practically everyone sooner or later—there are several maritime museums with information about and illustrations of sailing and steam vessels. The National Maritime Museum <www.nmm.ac.uk/> or The Museum of America and the Sea <www.mysticseaport .org/welcome.html> are two sites to begin your search for ship information. For other links to maritime museums on the Web, go to <www.execpc.com/~reva/html3e2.htm>. An ocean liner memorabilia Web site at <www.oceanliner .com> sells brochures listing steamships' schedules and fares.

WHEN TO STOP RESEARCHING

How much background research is enough? When do you call a halt to this phase of your project? For some topics there may be hundreds of sources. Do you need to check them all? I like writer Bob Reiss's gauge, as quoted in Philip Gerard's *Creative Nonfiction: Researching and Crafting the Stories of Real Life*: "If there's one more question to ask, you don't know enough, because the answer to that question, the fact that you *have* that question, means that you do not have a sense of the story yet." As you begin writing, more questions will inevitably pop up, which means you need to do a bit more background research. But once you have satisfied your curiosity about the themes you've identified in your ancestors' lives, then you've done enough research.

Reminder

Don't become Web-exclusive. There are also lots of great books on passenger ships, such as Eugene W. Smith's *Passenger Ships of the World Past and Present* (Boston: George H. Dean, 1978) and Arnold Kludas's five-volume set, *Great Passenger Ships of the World* (Cambridge, Mass.: Stephens, 1975–1977).

Gathering and Organizing Your Research

I love being a writer. What I can't stand is the paperwork.—PETER DE VRIES

R emember in the introduction I said my role was kind of like a midwife, to help prepare and assist you in giving birth to your family history book? Well, this is the part where you start to get the nursery ready for baby Belinda. You've already been shopping and bought the crib, the diapers, the powders and diaper creams, the blankets, the bibs, the pacifiers, and . . . well, you get the idea. Now you'll need to organize baby Belinda's room, so you can have things handy when that bundle of joy spits up, soils her diaper, won't stop crying, and makes you question why you wanted to have this baby in the first place—just as you may be questioning why you began to write your family history. Both are a lot of work, but like baby Belinda, the good times outweigh the bad (we hope!), and we have made a commitment to our baby and ourselves to see this thing through. You can't give up the writing project, any more than you can give baby Belinda back.

Like shopping for the nursery, you have shopped for genealogical data, books, and articles dealing with the themes you have chosen to write about in your family history. Now let's get the writing nursery ready by efficiently gathering your research from the social history sources first, then organizing it for your writing project.

Like any other research project, gathering data and or-

For More Info

If you need guidance on organizing your family history materials, consult Sharon DeBartolo Carmack's *Organizing Your Family History Search* (Cincinnati: Betterway Books, 1999).

ganizing it is an individual thing, meaning that everyone will have a method he or she is most comfortable with. So I will give you several options for gathering and organizing. Use one or a combination of several that suit you.

FOCUSING YOUR RESEARCH

For some themes, you'll find books that hit your topic right on the head, and you'll want to read the whole volume. For others, there may be only a chapter or a couple of paragraphs requiring your attention. Let's look at some examples.

For the Fearn family, I'm trying to learn what life at an army camp was like in the desert of Arizona Territory. The two books I found to begin my research on Arizona frontier life were Summerhayes' *Vanished Arizona* and Knight's *Life and Manners in the Frontier Army*. I read Summerhayes' book cover to cover because it focused on the woman's experience, which I wanted to write about in my narrative. But not everything in Knight's book was pertinent to my needs. Here is the table of contents from that book:

Case Study

1. Social History in the Army Novels of Captain Charles King
2. The Ladies of the Regiment
3. Cavaliers and Blackguards
4. The Garrison as Family
5. The Army Post
6. War Parties
7. Soldier and Citizen
8. Conclusions

I skimmed through all the chapters and decided that chapters two, four, and five were the most relevant to the overall theme I wanted to cover.

As another example, there were several themes I wanted to explore and address in *My Wild Irish Rose*. The narrative's primary focus was the life stories of two women, Rose (Norris) (O'Connor) Fitzhugh and her mother, Delia (Gordon) Norris, who emigrated from Ireland. As described in STEP 5, I looked for relevant themes based on the information I had gleaned from genealogical research and that I could develop and expand with additional social history research. On page 85 is the same chart as in STEP 5, except that I've added another column to indicate the sources I consulted. In some cases I read the entire book, but in others I just looked for specific information.

TAKING NOTES

Once you have a list of sources to research, you'll want to take notes as efficiently as you can.

If you are working from library books or those borrowed from a friend, you'll need to take notes. Using a computer or laptop comes in handy for this. The only danger is that you may lift too much of another author's work. So, consider taking notes by hand and paraphrasing.

If there are only short sections you find useful, it may be quickest and easiest to photocopy those and highlight relevant passages. In the margins of the photocopy, write the topic or theme so you can quickly identify it if you have collected many photocopies. The same method works for an article: photocopy the entire piece and use your highlighter.

If the whole book is germane to your study, you may want to consider purchasing it so that you can freely highlight or make notes in your copy. If your budget is tight, or if only a few chapters are relevant, then it's probably better to take notes.

I prefer to take notes by hand to avoid lifting too much of another author's work. It's better to paraphrase (restate the text or passage in your own words) and select insightful quotes. The two methods I suggest to my students for note-taking are using either a notepad or loose-leaf paper, or index cards.

Using a Notepad or Loose-Leaf Paper

At the top of a sheet of loose-leaf paper or in a notepad, write the title of the source and appropriate biblio-

Important

I know there are bibliophiles out there who are cringing at my recommendation to highlight and mark in books. If it's a rare book, of course, you shouldn't. But if it's a mass-produced book and there are copies still available, I see no harm in marking your own book.

DELIA/ROSE CHART

Date	Event	Theme & Questions	Sources
ca. 1885	Delia left Ireland and came to America.	Irish immigrant experience for women. What was it like to be an Irish woman immigrating to America? Is it likely that women came with family, friends, or alone? Why did they leave Ireland?	Hasia R. Diner, *Erin's Daughters in America: Irish Immigrant Women in the Nineteenth Century* (Baltimore: Johns Hopkins University Press, 1983), read entire book; Roger Daniels, *Coming to America: A History of Immigration and Ethnicity in American Life* (New York: HarperCollins, 1990), read chapters pertaining to Irish; Janet A. Nolan, *Ourselves Alone: Women's Emigration from Ireland, 1885–1920* (Lexington: The University Press of Kentucky, 1989), read entire book; Stephan Thernstrom, ed., *Harvard Encylopedia of American Ethnic Groups* (Cambridge, Mass.: Belknap Press of Harvard University, 1980), read chapter on Irish.
late 1800s– early 1900s	Delia lived in Greenwich, Connecticut.	Daily life in Greenwich, Connecticut. What events occurred in Greenwich during the time Delia and her family lived there that might have affected them?	Elizabeth W. Clarke, ed., *Before & After 1776: A Comprehensive Chronology of the Town of Greenwich: 1640–1976* (Cos Cob, Conn.: The Historical Society of the Town of Greenwich, 1976), looked at events from ca. 1885 through ca. 1925.
early 1900s	Rose was pregnant out of wedlock at age 17 in 1916.	Premarital sex in the early twentieth century. How common was premarital sex during this time? What kinds of stigmas were attached to "fallen women"?	Steven Mintz and Susan Kellogg, *Domestic Revolutions: A Social History of American Family Life* (New York: The Free Press, 1988), looked in the index under "sex, premarital," as well as read the chapter covering the 1910s.

DELIA/ROSE CHART

Date	Event	Theme & Questions	Sources
ca. 1920	Rose and her husband divorce.	Divorce after World War I. How common was divorce during this time? What kind of stigma was attached to a divorced woman?	Glenda Riley, *Divorce: An American Tradition* (New York: Oxford University Press, 1991), looked for information on divorce during the time of World War I.
early 1900s	Rose had only four children, whereas women in her mother's generation had double that number.	Reproductive control in the early twentieth century. Why were women of Rose's generation having fewer children? Why was the birth rate declining? What methods of birth control were available? Was the method used by one of the women in my story a common one?	Doris Weatherford, *Foreign and Female: Immigrant Women in America, 1840–1930* (New York: Schocken Books, 1986), read sections on family planning in general, but with specific eye for Irish or Catholic women; Linda Gordon, *Woman's Body, Woman's Right: Birth Control in America* (New York: Penguin Books, 1974), looked for information dealing with the time period of interest.
early to mid–1900s	Rose and her second husband lived in Harrison, New York.	Daily life in Harrison, New York. What events were happening in Harrison when my ancestors lived there that might have affected Rose and her family?	Marilyn E. Weigold, ed., *Westchester County: The Past Hundred Years, 1883–1983* (Valhalla, N.Y.: The Westchester County Historical Society, 1984), looked for information on Harrison in the 1930s–1950s.

DELIA/ROSE CHART			
Date	Event	Theme & Questions	Sources
1930s–1940s	Rose's nephew, who lived in her household, suffered from TB. He was also institutionalized in a tubercular sanatorium in up-state New York.	Treatment of tuberculosis patients. What were the symptoms TB patients suffered from? What treatments were available? What was life like in these sanatoriums?	Robert Taylor, *Saranac: America's Magic Mountain* (New York: Paragon House Publishers, 1988), looked for history of the Adirondack Cottage Sanatorium; Sheila M. Rothman, *Living in the Shadow of Death: Tuberculosis and the Social Experience of Illness in American History* (Baltimore: Johns Hopkins University Press, 1995), read chapters dealing with New York sanatoriums and patient treatment.
1920s–1940s	Rose's sister, Jane, was a victim of domestic violence.	Domestic violence. What were some of the causes of domestic violence? How common was it before it became "acceptable" to talk about it? How did family members respond when there was domestic violence in the household?	Linda Gordon, *Heroes of Their Own Lives: The Politics and History of Family Violence: Boston 1880–1960* (New York: Penguin Books, 1988), looked for general information on causes and effects of domestic violence on women.

graphic information (author, place of publication, publisher, and date). You might want to include the library's call number and, if it's a book you obtained through interlibrary loan, the name of the repository. If you obtained information from the Internet, include not only the URL, but also the date you accessed it; then if you need to refer to that source again, you can retrieve it more easily. As you find material to copy from the source, start a line with the page number, then the information. In the left margin, write the topic the note pertains to (see Figure 8-1 on page 89 for an example). Try to designate a separate notepad or notebook (if you're using loose-leaf papers) for your project, keeping all notes together. Start a fresh page for each new source you take notes from.

Using Index Cards

Buy two sizes: 3″ × 5″ and 4″ × 6″. Use the 3 × 5 cards as your bibliography cards (Figure 8-2 on page 90). For each source you check, make a separate 3 × 5 card, recording the bibliographic information, repository, and a call number (or URL and date for a Web site) in case you need to go back to that source.

The 4 × 6 cards will be your note cards (Figure 8-3 on page 90). You don't need to repeat the bibliographic information on each card, only the author's last name, an abbreviated title, and the page number. Put that information in the right corner; in the left corner put the topic you're researching, and in the body take your notes. With this method, take only one note per card, so that the material will be easy to organize when you begin writing.

For either method, if you are quoting material, be careful to quote it exactly as the author wrote it, and place quotation marks around it so you won't forget that it's a quote and mistakenly think that you paraphrased it.

ORGANIZING YOUR NOTES

It's important to organize while you gather sources and take notes, so that when the time comes to begin writing,

Hasia R. Diner, Erin's Daughters in America: Irish Immigrant Women in the Nineteenth Century (Baltimore: Johns Hopkins University Press, 1983)		
emigration	p. xiv	"In the decades after the Famine more Irish women than Irish men immigrated to the United States."
famine	p. 4	famines in Ireland also occurred in 1800, 1807, 1816, 1822, and 1839
work	p. 26	single and married Irish women might work outside the home as they liked the financial independence it gave them
Widowhood	p. 45	"Widowhood became an even more common life experience for Irish women in the United States than it had been in Ireland. . . ."
sex	p. 114	premarital sex, illegitimacy, and prostitution were rare among Irish women in Ireland and in America, although these did increase moderately once they immigrated to America

Figure 8-1
Taking notes on looseleaf paper. If using loose-leaf sheets to take notes from a book or article, put the subject in the left margin so you can easily find it while writing about that subject. Cross the item off as you use that information.

you can concentrate on that activity rather than hunting for the notes and sources you've spent the past few months gathering. In addition to your notepad, notebook or index cards, create file folders for the themes or topics you'll be covering in your narrative to keep track of other types of items. For example, you might create a file folder for the immigration experience, then use it to

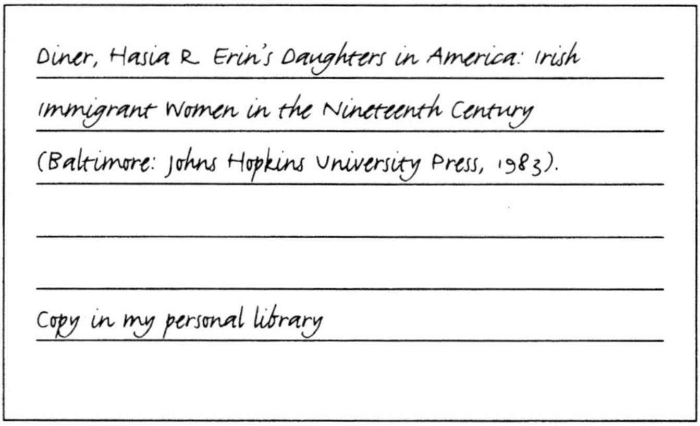

| Diner, Hasia R. Erin's Daughters in America: Irish |
| Immigrant Women in the Nineteenth Century |
| (Baltimore: Johns Hopkins University Press, 1983). |
| |
| |
| Copy in my personal library |

Figure 8-2
Use 3 × 5 index cards as your bibliography cards, copying all the information needed for a bibliography entry: author, title, publishing information.

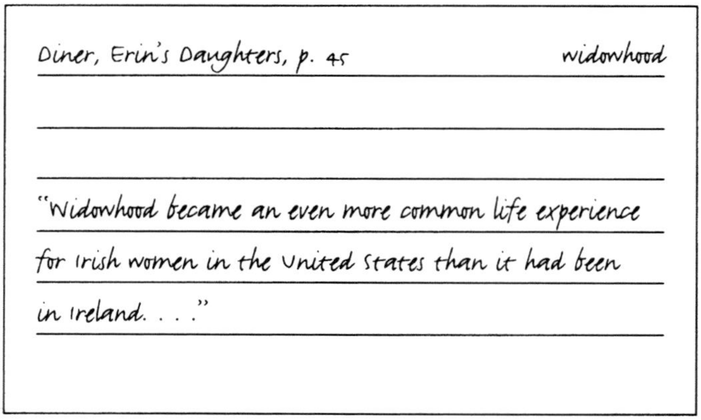

| Diner, Erin's Daughters, p. 45 | widowhood |
| |
| "Widowhood became an even more common life experience |
| for Irish women in the United States than it had been |
| in Ireland. . . ." |

Figure 8-3
Use 4 × 6 index cards to take notes from your sources. Put the author's name, an abbreviated title of the source, and the page number in the upper-left corner, and the subject in the upper-right. Take one note per card. Remember to use quotation marks around material you quoted precisely.

hold loose items such as articles, sheets of information downloaded from the Internet, photocopies of passages from books, pamphlets or brochures, and so forth. Keep your notes in the notebook or notepad you've designated for the whole project; or if you are using index cards, purchase a card file box to keep them together. If you have items that pertain to more than one topic, then put that item in one file and include a note to yourself in the other topic's file, so you will remember that this article also has information on another topic.

When you get to the point where you feel you have enough background research to begin writing, go through the notes that you've taken on note paper, and using different color highlighters, highlight similar topics, so you can quickly find them among your sources. If you are using index cards for taking notes, you can easily group the cards according to like topics. Then when you get to a particular subject in your narrative, you will be able to find all the appropriate notes quickly.

Tip

The same holds true if you photocopied pages, highlighted relevant parts, then wrote topic names in the margins. Use different color highlighters to mark like topics. If you feel comfortable highlighting and making marginal notes in a whole book, these marks will enable you to find quickly what you need when you begin writing.

As you write on a specific topic, pull out all your materials covering that subject, so you have everything you need at hand. When you have finished writing about that topic, put those materials away and get out the ones that deal with the next subject you'll be covering.

Assuming that you've either been making bibliography index cards or recording the bibliographic information on your notepad, you'll be able to cite the source easily in your narrative's foot- or endnotes and include all your sources in the bibliography (see STEP 15).

See, it wasn't as bad as you thought, this whole organizing business. Baby Belinda has stopped crying, her diaper is clean, her tummy's full, and she's sound asleep. Now you can get some writing done.

Making Choices About the Narrative

Use plain, simple language, short words and brief sentences. That is the way to write English—it is the modern way and the best way. . . . A wordy habit, once fastened upon a person, is as hard to get rid of as any other vice.—MARK TWAIN

[handwritten: pay attention you]

Now you're at the point where you are getting ready to spit out this family history narrative in no time. Here's what you should have accomplished so far:

- ☑ picked the type of family history you want to write
- ☑ defined the scope and structure of your writing project, and how many generations and family groups you'll cover
- ☑ transformed the data on your family group sheets into family summaries
- ☑ looked for the plot
- ☑ developed a thematic chronology and a checklist of localities and time periods
- ☑ revisited genealogical sources looking for broader information
- ☑ delved into social histories and other sources, taking and organizing notes on relevant details that will put flesh on the bones when you begin writing

As mentioned in STEP 1, this book's emphasis is on writing *creative nonfiction,* and the writing advice and techniques you'll learn about will apply whether you have chosen to write a life story (biography of one ancestor), a full-fledged family history, or a family history memoir where you are one of the "characters" in your story. We need to begin by defining *creative nonfiction*, then we'll look at some more decisions you'll need to make in telling your ancestors' stories.

WRITING CREATIVE NONFICTION

Creative nonfiction is factual writing using the techniques of a fiction writer rather than those of a traditional newspaper reporter. Creative nonfiction does not simply present facts; it features scenes and summaries intended to tell a good story. The author of creative nonfiction looks for drama, the human element, and deeper meaning in real-life events. But above all, the creative nonfiction writer stays true to the facts. "The importance of providing accurate information cannot be overemphasized," writes Lee Gutkind in *The Art of Creative Nonfiction*, "Names, dates, places, descriptions, quotations may not be created or altered for any reason, at any time." He further reminds readers: "The creative nonfiction writer may not employ 'literary license'—the writer may not alter truth to enhance the story or the dramatic narrative." Philip Gerard, in *Creative Nonfiction: Researching and Crafting Stories of Real Life*, agrees: "The hardest part of writing creative nonfiction is that you're stuck with what really happened—you can't make it up. You can be as artful as you want in presentation, draw profound meanings out of your subject matter, but you are still stuck with real people and real events."

\di'fin\ *vb*

Definitions

Creative nonfiction writing involves two primary writing devices: scene and summary. Remember the old cliché that writers should *show*, not *tell*; well, scenes show and summaries tell. Scenes allow your readers to feel like eyewitnesses to the events you describe. Review the scene in STEP 5 on page 55, about Janie, the victim of domestic violence. This scene shows the violence, allowing the reader to experience it along with Jane's niece, Kathryn. In *Blood Washes Blood*, Frank Viviano begins a scene with: "On a mild Wednesday morning in the second week of February, I read the death notice of the man who gave me my name. . . ." Viviano slows the story down here so we can experience reading the death notice along with the narrator.

Summaries, on the other hand, simply tell the reader what happened in a way that moves the story along in time more quickly. Viviano writes: "The republic was unseated on September 4, 1282, by Pedro of Aragon, the first in Sicily's six-century gauntlet of Spanish and Bourbon rulers. . . ." In this paragraph, he summarizes to keep the story moving. **While the history lesson is important for setting the stage for his ancestors, it's not the focus of the story,** so Viviano uses summary to convey the information without bogging down the narrative. Good, creative nonfiction writing will contain both scenes and summaries. Sometimes it may work to simply alternate the two, or the two devices can be meshed in one paragraph. As you read other family history narratives, try to identify which device the author is using at a given point: scene or summary.

Important

FOUR KEY PARTS OF YOUR STORY

Keep in mind that no one's family history is particularly exciting until the writer makes it exciting. Philip Gerard, in *Creative Nonfiction: Researching and Crafting Stories of Real Life*, says writers should ask themselves: "Why am I telling this?" If the answer is "because it matters," then you have found your passion, and "every detail of setting, every quoted line of an interview, every fact shows the reader why it matters in particular and right now." Your passion and enthusiasm for your family history will shine through, and your readers will find it contagious.

There are four critical aspects to consider with regard to your family history narrative before you even begin writing. All good stories have (1) a primary focus on people, not events (more on that in STEP 10); (2) a strong beginning; (3) a "keep 'em reading" middle; and (4) a powerful ending. It's these aspects that should command quite a bit of your attention as you're writing your family history.

PASSIVE VS. ACTIVE VOICE

Nothing can bog down your narrative more than using passive rather than active voice. Here are examples of passive voice:

- A notice was placed in the newspaper by James Neely Love.

- The area was settled in 1803.

- The will was recorded in the probate book.

Here are the same sentences written with active voice:

- James Neely Love placed a notice in the newspaper.

- Pioneers settled the area in 1803.

- The clerk recorded the will in the probate book.

Notice the difference? In the first set of examples, the subject of the sentence (the "actor") is either out of place at the end of the sentence or missing from the sentence entirely. In the second set, the "actors" show up and come where they should: at the beginning of the sentence.

There are occasions, however, where you may have no choice but to use passive voice. If you don't know who the actor was, for example, you will need to use passive voice. Here is a common situation in family history writing where passive voice is necessary: *Sally Collins was buried in Spring Grove Cemetery.* Passive construction is acceptable here because we don't know who buried Sally—although you could write: *Sally's family buried her in Spring Grove Cemetery.* In this case, however, because we want *Sally* to be the focus of the sentence, not whoever buried her, the passive structure is preferable.

Always grab the reader by the throat in the first paragraph, sink your thumbs into his windpipe in the second, and hold him against the wall until the tag line.—PAUL O'NEIL

Grabbing Your Reader

Sadly, many writers think they must begin their family history at the beginning: *Michael McMasters was born 7 May 1814 in a log cabin in Henry County, Kentucky. He married. . . . He died . . .* Now how many novels or movies begin like that? Not many, and there's a reason for it. The cradle-to-grave chronology doesn't grab the reader's attention. When we meet people in real life, they don't read us their vital statistics; so why should we meet your ancestors that way? There is no reason you can't use the same writing techniques that fiction writers and nonfiction journalists use even though you are writing nonfiction. **One of the most common techniques is to start in the middle of a story, then go back and tell the reader how we got to that point.** Look for something exciting, interesting, unusual, dramatic, or controversial in your ancestor's life experience and begin the story there.

Technique

Let's say you're writing about an immigrant family. Begin the story aboard ship, or at the moment they set foot on American soil. Or let's say you're writing about a family who made the overland journey from east to west; open with what it must have been like on the trail. Reel your reader in with an exciting, happy, or tragic event, or a conflict. If you have letters, diaries, or an interesting record, you can open by quoting that source. But remember: if you are writing nonfiction, it has to be a *factual* opening. Here's the opening from volume one of *Mills, Shoes and Skyscrapers: The Cannizzaro Family from Poggioreale to New Orleans* (privately published and distributed, 2002), by Elaine Trigiani:

Vito got the mule. His brother, Giuseppe Nicolò Cannizzaro, upon their father's death received part of their father's interests and indebtedness for what were lucrative, albeit highly taxed, leases on several mills in the area. The other part, along with the mule, went to his older brother Vito. . . .

See how Trigiani just plunged us right into the middle of the story? Then she flashes back to fill us in and answer the questions raised in the opening.

Now let's look at how the Fearn family narrative begins:

Lizards, snakes, tarantulas, scorpions, and black ants likely became dreaded creatures to the Charles Fearn family during their stay at Fort Grant, in the southern part of Arizona, in the early 1880s. The Fearns would find living conditions in the desert of Arizona challenging and quite unlike what they were used to back home in Ohio. Summer temperatures rose to more than 110° in the shade. In the evenings, the heat would dissipate only about twenty degrees, making it stifling to sleep indoors. Families moved their beds—iron cots with bedsacks filled with straw and a mattress laid atop—outside in the summer months for sleeping. To keep the ants from crawling on the bed, they set cot legs inside tin cans full of water, making it impossible for the ants to find their way onto the bed. Desert night sounds frightened many women and children unaccustomed to such noises. The Fearns would attempt to sleep through the howls of coyotes, the calls of wild cats, and the chirping of crickets and toads.

Notice that the narrative begins with conflicts and problems the family had to overcome:
- the move to Arizona from Ohio
- a new lifestyle and climate
- the need to develop coping strategies

Then the narrative flashes back to how and why the family moved from Ohio to Arizona. The reader keeps reading to see how and if this family survives their trials.

Look for problems, conflicts, interesting aspects, unusual circumstances, or controversies, and begin your story there. Raise questions, either in the reader's mind or on paper. Give the reader a reason to keep reading.

Keeping the Story From Sagging in the Middle

How do fiction writers keep you turning pages? They build suspense. Now I'm not talking Stephen King sus-

97

pense. All you need to do is leave something hanging, either within a chapter or at the end of each chapter. You don't need to give us everything you know all at once. Create an air of mystery. Here is a quote from a letter that I used to end a chapter in *A Sense of Duty*:

> I thought I could see the thing through, Grace, but I was a fool to think so. It's no go. The last few months have been pure hell, and I don't have to tell you to what silly, foolish little things I stooped in constantly trying to suppress the big thing, which I considered I had no right to say. . . . I've got to know whether I have a chance. As you probably know, I haven't anything to offer you; to ask you to marry me at present would be no compliment. . . . But if I'm ever lucky enough to be able to ask you with a clear conscience, will I have a chance? Will you write real soon and tell me, and tell me in words of one syllable, because nothing could be worse than uncertainty.
>
> I'm not saying the things that are usually said and that I want to say so badly, because I want to keep this letter as rational as possible, and I'm sure you know them anyway. But if I get a certain answer, oh what a letter I will write! Will you send it right away, you wonderful girl?

Now, be honest. Could you put the book down at that point? Even if you were late to pick up your kids from school, wouldn't you turn the page for a peek at Grace's answer?

As you are reading novels and family history narratives, be conscious of what is keeping you interested—or what is causing you to set the book aside. **Sometimes, it's not the lack of cliffhangers, but a lack of focus that causes a story to sag in the middle.** Have you gone off on a tangent that really has no bearing on the story? For example, let's say you're writing about an ancestor, and you mention the names of the witnesses from one of the ancestor's deeds. You've done research on the witnesses to see if they are

Warning

related to your ancestor. You found out that they were not, but, gosh, one guy led a pretty interesting life, and you want to share all this cool research with the reader. Unfortunately, you will probably lose your reader at that point. Or maybe you got so involved in researching a historical theme that now your book is turning into a history lesson. At best, your readers may skip over that part; at worst, they'll put the book down and perhaps never pick it up again. Stay focused on your characters and their story.

Remember, the goal is to unfold a story bit by bit. I'll cover building suspense in more detail in STEP 13, but for now, think about how you'll keep the reader engrossed in your book.

> *You don't initiate a story until you know how you're going to end it. You don't start a dinner party conversation—"A funny thing happened to me on the way to La Guardia"—and not know what happened in La Guardia.*—JOHN IRVING

Ending the Story

The beauty of writing nonfiction family history is that you know how it ends before you begin writing. But just as a family history does not have to begin with the day someone was born, a family history does not have to end when everyone in the story is dead. While that is a natural place to conclude, and appropriate in some cases, remember that you're writing *creative* nonfiction, so try to be creative about the ending.

Here's another eye-opener: your family history doesn't even have to have a happy ending. You certainly don't have to kill off your ancestors if you don't want to, nor does everyone have to live happily ever after. You can end the story with your great-grandparents in their old age. You can conclude with a tragic event. After all, throughout literary history, tragedies generally have stuck with us longer and have had more of an impact on us than comedies. A dramatic, sad event may be just the way to end the story of your ancestor's life.

CHOOSING A VERB TENSE

You'll probably find few family histories written in anything but past tense. Since we're writing about events of the past—things that have already happened—it's appropriate and best to write in past tense. Even if you write a family history memoir where you tell the story of finding your ancestors, it would be equally appropriate to write that narrative in past tense because those events have already happened. Here is an example of narrative written in past tense:

> Elizabeth Warren could not have anticipated how her life would be when she arrived in Plymouth. Her new home was the center of her sphere, and she tried to replicate her life in England as best she could. Elizabeth spent much of her time around the fireplace. It was there that she made meals for her family, warmed coals in a pan for the bed she shared with Richard, and kept the fire burning to warm her home.

Moreover, past tense comes naturally when we tell stories, and thus is simply easier to use when writing. When Kathy Sturdevant and I taught personal and family memoir writing classes for WritersOnlineWorkshops.com, we noticed that students who attempted to write in the present tense (as if the story were happening as they wrote it) frequently got into trouble as their verb tenses started to shift. After we pointed out about a dozen places in one assignment where a student had shifted verb tenses without even realizing it, the student understood why writing instructors advocate writing about past events in past tense. True, writing in the present tense lends immediacy to a story, making readers feel as if they are witnessing it as it happened; but unless you are an experienced and extremely skillful writer (who also happens to have a good editor who will catch tense lapses), I would recommend that you keep your narrative in past tense.

When I was writing the biographies of Jay Roscoe Rhoads and his wife, Grace, in *A Sense of Duty*, I didn't want Roscoe and Grace to die. I had grown fond of this couple, and I didn't want to think about their demise, even though in reality they had been dead for about fifteen years by the time I wrote their stories. So I didn't end their story with obituaries or death certificates; instead, I put family stories of their last days in an epilogue, and concluded the narrative with something more satisfying. On his eighty-fifth birthday, about two and a half years before he died, Roscoe had written a fabulous two-page reminiscence containing his life's philosophies. I transcribed the document verbatim, ending the book with Roscoe's own great closing sentence: "Well, so much for the ruminations of a tin horn philosopher, just turned 85."

Granted, I was lucky to have such a document to end the story with. But you might be surprised at what you find once you begin searching your family history for items that would make interesting and powerful endings. If it's a tragic ending, so be it. Another idea is to bring the ending back around to the beginning, so it makes a complete circle. This is the method I used to end the Fearn narrative:

Charles and Mattie Fearn experienced a way of life different from most families during the late 1800s. Because of Charles's military career, they saw and lived in Arkansas, Wyoming, and Arizona, but it was the desert of Arizona that brought the most challenges to the family. Perhaps more frustrating than the lizards, snakes, tarantulas, scorpions, and black ants were the wind and the dust. But despite the obstacles of desert military camp life, they endured and walked away with fascinating stories to tell their grandchildren.

The best endings resonate because they echo a word, phrase, or image from earlier in the story, and the reader is prompted to think back to that reference and speculate on a deeper meaning.—JAMES PLATH

TRANSITIONS

As you may recall from your English composition classes, each paragraph needs to flow into the next, and each scene needs to lead smoothly to the following one. Writers accomplish this by using transitional words or phrases, such as *however, furthermore, besides, in addition, a year later, the year before*, and so on.

Your narrative may require that you skip periods

of time. Sometimes several months or years of your ancestor's life may be unaccounted for in the records you have researched. If this occurs, you can make the transition in your narrative by writing something like: *James Collins purchased land in Clay County in 1862, but his name does not appear in any other public records until 1870, when the census taker visited him.* **Don't feel you have to account for every second of every day in your ancestor's life.**

Important

NARRATOR AND POINT OF VIEW

The *narrator* is the person telling the story. When writing your own life story, family history narratives, or family history memoirs, you will be the narrator. While that may seem obvious, I have seen writers try to turn one of their ancestors into the narrator, writing as if Great-grandpa Joe were telling the story. What's the problem with that? The problem is that unless Great-grandpa Joe really did tell the story of your family history, you are stepping outside the bounds of nonfiction and into fiction. For creative nonfiction, the writer is the most appropriate narrator. However, you do have some choice as to point of view.

First-Person Point of View

If you are writing a family history memoir, use the first-person point of view because the story is about your search for your ancestors. So you will use *I*, as in these two examples from family history memoirs:

> I felt seasick from scrolling through the censuses on the microfilm reader at the Minnesota History Center. Sitting hunched in front of the hulking gray machine, I grew queasy while I worked. The names of past generations, scrawled in the various delicate hands of the census enumerators, sailed past me like swells on a paper ocean.
>
> —MARY LOGUE, *HALFWAY HOME:*
> *A GRANDDAUGHTER'S BIOGRAPHY*

For days, I had been listening to stories about Edwina's relatives, each more intriguing than the last, and now she was showing me her sources. I like old things, and the office and its ancient files were to my eyes like a ship to the eyes of a castaway.

—EDWARD BALL, *THE SWEET HELL INSIDE*

When writing in first-person point of view, it is appropriate to refer to your relatives as *my grandfather, my aunt,* and so on; but be sure to include their names so it's clear to the reader about whom you are writing. When referring to distant ancestors, it is better to write: *my fifth great-grandfather* rather than *my great-great-great-great-great-grandfather* or *my five times great-grandfather.*

The danger with first person narrative is the tendency to use *I* too much, to the point that you become so self-focused that you exclude the reader. The focus of the story is the search and what you found, not you. Remember that you are just another character in the story.

Third-Person Point of View

You'll use this point of view when writing life stories (biographies) and family history narratives. Third person uses *he, she, they,* and so forth. There are two variations on the third-person point of view, which you may remember from your English-class days: omniscient and limited. In third-person omniscient, the narrator has unlimited knowledge about everyone in the story. English teachers like to use the God analogy to help students remember this point of view: it's as if God, who is all-seeing and all-knowing, is writing the story. In third-person limited, you tell the story from only one character's (or ancestor's) perspective. In other words, in a fiction story that uses third-person limited, the reader is privy to only one character's thoughts and feelings, so other characters must be revealed only through that character's eyes.

Third-person omniscient comes closest to the point of view that you will use in writing life stories or family history narrative. The problem with true third-person omniscient for creative nonfiction writers is that we can't know for sure what was going on in our ancestors' minds, and to write it as if you did is to fictionalize. So writing in true third-person omniscient is impossible for the family history writer. As Gerard reminds us in *Creative Nonfiction*, "The best the nonfiction writer can do is to present the *illusion* of interior lives, giving the reader insight and private information about real people, but stopping short of claiming to *know* what cannot be known—without making it up."

Technique

Here are two examples of presenting the *illusion* of knowing something about ancestors' "interior lives"—their thoughts or feelings. I've italicized words that prevent the narrative from crossing over into the realm of fiction.

No doubt Ann Townshend found her new life in the wilderness of Ohio unlike anything she knew in England. A new experience for immigrant *women like* Ann was dealing with a different race of people: Cherokee Indians. *Likely* she had heard stories, or *perhaps* had read some of the popular novels of the day, which spoke of frontier women taken captive by Indians. This *probably* induced a fear, real or imagined, of the dark-skinned natives who inhabited the area. Captivity narratives, published both as fiction and nonfiction, were popular reading, especially among women.

What went through Rebecca Allen's mind when she heard the news? Her husband Obed wanted to join thousands of other men headed to California, hoping to make a fortune in the gold mines. He *no doubt* assured her that he would return, that this was the opportunity of a lifetime—a chance to get rich quick. *But what would she and their three minor children do for money while he was gone?* Their oldest and only son still living at home was twenty, but he was going to marry soon and begin a family of his own. *Like most men* in Obed's situation—trying to convince his wife he was doing the right thing—he *probably* told Rebecca he would send money home to her as he made it.

In both passages, I've given the illusion of knowing the characters' thoughts and feelings by raising questions and speculating on what anyone's reaction to such circumstances might be. We'll cover speculating and making inferences more in STEP 14, but a good family history nonfiction writer also needs to have an understanding and appreciation of human nature and how most people would think and react to a given situation. As biographer Jean Strouse says in her essay, "The Real Reasons" (in William Zinsser's *Extraordinary Lives*), **"Good biographers combine the arts of the novelist, the detective work of the historian and the insights of the psychologist."** Put yourself in your ancestor's shoes for a scene and ask how you or any person might respond to the same events, given the time period. Just remember, you can never know for sure how an ancestor felt, so you must only give the illusion that you know.

Quotes

Narrator Intrusion

If you are writing your narrative in third person, you as the narrator need to stay out of the story. For example, you would not write paragraph after paragraph in third person, saying: *he did this*, and *she did that*, then, all of a sudden, switch to first person: *I was surprised to find my ancestors doing this.* That would be an inappropriate intrusion upon the story.

The narrator can unintentionally intrude upon the story in more subtle ways, however. Let's say you are writing about your ancestor who committed adultery in colonial Rhode Island. You report your findings from the records and the type of punishment she was to receive. Then you interject: *The punishment was well deserved, for this was not the type of behavior society wanted to condone.* You've just intruded upon the narrative by making a

Warning

judgment call: *The punishment was well deserved.* In whose opinion was it well deserved? Her contemporaries', or yours? Keep your opinions and judgments out of the narrative.

Similarly, be careful of twenty-first century hindsight. Don't insert things we know today that your ancestors could not have possibly known, such as the causes of certain diseases and recent medical discoveries. Also avoid using slang or today's trendy phrases in a historical narrative.

Write from the heart. Don't be too intellectual during the process. That leads to writer's block. And don't reread your material until after the first draft.
—JEROME COURSHON

Ready for the really fun aspects of writing family history narrative? In the next four steps, we get down to the nitty-gritty of developing your ancestor's character, describing the scene, using family stories and dialogue appropriately, and adding suspense, humor, and—my favorite—romance!

Bringing Your Ancestors to Life as Characters

*A writer begins by breathing life into his characters. But
if you are very lucky, they breathe life into you.*
—CARYL PHILLIPS

Quick! What's the first thing that comes to mind when
I say: *Gone With the Wind*? How about *To Kill a
Mockingbird*? Or *Death of a Salesman*? Or *Catcher in the
Rye*? Or *Star Wars*? If you answered: Scarlett O'Hara or
Rhett Butler; Atticus Finch, Scout Finch, or Boo Radley;
Willy Loman; Holden Caulfield; and Luke Skywalker or
Princess Leia, then you associated all of those titles with
a character from the stories. You probably didn't think:
the Civil War, prejudice in the South, tired working man
comes home to a complaining family, teenage boy coming
of age, or intergalactic battles. No, it's the characters,
above and beyond the story line, that stick with us. And
the characters should be what sticks with your readers
when they embark on the journey of reading your family
history. Once you make the decision to write your family
history narrative, memoir, or life story, your ancestors are
no longer names on a chart. They are now characters in a
story. The facts and events are secondary. **But as a creative
nonfiction writer, you can't create characters. You have real-
life people to portray in a manner that is as honest and as
accurate as possible.** Just as you searched records about
your ancestors to find the plot and look for themes for
your narrative, you also need to search with a writer's
eye toward what these documents can tell you about the
character of your forebears.

Important

107

Before we look at some examples, remember that your narrative should reveal characters bit by bit, not all at once—as if someone were reading us their vital statistics or resume. When we meet someone in real life, we learn about that person gradually. That's how the reader should get acquainted with your ancestors.

Also keep in mind Patricia Bosworth's words in "The Mysterious Art of Biography," (*The Writer's Handbook*, 1991, as quoted in William Noble's *Writing Dramatic Fiction*): "If one is lucky, one comes away with the essence of a character, a version of a life. But there is always more than one version." If you have any doubts about her statement, just take a look at how many biographies there are of Thomas Jefferson or George Washington, or of any ex-president or celebrity. "And it really can't be any other way," says William Noble, "because the writer, throughout the work, has made value judgments about what is or is not germane, what is or is not interesting, what is or is not supportable."

Carolyn G. Heilbrun, author of *Writing a Woman's Life*, agrees. In an essay titled "Dorothy L. Sayers: Biography Between the Lines," she writes, "Since no one's life can be really known, since what is recorded or remembered very much depends on chance, as biographers or readers of biography, we all choose among the relics to form the life we want to envision for our subject." So with these words of wisdom in mind, let's look at ways to bring out your ancestors' characters.

NOT JUST NAMES

Your readers are going to want to know what your characters were like: how they lived, how they might have felt, what they looked like. Readers want characters they can like (or hate), ones with whom they can empathize and identify. Obviously, it will be much easier to show character in your narrative for relatives you've known or interviewed. But you can do it with distant ancestors, too.

Many attributes reveal a person's character: speech, actions, behaviors, habits, body language, beliefs, secrets, likes and dislikes, clothing, food preferences, friends and acquaintances, (including which ones we admire or despise, and those we wish to impress), and so on. **Fiction writers use a character sketch list, and you might want to consider making one for each of your main characters.** List the following attributes:

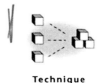

Technique

name	number of children
parents' names	hobbies
ethnic origin	health status
physical appearance, including dress	cause of death
	habits and quirks
profession or occupation	favorite expressions
education	favorite foods
economic status	positive traits
religious affiliation	negative traits
marital status	those admired
spouse's name	those despised

Don't worry if you can't fill in all the information. Get as much down as you can. The point is to examine your ancestors more closely, focusing on details that will bring them to life in your narrative.

Let's look at an example from Gay Talese's *Unto the Sons*. Talese is writing about his great-grandmother Ippolita Talese, presumably using information his father, Joseph, had told him about her.

Ippolita Talese had an aura of mystery about her that often puzzled her grandson, a detachment that sometimes made Joseph ill at ease in her presence; and yet he was oddly pleased that she was his grandmother. He was impressed by her. He was impressed by her well-groomed appearance, her delicate face and fair skin, which was remarkably unwrinkled for a woman of her age, and he was impressed with the fact that she changed her dress each evening before supper, or, at the very least, came to the table wearing a beautiful lace collar, and always emitted a slight but pleasant fragrance of perfume. She held her slim shoulders back when she walked, and sat upright during dinner in one of the high-backed chairs that had cushions and were much more comfortable than the furniture that Joseph was accustomed to at home.

Notice how this paragraph slowly *shows* us Ippolita's character. By describing her demeanor and traits— "well-groomed appearance," "changed her dress each evening before supper," "emitted a slight but pleasant fragrance of perfume," "held her slim shoulders back," "sat upright during dinner"—Talese is revealing her character. He could have written: "Ippolita was a proud woman who cared about her appearance," but that would be *telling*, not *showing*.

Try this: using only a few words, jot down some traits of one of the oldest relatives you remember. As an example, here are three traits of my Italian grandmother, Stella (Ebetino) DeBartolo, who immigrated to America when she was five:

proud
well groomed
practical

In my narrative about Grandma, I could write: *Stella was a proud woman who was well groomed and practical about life.* But has that described her character? Can you picture what kind of person she was in your imagination? Probably not. Those traits are too abstract and can mean different things to different people. Readers need something concrete to mentally latch onto, something that *shows* them *proud*, *well groomed*, and *practical*. Let's see what happens when I give examples of those traits in short anecdotes:

As I walked down the street side by side with Grandma, she would chide me for slouching. "Stand up straight," she'd insist. I'd look over at her posture.

Her back was rigid, yet not uncomfortable-looking. Perfect posture seemed to come naturally to this stout, five-foot-tall Italian woman with loosely-permed, short gray hair—but not to this pudgy, pubescent girl of twelve, who lacked any shred of confidence. Grandma's clothing was always meticulously clean and pressed, too: a reflection, no doubt, of the image she wanted and liked to portray at the fancy dress shop where she worked. . . .

Grandma had an extremely practical side to her. At one of the last family gatherings at her house that I remember, she served spaghetti. Everyone raved over her sauce and asked for the recipe. She shrugged off the request and said, as if it were the most obvious thing in the world, "What recipe? You just open a jar of Ragu. Why spend hours making spaghetti sauce, when these days you can just open a jar?"

In the first paragraph, I have shown *proud* and *well groomed* with an anecdotal episode that made me think she was proud and well groomed. I don't have to say it directly; readers can draw their own conclusions about her character from the anecdote I've told. In the second paragraph, I came right out and said that she had a practical side, but I followed it with an example that illustrates the point. This one anecdote out of many that I remember about her is what made me believe she was a practical woman. Again, people reveal their characters through actions, demeanor, and words (see STEP 12 for a discussion on how to include dialogue). It's up to you, the writer, to take notice of personality-revealing traits that you can then show the reader.

It's not that difficult to do. For example, say you think of your Uncle Sydney as *mean*. What did he do that made you think of him that way? Whatever that answer is, that's what you'll use as an anecdote to show his meanness to the reader. See? I'll bet you, too, can easily write a short character description like I've just done.

PHYSICAL DESCRIPTIONS

Whenever you introduce an ancestor into your story, give some physical description, if possible, but don't make it into an FBI wanted-poster description. Choose some significant details, then give them to us as you reveal character. Let's go back to the two paragraphs about my grandmother. While I haven't revealed things like eye color or complexion, you do know that she was a stout woman, five-feet tall, with good posture and loosely permed gray hair. Can you visualize an Italian woman who fits that description? I think almost everyone can. As readers, we envision characters in our minds by matching the written description to our own experiences and frame of reference. It's not important that you picture my grandmother precisely. Remember that even if you have a photograph of a person, the photograph can show only one aspect of a character; the description in your narrative, however, can reveal a more fully rounded personality.

Tip

If you have a photograph of your ancestor, use it to describe what he or she looked like. **Even if you plan to include that photo as an illustration in your book, a written description can bring to your readers' attention details they might not otherwise notice.** Clothing, for example, can reveal social status, occupation, and the time period. How it's worn can indicate whether the person is meticulous or careless. What style of clothing did he wear? How did she wear her hair?

Look at the photograph in Figure 10-1 on page 113. Here is how I described Delia in that photo:

Only one known photograph survives of Delia, with her hard life evident in her face: her eyes droop at the outer sides and appear weary. Though her face was pudgy and unwrinkled, she looked to be in her fifties when the photograph was taken. A stocky woman, Delia wore a half-smile. Dressed in a long, dark (perhaps black) dress, she stood in the yard, her left hand casually resting on an upholstered chair. Delia's dark, curly hair was pulled

Figure 10-1
Delia (Gordon) Norris (1859–1925). When you include photographs in your family history, be sure to work a description of the photograph into the narrative. You can point out details your readers may not have noticed.

back away from her face; no gray appeared at her temples or in her hair. Under her coat-style dress, she wore a print blouse with white collar and cuffs, and around her neck hung a long chain, which went to her waist. At first glance, one might think it was a crucifix; but upon closer examination, it appears to be a timepiece or magnifying glass. She wore no other jewelry except upon her left hand, where a wedding ring adorned her finger.

Remember, this is *my* interpretation of this photograph. Another researcher or family member might come along and describe Delia differently.

What if you don't have a photograph of your ancestor and don't know what he or she looked like? Then research the dress and hairstyles of other people from the same time and place as your ancestor, and describe that for the reader. Here's an example of how you might word your description

Men in Michael Carpenter's day did not wear their hair too closely cropped to their scalps, but it was not long either. Hair barely touched their shirt collars. Mustaches and mutton-chop sideburns were popular, and although no photographs have survived of Michael—if he had any taken—he may have worn his hair in similar fashion and grown facial hair as was the trend of the day.

PORTRAYING SYMPATHETIC CHARACTERS

Your characters should also be sympathetic ones, meaning that readers should be able to imagine themselves in similar circumstances and having similar feelings. In other words, your ancestors were human, with faults and failings; so show those faults as well as the good traits. If you write: *Matilda was a saint, perfect in every way. Everyone loved Matilda,* not only do we want to gag, but we can't relate to perfection because none of us is perfect. We need characters we can identify with, real human beings. On the other hand, if you were to write: *Matilda was a saint and everyone loved her. They loved her so much that no one had the heart to tell her she was a lousy cook,* then we can see that Matilda was just as human as we are. We can't create flaws, however; we can only look for them. By including even tiny ones, like being a lousy cook, we can ensure that an ancestor won't come across in the narrative as so saint-like that no one will believe she really existed. Remember, you're not writing a greeting card.

By the same token, we can't relate to total evil. Even those ancestral black sheep who were in and out of courtrooms for unspeakable crimes must have had a good side, too. In *My Wild Irish Rose,* when I wrote about Ralph, who abused his wife, Janie, I wanted to portray him as a three-dimensional character. Even though he beat his wife, he must have had some good traits; otherwise Janie wouldn't have married him in the first place. And indeed he did. One of his grandsons gave me stories about another side of Ralph, that of a kindly, loving grandfather, which I used to show another dimension to his character. Don't let someone's dark side cloud your view of him or her. Just as you might have to hunt for a tiny flaw just so you can portray that person as human, you might also have to search for some molecule of goodness.

CHARACTER MOTIVATION

People are consistently inconsistent. No one today does exactly what we expect them to do, so why should we expect our ancestors to be any more consistent than we are? Expect your ancestors to step out of character once in awhile: the aunt who never drinks may sneak a sip now and then to take the edge off a stressful situation; or the uncle who never loses his temper may have bopped a neighbor in the nose when the neighbor kicked your uncle's dog. You have the right to include these aberrations in your narrative, but the reader has a right to understand why the character is acting that way. Explain the behavior for the reader, if you can. If you can't, you may have to speculate, but base your ideas on research about why other people of your ancestor's day would have behaved in a similar fashion. Just be sure to make it clear that you are speculating (more on this technique in STEP 14); otherwise you'll be fictionalizing. "There's always danger in trying to get 'inside' a character with nonfiction," writes William Noble in *Writing Dramatic Nonfiction*, "because truth and reality may be elusive and incomplete. What a writer 'thinks' a character felt or didn't feel can only be as accurate as the source the writer uses for the information. An attempt to 'fictionalize' in the interest of adding drama can only lead the writer into trouble."

Reminder

CHARACTER GROWTH

Another aspect of characterization to look for in your ancestors is growth and change. For some ancestors, this will be obvious once you look at their lives from this perspective. Remember Ralph, the one who had a problem with spouse abuse? After his wife died, Ralph finally felt remorse for how he had treated her. Through interviews with my aunt, who witnessed his change in behavior as well as the violence, it was easy for me to show

Ralph's growth. For a seventeenth-century ancestor, however, finding evidence of growth will be more of a challenge, so be sure to notice when it does happen. Philip Gerard reminds us in *Creative Nonfiction* that "every good story contains a moment after which things can never be the same again. A moment of profound change: for the characters, for the reader." As mentioned in STEP 9, the best you may be able to do is to present the illusion of character growth. A way to do this without fictionalizing is to raise rhetorical questions, as in this example:

> Jacob Cohen had sold everything to bring his family to America. Although the first two decades were good and profitable—he was able to move them out of the Lower East Side tenement apartment into their own house—now that the Depression was upon the nation, he was behind on the mortgage. Did he wonder if he had made the right decision to come to America?

Jacob's *actions*—that is, what the records tell you happened next—will indirectly answer the question for the reader. Say, for example, that you find no evidence of Jacob losing the house; in fact, the family continued to live there until Jacob's death in the 1950s. The reader can surmise that he made the right decision to come to America after all. With your rhetorical question, you've suggested that Jacob may have experienced a profound change in his thinking (from doubt about his decision to confidence that everything has turned out fine) and thus you've given the illusion of character growth. But it's important that you word such illusions carefully, so you aren't crossing over the boundaries of nonfiction.

FINDING CHARACTER IN GENEALOGICAL SOURCES

Think about the records you've gathered on your ancestors. Do any of those records reveal something about an ancestor's character? **Here are some genealogical sources that might reveal character:**

- newspaper articles
- court records
- pension applications
- diaries and letters
- photographs
- wills and estate papers

Sources

Let's look at an example. Here's a transcript of a letter from an insurance agent to the Indianapolis pension office that was among the papers in Alfred Martin's Civil War pension file (WC 199257, National Archives, Washington, DC).

The voucher herewith attached of Hannah S. Martin, you will see I certify that she *did not* exhibit her pension certificate to me, this date, for the reason she has lost it or mislaid the same, she is a very old lady, and lives with her daughter and this pension is all she has for her support, she was very much worked up and nervous because she could not find her certificate, I told her that I would fix this up this way and send it to you, she was afraid the losing of the certificate would cut her means of support off. Now if this is not right return it to me with a new voucher and the necessary blank to proceed to get a new certificate, I never had a case like this before and I was at a loss just what to do or how to proceed in the matter, so I submit the voucher and this letter, to you and await your advices.

This document certainly tells us something about Hannah's character late in her life. You have two choices on how to use this letter in your narrative. You can insert a verbatim transcript of the letter and let her character come through as it is, or you can use the details given in this letter to give your narrative more drama and action, as in this example:

In 1904, Hannah Martin was eighty-two-years-old, and since 1879, had been living off of her third husband's Civil War pension. Nervous, agitated, and afraid of losing her one means of support, Hannah had mislaid or lost her pension certificate and could not find it anywhere. Without it, the pension agent in Indianapolis could stop her payments. Fortunately, Walter Hughes, the resident agent for the Phoenix Insurance Company, came to her rescue. Hughes reassured Hannah he would handle the problem and wrote the pension office on her behalf. . . .

You could then follow this introduction with a transcript of the letter, although it might appear redundant. When you have documents rich with details that show an ancestor's character, be sure to make the most of them in your narrative.

Now think setting. When I say *Dr. Zhivago* what comes to mind? Cold? Snow? Russia? How about *South Pacific*? Warm, sandy, white beaches? Good. Let's immerse ourselves in our ancestors' setting—but I have dibs on the sandy, white beach!

Describing Your Ancestors' Setting

Setting . . . contributes enormously to the general feeling or tone of a story.
—JACK M. BICKHAM, *SETTING*

I was born in Port Chester, New York, in 1956. That's enough information, right? That's all you need to know about the time and place into which I was born. From that information alone, you know exactly what Port Chester is like and what the year 1956 is all about. No? You need more information? From reading some family histories, you'd think that's all a writer needed to do to give the story a setting. Ah, if only it were that simple.

Where does your family history take place? What's the time period? You'll need to know a lot about both of these to describe them for your reader, but as Noble says in *Writing Dramatic Nonfiction*, "the emphasis is on 'sense,' not place." If you state in your narrative that an ancestor lived in Philadelphia, that identifies for the reader the place, but we don't have a "sense" of it. What was it like to live in Philadelphia in your ancestor's day? If you write, "The year was 1850," you've identified the time period, but not a sense of what life in 1850 was like.

Instead, describe what Philadelphia in 1850 looks like. **Remember, your readers may have little or no knowledge of the way people lived then and how the city looked.** Also, bare dates lend a dry, academic textbook style that you are trying to avoid. Show us the time period through the typical clothing people like your ancestors wore, the

Reminder

forms of lighting in houses and on city streets, the types of furniture people had in their houses, and the modes of transportation—the social details.

Don't overwhelm your reader with description, however. When we tour Philadelphia, we don't have a bird's-eye view; we see the city piece by piece. Show readers the setting little by little in your narrative. Readers don't want a geography lesson or to feel like they are reading an almanac. Let the reader visualize the setting by describing social life in detail.

> Philadelphia was a bustling metropolis when, by 1849, the Zesingers made the area their home. The city was in a state of constant change during the mid-nineteenth century. Philadelphians were tearing down old buildings and replacing them with imposing new structures made of red sandstone, granite, and iron. More than one hundred miles of gas lines fed the city's 1,718 street lamps. Iron water pipes replaced wooden ones, so that indoor plumbing was commonplace for better housing. In poorer districts, families received their water supply from public hydrant pumps. The only way in which Philadelphia lagged behind other urban areas was in its transportation. Citizens were not in favor of introducing streetcars for fear of "increased congestion, noise, and accident hazards." In the 1850s, people traveled by hacks, cabs, and horse-drawn omnibuses. During deep winter snows, people used large, open sleighs drawn by four-horse teams.

IT'S ALL IN THE DETAILS

Remember those county and local histories I suggested you revisit back in STEP 6? To describe the setting, you'll be using the notes you took on topography, climate, buildings, and community. Here are some items to consider adding to your narrative:

- place (describe the countryside, town, community, topography)

- time and season (describe the climate and seasonal appearance)
- architecture (describe the interior, exterior, and landscaping of homes, public buildings, and outbuildings)
- artifacts (describe household furniture and objects)

If the story involves a setting where you have never been, the best case is to visit it and walk the streets, fields, and neighborhood. If that's not possible, research it. Interview someone who has been there. Remember, you don't need to break a leg to know that it would hurt; likewise, you don't need to visit an area to be able to write about it. But you do need to do thorough enough research to make sure you have accurate information. Some things you just can't experience first hand—like crossing the Atlantic in the 1600s on a sailing ship from England to America—yet you can still convey the sense of the experience by researching historical accounts of people who were there and experienced the things you want to write about.

You'll find many sources beyond county histories that will give you the type of material you need to give your readers a sense of the time period and place:

- historic photographs of the area in local history collections, and in the vertical files of libraries and archives
- genealogical sources (land and tax records, city directories, agricultural schedules, manufacturing schedules, family stories)
- social histories
- travel guidebooks that offer historical information
- books on historic homes, architecture, and antiques
- books on an area's geography and topography
- maps (Sanborn fire insurance maps, topographical maps, bird's-eye view maps)
- farmer's almanacs
- newspapers

Reminder

USING SENSORY PERCEPTION

When you describe the setting, try to involve the reader's five senses: sight, sound, taste, touch, and smell. Think about the setting in terms of how it looks, the sounds you would hear, how it feels during a particular season, what it smells like, and even what you might taste (ethnic specialty foods, for example). By telling readers what they can see, hear, smell, taste, and feel, you will have "shown" them the setting.

One of my favorite examples of a vivid sense of place comes from Frank McCourt's *Angela's Ashes*:

> My father and mother should have stayed in New York where they met and married and where I was born. Instead, they returned to Ireland when I was four. . . .
>
> Out in the Atlantic Ocean great sheets of rain gathered to drift slowly up the River Shannon and settle forever in Limerick. The rain dampened the city from the Feast of the Circumcision to New Year's Eve. It created a cacophony of hacking coughs, bronchial rattles, asthmatic wheezes, consumptive croaks. It turned noses into fountains, lungs into bacterial sponges. . . . From October to April the walls of Limerick glistened with the damp. Clothes never dried: tweed and woolen coats housed living things, sometimes sprouted mysterious vegetations. In pubs, steam rose from damp bodies and garments to be inhaled with cigarette and pipe smoke laced with the stale fumes of spilled stout and whiskey. . . .

So, who's ready to jump on a plane and head to Limerick? What senses has McCourt awakened in you, the reader? Sound ("hacking coughs, bronchial rattles, asthmatic wheezes, consumptive croaks"), sight ("the walls of Limerick glistened with the damp," "steam rose from damp bodies"), smell ("garments to be inhaled with cigarette and pipe smoke," "stale fumes of spilled stout and whiskey"), and touch ("clothes never dried"). He aroused four out of the five senses in one paragraph. No wonder he won a Pulitzer!

Let's say you discovered from a farmer's almanac that it rained the day your ancestor was born. What does rain sound like? What would it sound like on the canvas of a covered wagon? In a structure with a tin roof? In a sod house? Is it a heavy rain or a drizzle? What does rain smell like? On a open field? On pavement? As we do when imagining characters, we associate sounds and smells (and the other senses) with our own past experiences.

Smell, in particular, is a powerful sense. Fragrances and odors immediately trigger memories, good and bad, of an event or experience. Write about the smell of burning leaves when your grandpa raked them in the fall. Write about the aroma of that apple pie your mom always made, or the spaghetti sauce simmering on the stove. These are smells most of us know, and they bring back memories of our own experience with them. Did your ancestors live by the ocean or a lake? On a farm? In the heart of a big city? What smells would they have smelled? Here's an example from one of my narratives about the rotting potatoes at the outbreak of the famine in Ireland. According to numerous personal accounts from all over Ireland, the odor was prevalent throughout the country.

One morning in 1845, between about July and September, Hugh and Mary McGuire woke up to the strangest odor. It was hard to identify at first. The smell reeked of something sickly or decaying. "What *was* that smell?" families all across Ireland were wondering. It seemed to linger and hang heavy with the fog. What could be rotting in such mass quantities that it would cause this malodorous, sewerlike smell?

Keep in mind that many of your readers are reading your family history narrative to experience what life was like in your ancestors' days, something they wouldn't be able to

Reminder

experience personally. Your job is to make your readers forget that they are reading and to give them the illusion of being in the story with your ancestors, seeing and hearing and smelling and feeling what's happening to them. When I read *The Grapes of Wrath*, I want to feel the grit of the dust bowl in my hair and teeth. When I read *The Haunting of Hill House*, I want to be scared. When I read your family history, I want to experience the same things your ancestors did. If it's a famine, I want to feel hunger and the need to get up and get something to eat. If it's a flood, I want to shiver, feel cold and wet, and the desire to get dry and crawl under the electric blanket. Give your readers a *sense* of the setting, not just the facts.

Using Family Stories in Your Narrative

We are basically storytellers, descendants of the old men who sat around the fire and told us legends, fairy tales, exploits, or maybe just how funny Og looked when he fell into the tar pit.—SOL SAKS

Everyone has some kind of family story or legend that they can include in their family history narrative. Some of these stories may be only colorful myths that have been perpetuated through the generations. Others may have good substance for your narrative. Many of these stories you may have heard repeated throughout your lifetime; others you might have gleaned from an oral history interview. Even if you've already interviewed your relatives, you may want to consider doing additional interviews now that you have the book's scope in mind. So let's begin with a brief overview of oral history interviewing, then we'll look at how to edit and use the interview material in your narrative.

Oral History

For more advice and instruction on conducting oral history interviews, see Katherine Scott Sturdevant's *Bringing Your Family History to Life Through Social History*, and Emily Anne Croom's *Unpuzzling Your Past*, 4th edition.

THE NEW FOCUS

If you've interviewed your relatives in the past, your focus at the time may have been on obtaining genealogical facts rather than on trying to get stories that reveal character, setting, and the drama of your family history. Getting those names, dates, and places was important as you began your research, but now that you're winding down researching and preparing to write, you may want to revisit the relatives. Ask questions that will get you the stories of real people that will give your family history that human element we've been talking about.

In *Creative Nonfiction*, Philip Gerard reminds us of these three facts about human nature:

1. People love to talk about themselves to someone who seems genuinely interested.
2. If someone talks long enough, he or she will inevitably tell you something they didn't intend to tell you.
3. People have a strong aversion to long pauses in a conversation . . . [so] without even asking a question, they will usually talk to fill the silence.

My favorite book for preparing questions for oral history interviews is William Fletcher's *Recording Your Family History: A Guide to Preserving Oral History Using Audio and Video Tape* (Berkeley: Ten Speed Press, 1989). He suggests hundreds of questions to ask relatives to get the type of stories you're after for your family history narrative. The book's chapters are broken down by the life cycle, and by specific national events as they relate to the everyday person: family history, childhood, youth, middle age, old age, narrator as parent, grandchildren, historical events, general questions, unusual life experiences, and personal philosophy and values. In addition, there are special questions for interviewing Jewish, black, and Hispanic relatives. Other books, such as Croom's *Unpuzzling Your Past*, have similar questions, but if you can latch onto a copy of Fletcher, too, you'll have a broader variety.

People to Interview

While older relatives will be your priority and the best source for stories, don't neglect younger relatives, especially if the older ones are gone, or aren't accessible because of distance or health problems. They are likely to have heard their elders recite family stories, too.

If you're running into a shortage of relatives, remember there are many other people you can interview for stories and background information:

- your parents' and grandparents' friends and neighbors
- the town historian
- someone of the same generation, same ethnic background, and from the same area as your relatives

Oral History as a Reliable Source

For too long, I'm afraid, many genealogists and even some historians have discredited the use of oral history, becoming document-oriented researchers. **Oral history, however, is no less reliable a source than any document we might consult.** All sources are prone to errors and discrepancies, even those carved in stone. If you've traced your ancestors in all censuses for their lifetimes, then you know what I'm talking about. There are inconsistencies and errors from one census to another.

Important

Yes, one person's version of an event will differ from another's. And, yes, people's memories are prone to lapses and inaccuracies. On the other hand, consider that "oral sources tell us not just what people did, but what they wanted to do, what they believed they were doing and what they now think they did." You won't find the *how, what,* and *why* in genealogical sources. From oral histories we get more than just eyewitness accounts that could be accurate or inaccurate; we get themes and personal interpretations of events. Like many historians, we can recognize oral history for what it is and consider its unique, valuable role in family history: that is, someone's personal recollections and interpretations of his or her own experiences.

The quote in this paragraph came from Alexander Stille, "Prospecting for Truth in the Ore of Memory: Oral History is Gaining New Respect Through Insights into Its Distortions," *The New York Times,* Arts and Ideas Section, 10 March 2001, pages B9, B11.

I never knew my mother's mother, my grandmother Rose, about whom I wrote in *My Wild Irish Rose.* She died when I was six months old. I have come to know her through research, but mostly from the stories my mother and aunt shared with me. That is the way of researching and writing our family histories. Many of the ancestors we hope to discover the most about we never knew personally. We learn about their lives through piecing together bits from a variety of sources, and oral history can form a large part of that overall picture. So, should you hesitate to use oral history material in your family history? Heavens no!

Can You Use Everything Someone Tells You?

There are some ethical and legal considerations when conducting oral history interviews with the intent of publishing them. Assuming you have written out questions and that you are taping the interview (with the person's permission, of course), legally, you own the copyright to the questions you pose, and the person you are interviewing would own the copyright to the answers. This means that you will need written permission from your interview subject granting you the right to use those answers in your book. The fact that the person consented to the taped interview, even if you got the person's agreement on tape, may not be enough. Sturdevant's *Bringing Your Family History to Life Through Social History* has release forms you can use or adapt.

Important

An additional courtesy, as well as an ethical consideration, would be to run what you plan to publish by the person who contributed the stories. Remember Gerard's second point: that the longer someone talks, "he or she will inevitably tell you something they didn't intend to tell you." You don't want to spend hours weaving interview material into your narrative, only to have your interviewee ax a great story because he or she had second thoughts about it being in print. In all fairness, you need to check with your interviewee before you go to press. I usually have the person review a transcript of the interview before I even begin writing, so I'll know what I can use and what I can't. When you send the transcript for review, include a copy of the release form for your interviewee to sign and return with the edited transcript. But so the release doesn't take your relative by surprise, it would be a good idea to discuss it before the interview, leaving him or her a copy to look over.

BLENDING ORAL HISTORY IN THE NARRATIVE

You may have an oral history transcript of forty or more pages, but you'll use only a fraction of it. You do not include transcriptions of every single document you found on an ancestor in your narrative; you use them as sources. An interview transcript is simply another source. You will select portions to use in the narrative

WRITING ABOUT LIVING GENERATIONS

If you're writing the life story of a living person, or plan to include information about living generations in your family history, there are some issues you need to consider. Just as you do not own a person's words from an oral history interview and cannot use them freely without the interviewee's permission, the same is true when it comes to writing about a living person's life. Everyone has the right to privacy, so if you plan to publish anything about someone living, I recommend that you get that person's permission. Even an e-mail exchange—you tell Cousin Betty that you're writing the family history and are planning to include vital information about her and her family; she replies that that's okay—is better than nothing. At least you have something in writing, and Cousin Betty has been forewarned.

As you should do when converting oral history interviews to narrative, consider allowing your subjects to read what you have written about them before publication. This will ensure that your information is accurate and that your subject knows what you have written. While you may not think that your cousin's first marriage—which took place several decades ago while he was in his late teens and ended after only three weeks—is a big deal, he may not want anyone to be reminded of his big mistake in print.

Also, be cautious about including information about living children in print or online. While the odds of someone reading your family history and seeking out a child for sinister purposes are slim, the chance remains. Consider this scenario: Cousin Marty, who is new to genealogy, creates a home page on the Internet that includes excerpts from your book. He doesn't realize that he's violating your copyright, nor does he realize that he's endangering your children by posting their birth dates and other identifying data. It happens, and one way to prevent it is to list living children in your book by name only, without any other identifying information.

129

that are relevant to the plot, themes, characters, and setting. And you probably will not use the interview material in the order it was told to you. You as the writer have the flexibility to place quotes or paraphrases in whatever order seems natural to your story. Philip Gerard, in *Creative Nonfiction*, puts it this way:

> You have to choose carefully from everything your subject said and present his or her words in a dramatic context—which usually means in a different order from the one in which they were actually said. More often than not, you leave out much of the interview, choosing only the best, most telling stories.

Moreover, you'll want to work in the interview material smoothly and seamlessly. Do this as you would with any source: by mixing quotes and paraphrases in the narrative. For example, here are the notes from an oral history interview:

> Jane and Ralph had two children, Ralph and Donald. Donald was the oldest. Ralph had TB. . . . They sent him to a sanatorium in upstate NY. . . . This was when he was about 18, and he was there most of his 20s. Possibly in his early 30s when he died. Doesn't remember the name of sanatorium. "We used to visit him in the sanatorium. It was like a hospital, and because we were too young and it was a contagious disease, we weren't allowed to go up and see him. But he used to wave to us from the window as we played on the grounds."

Using the notes from the interview, direct quotes, and Ralph's death certificate, I wrote this paragraph:

> Mary remembers visiting her cousin Ralph, who had tuberculosis and was sent to a sanatorium in upstate New York in his late teens. "We used to

visit him in the sanatorium. It was like a hospital, and because we were too young and it was a contagious disease, we weren't allowed to go up and see him. But he used to wave to us from the window as we played on the grounds." Tuberculosis was the leading cause of death in the nineteenth century and into the twentieth century. Ralph died from the disease in 1946 at the age of thirty-two.

The beauty of using oral history interview material is that it brings life to your narrative. We have real people talking and remembering. It also gives the illusion of dialogue, a subject I'll give more attention to on page 134.

Treat material from oral history interviews in your narrative as you would material from diaries and letters: **You will need to annotate items that aren't clear to the reader, identifying people, events, and places or explaining archaic or slang terms.** You'll also want to add historical context. In the above example, to augment the interview story, I'll turn to social histories on tuberculosis and give the reader some background on the disease and why people were sent to sanatoriums.

Reminder

Citing Oral History Interviews

While citing sources of information is covered in more detail in STEP 15, it's relevant to discuss citing oral history interviews here. If you're using only one or two quotes from an oral history interview in your narrative, then cite it as you would any source, with enough details so that your reader knows where the information came from.

Citing Sources

[1]Oral history interview between the author and Mary _____ on 31 October 1997. The interview was conducted in her home at _____ Avenue, _____, when she was sixty-six years old. The oral history tapes and a transcript are in the possession of the author.

On the other hand, if a substantial portion of your narrative is based on an interview, then it would be overwhelming to keep citing it for every quote. Instead, it is appropriate and acceptable to cite it like this:

[1]Unless otherwise noted, all specific information pertaining to the _____ family was obtained from an oral history interview with Mary ____ by the author on 31 October 1997. The interview was conducted in her home at ____ Avenue, _____, when she was sixty-six years old. The oral history tapes and a transcript are in the possession of the author.

HANDLING ORAL HISTORY DISCREPANCIES

I once interviewed two brothers separately. When I asked the first brother if his mother was the emotional type, he responded, "Oh, yes. She cried over everything." When I interviewed the second brother and asked the same question, he responded, "No, she didn't cry very often." I had to temporarily stop the interview and laugh because the versions were so different. I looked at the second brother and asked, "Were you raised in the same household as your brother? Because he said the totally opposite thing about your mother, that she cried over everything." The brother looked puzzled, too. This wasn't the mom he remembered. Memory is all about a person's perception. The first brother perceived his mother as emotional; to the other, she wasn't. Maybe she let her guard down more with one than with the other. Or maybe to the first brother, seeing his mother cry was so upsetting that it made a bigger impact on him. Who knows?

Clearly, when interviewing family members you may find slight discrepancies or even glaring conflicts. Now what do you do? Newscasters and journalists have to deal with this type of problem every day. As you are probably aware, when three people witness the same accident, each one may walk away with a different version of the story. Who's right? They all are. No amount of convincing will make Grandpa change his mind that Aunt Martha's version is the correct one, so why bother? Do what reporters do:

1. Give multiple versions of the same story ("According to Aunt Martha. . . ." "On the other hand, Grandpa Miller's version of the story . . .").
2. Select the one that most closely corroborates what your other sources are telling you.

As with everything about writing a family history narrative, memoir, or life story, you as the writer have to make judgment calls. Remember what Carolyn G. Heilbrun said: (STEP 10, page 108) "[W]e all choose among the relics to form the life we want to envision for our subject." Another author will have a different interpretation, but this is your book; this is the story you are telling. Explain any judgment calls in the introduction to your book, so readers will know what decisions you've made and why.

THOSE COLORFUL FAMILY LEGENDS

What about those colorful stories about your sixth great-grandfather being kidnapped in Europe, put on a ship to America, and sold as an indentured servant? Or how your great-great Uncle Willy rode shotgun with Jesse James? Or how you must be related to President John F. Kennedy because your last name is Kennedy and you had family living in Boston at one time? These colorful family legends—the ones you haven't been able to prove or disprove in the course of your research—also have a place in your family history narrative. **Use and acknowledge them exactly for what they are: family legends.**

Tip

According to family lore, Johannes Schneider was a young boy of eleven when he was kidnapped from the field where he played in Germany and was brought to America to be sold as an indentured servant. No documents have surfaced to confirm or negate this legend. . . .

Deborah Navas had to deal with many ancient family legends in her narrative *Murdered by His Wife*. The murder of Joshua Spooner took place in 1778, and many tales were written about the case in the years that followed. Navas had to separate probable fact from romanticized versions of people's lives. Here's how she handled one legend:

> Bathsheba Newcomb Ruggles . . . reputedly served her husband's favorite dog to him in a pie. Given that Timothy Ruggles was a vegetarian, this incident is most likely apocryphal, typical of . . . the exaggerated accusations leveled at both Ruggleses.

What would you do with the following family story?

> When Hugh McGuire left Ireland, his mother gave him a hug and handed him two baked potatoes for the journey, which he put in his pockets. He walked down the hill from the house, turned to look back at his mother one last time, but regretted it. She was weeping, and it was all he could do to keep walking toward the dock and head for America, knowing he'd never see her again.

It's a priceless family story, but can it be documented or proved in records? No way. Does that mean you should leave out the story? No way. Again, you can preface it with "According to the family legend . . ." or, since it was a story told during a family history interview, you can simply quote the narrator. Don't omit family tales; include them for what they are. They add color and drama to your family history.

USING DIALOGUE

Now it's time to discuss the dreaded "*D* word" in nonfiction family history writing: dialogue. Can you use it, and if so, how can you use it so your work doesn't cross into the realm of fiction? Certainly, you can use dialogue in your nonfiction narrative! **But under no circumstances should you *create* dialogue. You can't put words in your ancestors' mouths that they might not have uttered.** As William Noble warns in *Writing Dramatic Nonfiction*: "When made-up dialogue is attached to a factual situation the entire issue of veracity comes into question." Simply put: the use of obviously made-up dialogue, no matter how many disclaimers and explanations you give in the introduction and footnotes, will cast doubt on the veracity of your whole narrative.

Warning

Having said that, let's look at some acceptable ways for a nonfiction writer to use dialogue.

1. **Quotes from an oral history interview.** We discussed how to do this on pages 130-133. Use direct quotes from interviews, but don't overwhelm the reader with them. Paraphrase interview material, in addition to augmenting and transitioning with information from records and background sources.

2. **Quotes from diaries, letters, affidavits, or other documents.** You can use these to give the illusion of dialogue in your narrative. (More precisely, this would be called *monologue* rather than *dialogue*.) Here's an example using material from the Revolutionary War pension file of Thomas McQueen (S33080, NARA Microfilm M804, roll 1700), where Thomas McQueen narrated his experiences: "About the time the [officers] broke up," said Tom, "a horseman rode up and gave information that the enemy was close by. We men immediately formed in order of battle and pressed forward to meet the enemy. About 12 o'clock, we came in contact with the enemy." Now turn to the excerpts in Appendix A, page 227. The quotes about Charles's final days all came from affidavits in his pension file. But rather than just reporting the facts or giving verbatim transcripts, I've woven the quotes into the narrative so they give the illusion of conversation.

3. **Remembered conversation.** Let's say you remember your father telling you a story about his grandfather. You remember it vividly, but of course you can't recall the conversation verbatim. It would be acceptable to recreate your

conversation with him or his comments, but make it clear in your narrative that this is remembered conversation. If the narrative is in first person, you could write: *I remember Dad talking about his grandfather....* Or if you are writing in third person, recast it as: *Dad [or use his name] used to tell the story about his grandfather....*

4. **Habitual or typical dialogue.** This would be the kind of conversation your parents or grandparents would have had that you would have witnessed: *Mom and Dad had the same conversation every night at the dinner table. Mom would* usually *ask Dad how his day went, and he* always *replied, "Same old, same old."* When using habitual or typical dialogue, you must give the reader clear signals that the dialogue is merely capturing the essence of conversations that happened in real life, hence the use of words like *usually* and *always*.

You should explain in the preface or introduction to your book that you are using dialogue deliberately, but only conversations or monologues that actually happened. I like what Dan Kurzman, author of *Blood and Water*, a creative nonfiction work about World War II, wrote in his preface (as quoted in Noble, *Writing Dramatic Nonfiction*):

> All quotations, thoughts, and feelings presented here appear precisely as these individuals expressed them to me, or as they recorded them in their diaries, memoirs, letters, or war records. Let me stress that nothing in this book is fictionalized....

Readers will want that added assurance that you know what you're doing, and that the narrative they are about to read is completely factual.

Including Suspense, Humor, and Romance

It's hard enough to write a good drama, it's much harder to write a good comedy, and it's hardest of all to write a drama with comedy. Which is what life is.
—JACK LEMMON

The best-loved stories make us laugh or cry and keep us on the edge of our seats. Can you evoke those same feelings in your readers as they read your family history? Sure, you can. Can you do it without fictionalizing? Certainly! Just as you had to look for the dramatic plot and determine the best way to grab the reader's attention in the opening paragraph, now you need to look at your family history to see what parts lend themselves to suspense, humor, and romance.

KEEP 'EM READING

After you grab the reader's attention in the opening paragraph, you need to keep the reader going. In the section on "Keeping the Story From Sagging in the Middle" (page 97), there was one example of how to use suspense to keep the reader engrossed in your family history. Remember, suspense isn't always the Stephen King type. **Just deliberately leave things hanging at appropriate places throughout the narrative, so that the reader will want to keep reading in order to find out what happens next.** But if you do leave things hanging, you must be sure to eventually answer anything left unanswered. When you use suspense as a writing technique, you promise readers that you will come back to what-

Technique

137

ever you dangled in front of them and will draw a satisfactory conclusion later on. The first time you don't, you lose the reader's trust.

Although they're overly dramatic, think of how soap operas and some prime-time television shows keep you tuned in. They reveal pieces of a story bit by bit, and in the process they build suspense. Do the same with your family history by looking at the events you've uncovered in your research, and thinking about which ones lend themselves to becoming cliffhangers. Remember Roscoe's letter asking Grace if she felt the same about him as he did about her (page 98), which I used to close a chapter? Even if a reader doesn't have time to completely read the next chapter, you can be sure that he or she will turn the page and peek at the first few sentences to see how Grace answers. Here is the ending of another chapter from that same narrative:

> Roscoe wanted to go to the front. He was in the Army, in France, and ready to fight for his country. But Grace did not look at the situation the same way Roscoe did. "I'm afraid we are hoping in opposite directions, along one line, sweetheart," wrote Grace. "Because, I'm hoping, as hard as I can ever hope, that you will never see the Front. Do you think I am very, very mean, honey? I don't want to be, but I just can't help it. . . . I'm sorry dear but I am hoping that you are still many miles from the Front. But if you are going to be a little bit unhappy for the risk of your life if you do not get there, why, maybe I'll allow you to go for a couple of weeks, but no longer." (November 2-3, 1918) What Grace did not know was that Roscoe's regiment had already received orders to go to the front.

Here I've left another aspect of the family history hanging. The reader now wants to know what happens to Roscoe at the front. Does he survive? What will Grace's reaction be to the news? The reader turns the page to find out what happens.

In Appendix B, page 234, there's another cliffhanger in the middle of the narrative to lead into the next section: "It appeared the McQueen men had a history of violence and rebellion, starting at least with Philip's fifth great-grandfather, Dugal McQueen, in Scotland." Readers keep reading to find out what Dugal McQueen did. It doesn't take much to create suspense. Be careful, though, not to overdo it; otherwise, you'll just frustrate your readers. The best and most appropriate places for suspense are at the end of a chapter or section; then you can resolve the question in the next paragraph.

MAKE 'EM LAUGH

Humor is a complex quality, and it can be tricky to include in your family history. What's funny in spoken words may not be as funny—or funny at all—on paper, partly because you can't hear inflections in the voice or see facial expressions and body language. **Think about the two main elements of comedy:**

Notes

1. **The unexpected.** Often we find things funny because the punch line is something we don't expect. A recent TV commercial for household appliances provides a good example: A husband and wife are sitting at the table eating lunch. The wife calmly reports to her husband, "Honey, I think I broke the washing machine today." He looks puzzled, and asks, "Really? How did that happen?" She calmly replies, "I hit it with a sledgehammer." That's not the follow up line you were expecting, was it? That's what makes it funny.

2. **Common knowledge.** Poking fun at a president or other famous person is usually funny because we all know that person. Telling a funny story about Granddad may be funny only to those who knew him. Have you ever had a funny story bomb, and you saved face by saying, "Well, you had to be there," or "You had to know Joe to get it"? That's what I'm talking about.

If you have readers who didn't know Granddad and
that he always pointed his arthritic finger at the dog
when he talked to the animal, they may not see the
humor in it. On the other hand—and here's where
common knowledge comes in—if you tell us that
Granddad always wore his baseball cap with the brim
bent up, we've all seen what someone looks like in a
baseball cap with the brim bent up, so that is a humor-
ous image that makes us chuckle.

Anecdotal family stories and quotes from letters, diaries, or other papers are the best places to find humor to
add to your family history. It may not be laugh-out-loud
humor, but it can lighten the mood of the narrative in
spots and show how people interacted. Here's an example from *A Sense of Duty*. World War I had just ended,
but Roscoe was still in France with his military unit.

This morning they held a special mass at the Cathe-
dral here [in Tulle] for "La Victoire." They put us
on the front row among a lot of French generals
and other things. . . . In a Catholic Church I like to
have someone in front of me so that I can see how
they handle themselves and act accordingly. There
is one officer with us who is a Catholic, and he
claimed to have all the dope on the situation, but
he certainly gave us a "bum steer." I noticed that
we were usually up when the rest of the people were
down, and down when they were up. But I was the
prize boner, when the archbishop came along and
shoved out his ring to be kissed. I thought he
wanted to shake hands. It didn't look quite right
to me, but just to show there were no hard feelings
I was going to be real cordial, and I was saved just
in time. . . . [17 November 1918]

MAKE 'EM SWOON

Love stories, of course, are as old as time, and there's
nothing like a good romance. It doesn't have to be

"mushy" or risqué. Here's an example of adding romance to a family history:

> Both Tom and Iva grew up near Rochester in Fulton County, Indiana, having attended the same one-room schoolhouse together. A family member recalled that Tom and Iva knew each other from school. When she was ten and he was fourteen, Tom would pat Iva on the head. Though it is doubtful this was the beginning of a budding romance at that age, it grew into life-long friendship that culminated in love. On the bricks of the Mt. Vernon school, there remains an inscription, "Tom Loves Iva."
>
> In past generations, the social circle for young people extended around family, work, and church; while Tom and Iva were growing up, a new realm was added: school. Compared to their parents' and grandparents' sphere for finding mates, Tom and Iva spent more time in school and had a wider choice of marriage partners. Boys and girls grew up seeing each other every day at school, which led to genuine friendships between the sexes. . . .
>
> No longer did men look at potential mates for their virtue, purity, and domestic skills. Men who came of age when Tom did were seeking a woman who was familiar, and this was certainly the case when Tom began courting Iva.

Like humor, romantic stories will more than likely come from oral tradition and notations in letters, diaries, and other papers. But you can also add an element of romance to your narrative by discussing how people in a particular time period would have courted. (More on speculation in STEP 14.)

ADDING EMOTIONS

Warning

Of course, you cannot attribute emotions to your ancestors without specific evidence; otherwise you are fictionalizing. Here is an example of fictionalizing emotions:

Alfred died of heart problems a week before his fiftieth birthday, and the family buried him in Fulton Cemetery. Because of his sudden death, he had not prepared a will. His wife, Hannah, was so distraught, she waived her right to administer the estate.

We don't know that Hannah was distraught over her husband's death, although it's a likely possibility. Maybe she wasn't confident about handling the role of administratrix, or perhaps she was too busy making plans to take a trip to Europe and buy a new wardrobe from whatever money Alfred left her. Here is a way to write it as nonfiction:

Alfred died of heart problems a week before his fiftieth birthday, and the family buried him in Fulton Cemetery. Because of his sudden death, he had not prepared a will. His wife, Hannah, *no doubt distraught*, waived her right to administer the estate.

Here we're suggesting this is the likely reason she waived her right to administer the estate, but we aren't saying that it *is* the reason.

Suppose you want to show your great-grandmother's probable excitement over graduating from college, since she was the first woman in the family to get a college degree, and it was unusual for many women of her day even to go to college. How can you do that and keep it nonfiction? You can write: *Imagine how excited she must have been to receive her college diploma* or, *What woman of her day wouldn't be excited to receive a college diploma?*

Let's say your sixth great-grandparents, William and Effie, lost six out of twelve children, all before the infants were two years old. How can you express how they must have felt to lose so many children? The same way as you would for your great-grandmother getting her diploma:

The loss of any child is traumatic for a couple, but to lose six infants before they each reached the age of two must have been heartbreaking for William and Effie.

Don't be afraid to add emotions to your ancestors, but be especially careful how you do it. You will need to make it clear that you are speculating, basing your ideas on typical human responses in such circumstances.

Okay. I keep mentioning the role of speculation in your family history writing. Let's look at how it's done.

Blending Social History With Family History

The more you read, the more you become aware of the techniques that are special to every genre, and the more you begin to see ways to meld the strengths of the genres into a whole that is, one hopes, more than the sum of its parts.—DEAN KOONTZ

L et's return to the amusement park analogy. (It was that or baby Belinda, and frankly, she scares me. You've seen *Child's Play*, right?) At Playland, there were a lot of the typical rides that you'd find at your neighborhood come-and-go carnival. But at Disneyland, they jazz up the ordinary rides with the Mickey Mouse and fairy-tale themes. You'll be doing the same with your family history: jazzing up typical family history data with the general but relevant theme information you've gathered from a variety of background sources. Disneyland successfully put the two (typical rides, special theme) together; now it's time for you to try combining the typical facts from your family history with social history themes.

Technique

To practice, one easy way to bring the two together is to write the general information first, then plug in your ancestor's information. Let's pick the topic of food in colonial Virginia, and say that your ancestor was William Fitzhugh, a fairly prosperous planter. We've done some background research and discovered what kinds of foods the wealthy planters of Virginia ate. Don't worry about your ancestor for the moment; just write a sentence or two about the general topic.

Prosperous planters of Virginia ate the same foods as the gentry in southwestern England. They loved red meat, roast beef in particular, and preferred it and fresh game over the abundance of seafood the Chesapeake had to offer.

Now let's plug in William Fitzhugh. I've italicized the inserted text:

Although there are no surviving records that tell what William Fitzhugh ate, his diet was probably similar to that of other Virginia elite. Prosperous planters of Virginia ate the same foods as the gentry of southwestern England. They loved red meat, roast beef in particular, and preferred it and fresh game over the abundance of seafood the Chesapeake had to offer.

See how easy that is? Let's look at a few more examples of writing the general, relevant social history first, then inserting what we know about the ancestor.

- *Social history research before blending:*
  In colonial Virginia, many children lost at least one parent to death before reaching their eighteenth birthday.
- *Combined social and family history:*
  In colonial Virginia, many children lost at least one parent to death before reaching their eighteenth birthday, and this was the case with Henry Fitzhugh, whose father, William, died when Henry was fifteen.
- *Social history research before blending:*
  Most of the newcomers to the Chesapeake colonies were young men who arrived as indentured servants.
- *Combined social and family history:*
  Most of the newcomers to the Chesapeake colonies were young men who, like Richard Hutchinson, arrived as indentured servants.

- *Social history research before blending:*
  Colonial Virginia elite loved to celebrate. At any occasion—weddings, baptisms, religious holidays, and when family members or newcomers visited—an elaborate feast was prepared, sometimes on short notice.
- *Combined social and family history:*
  Colonial Virginia elite loved to celebrate. At any occasion—weddings, baptisms, religious holidays, and when family members or newcomers visited—an elaborate feast was prepared, sometimes on short notice. Colonel William Fitzhugh was no different, treating guests "royally, [with] good wine & all kinds of beverages." (Quote from Richard Beale Davis, ed., *William Fitzhugh and His Chesapeake World, 1676–1701* [Chapel Hill: University of North Carolina Press, 1963], 18.)

Important

Your goal is to blend the two types of information (general, social history and your family history), into one flowing, cohesive narrative. You do this by discussing the social history subject matter, then connecting it to your family history. Or, you can do it in reverse. Write about your ancestors from what you discovered in the records, then weave in the social history. Here is an example:

Roscoe entered Princeton University in the fall term of 1912. He was sixteen then, turning seventeen on October third. . . . A growing number of young men were college bound by the turn of the twentieth century. Enrollment in colleges and universities surged between 1900 and 1930, caused in part by an increase in extracurricular activities. Clubs, organized athletics, fraternities, and other social events attracted youths, in addition to a new direction of academic instruction. It was now possible to get an education in modern technologies: economics, management, and engineering. This change in higher-learning institutions also helped bring about the emergence of adolescence as a distinct period of life.

Beginning with what I knew specifically about Roscoe, his age and when he entered Princeton, I then filled in the social history of why young men were beginning to attend college during this time period. Write your narrative in whichever way is easiest for you. Eventually, it will come automatically.

WHAT TO PUT IN AND WHAT TO LEAVE OUT

Perhaps equally difficult as deciding when you've done enough research is deciding what you'll include in the narrative and what you'll leave out. After all, you don't want to lose your reader by detailing the manufacture and workings of the grandfather clock that sat in your aunt's house, no matter how fascinating you think it is, when it's not relevant to your story. So what was the point of doing all of that research, if it's not all going to go into your family history? Although Rhona Martin's *Writing Historical Fiction* was intended for fiction writers, her advice applies to nonfiction historical writing, too: "If you haven't done [all the research], if you don't have all that back-up information at your fingertips, what you do put in is likely to be wrong." Martin uses this analogy: "Research . . . is like an iceberg. Only the tip must show, but the rest of it, the great bulk that lurks invisibly under water, has to be there for support."

Unfortunately, there is no hard-and-fast rule when it comes to determining how much social history information to put in or to leave out, except to keep the focus of your book in mind. If you find you are writing pages upon pages of how grist mills were operated, it's probably not moving the story along and is therefore too much. That's not what your book is about. Yes, you want to give your readers enough detail to show them how a grist mill like your ancestor's was run, but your narrative isn't a history of grist mills. A good example of staying focused comes

Technique

147

from Deborah Navas's *Murdered by His Wife*. This life story revolves around the murder of Joshua Spooner in 1778. His wife, Bathsheba, was convicted of the crime, along with three accomplices. One was Ezra Ross, who served in the Revolutionary War. While Navas could have devoted a whole chapter or more detailing the battles Ross fought in, she kept the focus of her narrative in mind and just summarized these events. (See page 93 in STEP 9 for more on summary and scene.)

If after studying examples from other narratives you are still having trouble determining whether you have included too much social history information or not enough, enlist a couple of impartial friends or your spouse to help you. Have them read the section in question. If they find they are getting bored or skipping over parts, then you know you've put in too much detail. If, on the other hand, they start asking you questions about what you've written, this shows they want more information and that you haven't included enough.

To decide what you'll put in and what you'll leave out of the genealogical data on your ancestors—that is, what's truly relevant to your story—ask yourself if the information you plan to include is moving the story along or bogging it down. Let's say your ancestor Peter Turner bought and sold land as frequently as some people buy computers. Is it necessary to enumerate all these transactions in the narrative, or will it just slow things down? Can you *consolidate* the land-buying and -selling activities in the narrative so that the story will keep moving? Sure you can, especially if you are doing what I suggested in STEP 2, that is, dividing your family history into two parts: a narrative, followed by the family summaries. In the family summaries, you can enumerate to your heart's content all of Peter's land transactions. Or, you can do so in a foot- or endnote to the narrative where you have consolidated Peter's activities.

This second part of your family history also gives you a wider comfort zone for including some material that may not fit conveniently into the narrative, such as details on census enumerations, city directory listings, tax rolls, or even full dates. The narrative might flow more smoothly if you write: *Polly gave birth to her first child in the fall of 1873*, rather than *Polly gave birth to her first child on 23 October 1873*. But you won't have to worry that precise information isn't given in the narrative because it's given precisely in part two of your book.

SPECULATION

Genealogists make speculations all the time. You've no doubt seen other family history books or scholarly articles that contain statements like: *He was almost certainly the son of Jacob Jones*, or: *He probably left Oklahoma about the time of the dust bowl*, or: *Robert and Sallie likely had these children*, or: *Thomas may have married as his first wife, Lucinda Strong*. These speculations aren't pulled out of thin air. Researchers suspect these might be true scenarios based on their research findings, but they aren't 100 percent sure, so they use what some people call "weasel wording," such as *almost certainly, probably, likely*, and *may have*, to indicate that they are speculating. **Thus, you can use the same technique in your narrative family history, because you will be basing your speculations on your research into social history sources.**

Let's look at some examples. This first one is from historian and Pulitzer Prize-winner Laurel Thatcher Ulrich's *Good Wives: Image and Reality in the Lives of Women in Northern New England, 1650–1750* (New York: Vintage Books, 1982). I've italicized words and phrases that show where she is speculating.

Technique

The house over which Beatrice presided *must have looked* much like surviving dwellings from seventeenth-century New England. The best bed with its bolster, pillows, blanket, and coverlet stood in the parlor, a second bed occupied one corner of the kitchen. . . . (page 18)

The contents of her inventory *suggest* that Beatrice Plummer was adept not only at roasting,

149

frying, and boiling but also at baking, the most difficult branch of cookery. *Judging from the grain* in the upstairs chamber, the bread which she baked was 'maslin,' a common type made from a mixture of wheat and other grains, usually rye. . . . (page 20)

Unfortunately, there is little in [Magdalen Wear's] inventory and nothing in any other record to document the specific strategies which she used [for raising a family and running a household], though the general circumstances of their life *can be imagined.* . . . During the spring corn famine, an almost yearly occurrence on the Maine frontier, *she might have gone* herself with other wives of her settlement to dig on the clam flats, hedging against the day when relief would come by sea. . . . (page 31)

Here are a few more examples from historian Gerald McFarland's *A Scattered People*, again with phrases indicating speculation in italics:

Indeed, *immigrants like* Benjamin Adair left Europe in search of something different and better, and it was aspirations not unlike those that caused them to cross the Atlantic before 1800 that led many, Benjamin Adair included, to cross the Appalachian Mountains in the early nineteenth century. . . . (page 41)

The Adairs . . . *were typical* of Ohio's early settlers in that they traveled to the frontier in multifamily groups, rather than as individuals or as a single, nuclear family. . . . (page 49)

Keys's migration narrative . . . may therefore be taken as a fair approximation of what the Adairs *probably encountered* on the road to Ohio. . . . (page 46)

If McFarland had written, "Indeed, Benjamin Adair left Europe in search of something different and better . . . ," he would have been writing fiction, because how would he know that this was the reason Benjamin left, unless Adair had left some written account of his decisions? So McFarland speculates on why Benjamin left, based on the reasons thousands of other immigrants—*like Benjamin*—left. The crucial element that separates fact from fiction in family history writing is the wording, and it can be just a simple, one-word difference.

Finally, here are some examples from professional genealogist Donna Rachal Mills, who wrote *Some Southern Balls: From Valentine to Ferdinand and Beyond*. Once again, I've italicized the words that make it clear Mills is speculating.

> There at Eleanor Hook's plantation on Bayou de Siard . . . Margaret *apparently* met James Ball during his enforced stay in the area. . . . (page 123)
>
> Ball's interest in the Cove Creek property *may well have stemmed* from the unquenchable lure that Arkansas's precious minerals held for him. . . . (page 125)
>
> . . . life dealt unlucky draws to Sally Lacombe and her daughter Margaret. . . . Their faces *must have worn* the ravages of their labor, making them old long before their time. . . . (page 200)

Important

When you write a statement of fact, ask yourself: *How do I know this?* If you have a document that says it's so, then great. If not, then you need to reword what you've written and make it clear that you are speculating.

MAKING INFERENCES

Genealogists make inferences all the time, too. To infer means that you are drawing a conclusion from facts. If you see smoke, there must be fire. That's an inference. You have no proof that there is a fire, but you are drawing a conclusion based on the fact that there's smoke. The Board for Certification of Genealogists calls making inferences the "genealogical proof standard" or GPS. According to the *BCG Genealogical Standards Manual* (Washington, D.C.: The Board for Certification of Genealogists, 2000, page 2), the fifth process in meeting the genealogical proof standard is: "We arrive at a soundly reasoned, coherently written conclusion" based on exhaustive research that we have analyzed, correlated, and documented. The *Manual* further states:

> Meeting the GPS does not require, or ensure, proof beyond the shadow of a doubt, but an objection that 'something else *could* have happened' is insufficient to discredit our own or another person's conclusions. Genealogists recognize, however, that any statement about ancestors, even if it meets the GPS, is not absolute or everlasting. When new evidence surfaces or flaws in the conclusion are found, we re-examine the statement to determine if it remains valid.

In other words, there is no final word when we compile a genealogy or write a family history. A new source or more research tomorrow, next week, or twenty years from now may uncover new evidence that changes everything. That's why authors write revised editions. But in the meantime, we write our family histories based on our present knowledge and research, making inferences as we go.

Quotes

One's perception of the past is changeable, reshaped by new information and new insights.—DEBORAH NAVAS

Let's look at some examples of making inferences in writing your narrative.

For many years, Elizabeth Goss suffered probably from tuberculosis, also known as consumption. Her obituary stated that her "health had been delicate and she went west in [18]76 and rergained [*sic*] some strength, and again in '81 but temporary relief, only, was the result." She had gone to Oregon with her daughter Dolly Alspach "with the hope of improving their physical condition." One of the most popular treatments for tuberculosis between the 1840s and 1920s was to go west. The arid climate and fresh air were thought to promote healing. Although more men than women took the opportunity to seek a cure in the western states, some women also visited the West in hopes of regaining their health. The open-air living that physicians prescribed in the West seemed to work for many and put their disease into remission. Upon returning east, however, their symptoms usually reappeared. Apparently this was the case with Elizabeth. A lingering and wasting illness, tuberculosis struck all classes of people, causing them to suffer for many years before it ultimately took them to the grave. Elizabeth was not so fortunate to find a total cure in the West; she died from "lung trouble" in 1892 in Fulton County, at the age of sixty-seven.

I don't know for a fact that Elizabeth Goss died from tuberculosis, but all the evidence—delicate health, going west, and dying from "lung trouble"—points to that diagnosis; thus I inferred that this is what she actually died from. Here's another example:

The Revolutionary War brought new and disturbing fears to women like Sarah Collins. Smallpox incubated and spread among soldiers and to those with whom they came into contact, inspiring new interest in an earlier inoculation against the disease. The decision to inoculate oneself and one's children was not an easy one for most women, however, considering it required being deliberately infected with the disease. Sarah Collins would have faced this decision. Infected soldiers had brought smallpox to Tyringham where Sarah and her family lived, causing an epidemic. In a town meeting held in March 1777, the officials voted to table all issues except for the issue of smallpox. They also voted to stop inoculating for the present, apparently fearing that this was contributing to the numbers contracting the disease. The message was then carried to all the households in the town that were infected. The Collins household was not mentioned in the town minutes among the ones that had been infected, however.

Eight years later, in 1785, the town was still battling the disease. . . . Deaths from smallpox were reported on a daily basis. One of Sarah's children, her first-born child Rodalphus Collins, died in Tyringham on 2 March 1783, at the age of thirteen. Although his cause of death was not recorded, he may have been a victim of the smallpox epidemic.

For More Info

For more on historical inference, see Sturdevant's *Bringing Your Family History to Life Through Social History*, pp. 187–188.

Once again, I've drawn a conclusion based on the evidence. Rodalphus could have died from any number of things, but because he died in Tyringham during the continuing smallpox epidemic, there is a strong possibility he succumbed to that disease. But, notice that I did not say he did for a fact, nor did I say for a fact that Elizabeth died from tuberculosis. I made an inference in both cases, drawing a speculative conclusion based on the evidence.

RESEARCH ANALYSIS

A big part of credible genealogy is the analysis and correlation we do with historical documents. As just mentioned, we often make speculations or inferences based on our research findings; the reader needs to know how we arrived at those conclusions. It's not enough to say: *Donald was probably the son of Michael.* How did you arrive at that conclusion? Should your analysis go into the family history narrative? Yes, but maybe not in the narrative per se. If the analysis becomes distracting to the reader—in other words, if the story suddenly begins to sound like a research report—the effect is the same as with narrator intrusion. When that happens, remove the analysis from the narrative and put it in a foot- or endnote (see page 163). Some analytical explanations may be lengthy, however, and it would look silly to have a note several paragraphs long. Assuming you are doing a two-part family history with the narrative as part one and the family summaries as part two, put your analysis in the text of part two where it more logically fits.

Another important aspect in narrative writing is to make it perfectly clear which is verifiable information about your own family and which is historical background information. This can be accomplished either through the wording or by citing your sources. While the blended information should be seamless in the narrative, the annotation should allow your reader to identify the source of each piece of information. Think of it this way: if you were to strip off the layers of Space Mountain at Disney World, you'd see that the core is nothing more than a roller coaster ride. The core of your research has to be evident under the layers of your story, too. So let's now look at how to properly cite sources of data.

Including Documentation

When you take stuff from one writer, it's plagiarism;
but when you take it from many writers, it's research.
—WILSON MIZNER

Citing Sources

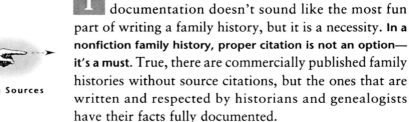 know you're tempted to skip this step. I admit, documentation doesn't sound like the most fun part of writing a family history, but it is a necessity. **In a nonfiction family history, proper citation is not an option—it's a must.** True, there are commercially published family histories without source citations, but the ones that are written and respected by historians and genealogists have their facts fully documented.

If you've read any other genealogical guidebooks or taken any genealogy classes, you've no doubt heard the lecture on the importance of documentation in genealogical research. Simply put, for each piece of information you note about your family, you need to record where the data came from. The same is true for each piece of historical information you gather.

But I'm just writing this for my family, you may say. *They want me to do a book, and my relatives aren't going to look at the endnotes or even care.* If this is what you are thinking, go back and reread page 14 about who your audience will be. Somehow, somewhere that book "just for the family" will end up in a library, and another genealogist or historian will use your book for their own research. If it's not documented, they might think it's fiction and would take your work with a grain of salt. That's not what you put all those hours into it for. Besides, you want to *show off* to your family all the work you put into this project!

Another excuse I hear for not documenting is that it's off-putting to the average reader. It looks intimidating and academic. Come on. I find it hard to believe that a teeny-tiny number at the end of a paragraph is that frightening to people. Just because the work has endnotes and a bibliography doesn't mean that it has to read like an academic textbook. There are a couple of methods of citing your sources in a family history narrative that will make them as unintrusive and unintimidating to the reader as possible.

WHAT NEEDS A CITATION?

Before I get into how to cite sources, let's explore what type of information requires a citation to begin with. In short, anything that is not common knowledge and is specific information about your ancestors needs a citation: that is, an endnote. Obviously, if you write: *Constance Cooper was born in Illinois on 16 March 1878*, this is a specific fact that demands documentation describing where you found her precise birth date and place. Whether the source is family knowledge, a family Bible, or a tombstone inscription, tell the reader where you got the information.

Common knowledge, however, is a bit trickier. **Common knowledge doesn't mean knowledge common to the general population.** Lord knows if you were to ask a dozen people on the street who the vice president of our country is, only a few would be able to answer correctly. One late-night talk show host, who regularly asks people on the street such questions, asked some people to identify Chernobyl (the power plant in the Ukraine that exploded in 1986). One response was, "That's Cher's real name." Okay. So we don't want to rely on *that* type of common knowledge. Common knowledge means *common to the sources you examine*. If all of the sources on the topic of westward migration say that the Homestead Act was passed in 1862, then you don't need to cite that

\di'fin\ *vb*

Definitions

piece of information. Or, if all the sources on the topic of immigration say that heavy Greek emigration to America began in the 1890s, then you don't need to cite that either. But if you are writing about a battle in the Revolutionary War and you give details about the engagement and losses, you would need a reference, since these statistics aren't necessarily the same from one source to the next. When in doubt about whether a certain piece of information requires a citation, it's better to err on the side of too much documentation than too little.

End- or footnotes can also be used to explain a discrepancy among sources. Rather than interrupting the narrative to tell the reader why you believe one record is more reliable than another, or that you know from all your other research that a particular record contains an error, put this analysis in a note.

Other items requiring citations are archaic or obsolete popular terms. You may have a document, letter, or journal entry that uses words or phrases that we no longer use today. For example, will your readers know what a World War I "doughboy" was? Do you know? If not, that's something you'll have to research and provide an explanation for in a foot- or endnote. (*Doughboy* was a nickname for a U.S. infantry soldier, derived from descriptions of the pasty faces of mere boys who were drafted or enlisted.) Examine the narratives in the appendixes to see what types of information have source citations.

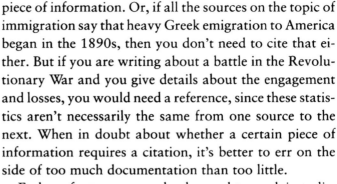

For More Info

For the finer points on citing sources and evaluating evidence, see Emily Anne Croom's *The Sleuth Book for Genealogists* (Cincinnati: Betterway Books, 2000), and Elizabeth Shown Mills' *Evidence! Citation and Analysis for the Family Historian* (Baltimore: Genealogical Publishing Co., 1997 or current edition). Also see Katherine Scott Sturdevant's *Bringing Your Family History to Life Through Social History* for citation examples of home sources, photographs, artifacts, and oral history interviews.

CARMACK RULE FOR CITING SOURCES

Unfortunately, for family history documents such as censuses, land records, passenger lists, vital records, and so forth, there is no consensus among genealogists (professional or hobbyist) on how to "properly" cite such sources. Each author on the subject may cite a census, for example, just a little bit differently. Here's how Elizabeth Shown Mills, in the 1997 edition of *Evidence!* (page 73), recommends citing a federal census found on microfilm in an endnote:

Mortimer Edwards household, 1880 U.S. census, Winona County, Minnesota, population schedule, town of Winona, enumeration district [ED] 289, supervisor's district [SD] 1, sheet 19, dwelling 172, family 182, National Archives micropublication T9, roll 637.

Here's how Emily Anne Croom, in *The Sleuth Book* (page 235), suggests you cite the same reference, also in an endnote:

Mortimer Edwards household, U.S. Census of 1880, Winona County, Minnesota, e.d. 289, sheet 19, dwelling 172, family 182, National Archives microfilm T9, roll 637.

Census

Here's how I would cite that same federal census found on microfilm in an endnote, if it's not clear from the text who the head of household was:

Mortimer Edwards household, 1880 U.S. census, Minnesota, Winona Co., ED 289, sheet 19, #172–182, National Archives Micropublication T9, roll 637.

If the text makes it clear that Mortimer was the head of household, then I eliminate "Mortimer Edwards household" in the citation. But, if the head of household's name was misspelled on the census, then I include it in the citation as it appeared in the document, thus "Mort Edward [*sic*] household, . . ."

Now let's look at how some scholarly genealogical journals cite censuses. Again, I'll use that same census reference, but write it based on the style each journal uses. From the *New England Historical and Genealogical Register*

1880 U.S. Census, Winona County, Minnesota, roll 637, ED 289, sheet 19, line 15, dwelling 172, family 182.

From *The American Genealogist*:

1880 Federal Census, Winona Co., Minn., E.D. 289, sheet 19, line 15, #172/182.

And, finally, from the *National Genealogical Society Quarterly*:

1880 U.S. Census, Winona County, Minnesota, population schedule, town of Winona, sheet 19 (taken 14–15 June), dwelling 172, family 182, National Archives microfilm T9, roll 637.

Notice that each citation has slight variations. Is one right and the others wrong? No. They are merely different format styles, and you will find many others besides these if you start looking carefully at published genealogies and scholarly genealogy journals. While genealogists may not totally agree on a style for citing a source, they do agree that it is crucial for each citation to contain all of the information you would need to find that source. But this is just one important aspect to citing sources. The other is consistency: use the same style for each record type you cite. If you choose to follow the Mills format for citing censuses, for example, then follow it for all of your census citations. Or if you choose to follow Croom's or my style for citing censuses, then do so for all of your census citations. **So here's the simplified Carmack Rule for Citing Sources: A citation must have complete identifying information, and each record type should be cited consistently.** Or as my colleague Robert Charles Anderson says even more succinctly, "Be clear and consistent."

Important

The same would be true with your social history sources, although they are easier to keep consistent because the majority of your citations will be of published books and articles. Fortunately, there is more of a consensus among genealogists for citing publications. Most genealogists and historians use *The Chicago Manual of Style*, 14th edition (Chicago: The University of Chicago

Press, 1993) as a guide. So, for example, your endnote citation from a published social history book would look like this:

¹Wayne E. Fuller, *The Old Country School: The Story of Rural Education in the Middle West* (Chicago: University of Chicago Press, 1982), 53-54.

And an article would look like this:

¹Elizabeth G. Messina, "Narratives of Nine Italian Women: Childhood, Work, and Marriage," *Italian Americana* 10 (Spring/Summer 1992): 186-202.

FOOTNOTES VS. ENDNOTES

Footnotes are the references at the bottom of a page. In the days before computers, typing these was a nightmare, but now your word processing software will do it automatically for you. The advantage of using footnotes in your family history is that the reader doesn't have to turn any pages to find out where the footnoted text comes from; it's right there at the bottom of the same page. The disadvantage is that many readers really don't care to read footnotes and find them intrusive and intimidating. For scholarly texts, footnotes are preferred; but for a readable family history narrative, I would avoid this type of citation.

With endnotes, you still have that superscript number after the text you want to reference, but the reader has to flip to the back of the book to find out where the information came from. Readers who just want to enjoy the story and don't care where you found your facts will prefer this method because they can ignore the note number if they choose. This format for citing sources is less intrusive on the narrative and more acceptable to the average reader.

A newer trend in the style of endnotes is what I call "blind citations." No superscript note numbers appear in the narrative; instead, the endnotes are keyed to page numbers in the text. This method seems to be popular among commercial publishers who are now publishing family histories. Here's an example of this citation style from Edward Ball's *Slaves in the Family*. On page 22 of the narrative, there is no indication that the reader should look for a citation, other than that specific information—"Elias Ball . . . was born in 1676 in a tiny hamlet in western England called Stokeinteignhead"—has been included. Obviously, this is not common knowledge and deserves a reference. Turning to the back of the book, the reader finds a section called "Notes," which is broken down by chapter. The text on Elias was in chapter two; so under that heading, the reader finds

> Page 22. **Elias Ball . . . was born:** Nan. S. Ball, *Ball Family of Stoke-in-Teignhead, Devon, England,* pamphlet (Charleston, S.C.: 1944).

Thomas Keneally's family history, *The Great Shame,* uses this same method, except that the notation format is slightly different, with the page number in the margin:

> 4   Hugh's marriage and children: Ship's Indent, *Parmelia,* AONSW; Returns of Applications, 1837–43, 21 December 1841, 4/4492, MF reel 700, AONSW . . . [Abbreviations are spelled out at the beginning of the notes section.]

While readers who don't care to read notes will love this blind-citation method, those of us who do like to know where the information came from find this technique frustrating. It's actually more interruptive and intrusive to read, because now readers think as they're reading, "Gee, is there a reference for this?" Then they have to check what chapter and page number they're at, flip to the back of the book, find that page reference, and match the topic or keywords in the text. I recommend you stick with the standard endnote citation, with superscript numbers in the text, and all references grouped together at the back of the book.

Oh, No! Endnote Number 20,937?!

Obviously, even if you use the standard endnote method for citing sources, you still need to break it down by chapter, starting with note number 1 with each new chapter—so you don't end up with a note number of 20,937 by the end of the book. You can reduce the number of notes within each chapter as well. **Rather than including a note after every fact in a paragraph, you can consolidate sources so that you end up with only one note per paragraph.** Be sure, however, to cite multiple references in the order you discussed them in the paragraph so the reader can follow along. You can also help the reader by adding information. Here is a sample paragraph with its one citation:

Technique

Sometime between 16 June 1900 and 31 March 1901, David and Delia Norris and their children returned to Ireland, where they lived in David's home townland of Tamlaghtmore. Located in Northern Ireland in County Tyrone, the parish of Arboe, and barony of Dungannon Upper, Tamlaghtmore consists of a little more than 261 acres. Arboe parish covers about 33,500 acres, but 21,000 of those form part of Lough Neagh. In the parish, there are about fifty acres of woodland, with a thousand acres of bogland.[1]

Notes

[1] David and Delia appeared on the 1900 federal census in America, which was taken on 16 June 1900, and they appeared on the 1901 Irish census, taken on 31 March 1901. 1900 federal census, Connecticut, Fairfield Co., Greenwich, ED 72, Sheet 23A, #391-457; 1901 Census of Ireland, Co. Tyrone, Cookstown Poor Law Union, Killybolpy District, Barony of Dungannon Upper, Paish of Arboe, Townland of Tamlaghtmore, form 10, FHL #855982; death certificate, David Norris, Town of Greenwich, Connecticut, gives his place of birth; *General Alphabetical Index to the Townlands and Towns, Parishes and Baronies of Ireland Based on the Census of Ireland for the Year 1851* (originally published, Dublin: 1861, reprint Baltimore: Genealogical Publishing Co., 2000); *Topographical Dictionary of Ireland* (originally published London: 1837, reprint Baltimore: Genealogical Col, 1984).

The examples in this step show complete source citations within the notes. Typically, repetitive citations are abbreviated after the first complete reference. For style guidelines on shortened citations, see Mills's *Evidence!*, Croom's *The Sleuth Book for Genealogists*, or *The Chicago Manual of Style*.

The sources in the note are listed in the order in which I discussed the topics in the paragraph.

In the previous step, I had mentioned putting short analyses in notes, rather than as part of the narrative. Notice that I did that in this note. In the text I gave a conclusion from my research: "Sometime between 16 June 1900 and 31 March 1901, David and Delia Norris and their children returned to Ireland, where they lived in David's home townland of Tamlaghtmore." How did I know that? It would have interrupted the flow of the narrative to give my analysis at that point, so I put it in the note as the first item, since it was the first thing the reader encountered in that paragraph. Then I cited my sources in order.

THE BIBLIOGRAPHY

Can't you do away with all those pesky notes and use just a bibliography? I'm afraid not. The notes and bibliography serve two distinct purposes, and one can't be substituted for the other. The notes tell your reader precisely where you found facts and information. The bibliography is merely a listing of all the sources—usually just the published ones, not genealogy records—that you consulted. The bibliography may also include sources you looked at but didn't use any specific information from. While it is possible to get away with not having a bibliography, presumably because the citations in your notes are complete, it doesn't work in reverse.

The bibliography, however, serves as a quick reference for your readers. Typically, after you've fully cited a book in an endnote, the subsequent citations are shortened. For example, the complete citation may be "Hasia R. Diner, *Erin's Daughters in America: Irish Immigrant Women in the Nineteenth Century* (Baltimore: Johns Hopkins University Press, 1983), 4." The next time you cite that work you would shorten it to just the author's last name, an abbreviated version of the title, and the page number: "Diner, *Erin's Daughters*, 28." So the reader doesn't have to hunt back through the endnotes to find that first complete citation, it's more convenient to go to the bibliography, which should list all the books and articles that are referenced in the notes. Some authors choose to never put a full citation in the notes, because the reader can go to the bibliography to find the complete reference.

Bibliographies are arranged alphabetically by the author's last name, then the title of the work, and the publication information. Look at this book's bibliography for examples.

Whew! Okay. We got through the worst part. It's all downhill from here. Well, until we get to the section on indexing in STEP 17. But for now, let's take a break from the hard stuff and think about a more enjoyable part of putting together a family history book: finding photographs and illustrations.

Adding Illustrations

*Drawing is not what you see, but what you must make
others see.*—EDGAR DEGAS

Our love of illustrations stems from childhood. We like books with pictures in them. Go to a bookstore and watch people as they flip through books they're thinking about buying. They're looking for pictures or illustrations, and they stop when one catches their eye. After examining the picture, they read the caption, then they flip through the book again to find more.

Illustrations add to a book, and one of the most enjoyable parts of writing and publishing a family history is finding and choosing illustrations, such as photographs, maps, historical documents, and drawings.

PHOTOGRAPHS

The first type of illustration that will probably come to mind is family photographs. This is the time to bug your relatives once again, asking them if they have any photos of ancestors that you might include. But consider more than just the head-and-shoulders or full-body portraits that studio photographers took. Are there photographs in your or your relatives' collections that are candid shots of family members, or pictures of houses, pets, cars, or other treasured items? These will add more variety to your illustrations.

Some families either didn't take or didn't keep many photographs, or those they kept aren't identified. What's a writer supposed to do in a situation like that? If your ancestor's house is still standing, take a photograph of how

Figure 16-2
The DeBartolo House, 90 Theodore Fremd Avenue, Rye, New York, as it looks today. If you don't have a photograph of an ancestor's house taken during his lifetime, use a current photograph if the house is still standing.

Figure 16-1
Red French's cat, circa 1940. Photographs of family pets are just as important as photographs of people.

the house looks today to include in your book. (If you can't make the trip, ask a relative or someone who will be visiting the area to take a photograph for you.) **Be creative and think of items you could take photographs of that would be relevant to your family history.** Here are the subjects of some photographs that I'll be including in a client's family history, since his family is one of those that didn't keep many:

Idea Generator

- the church where the client's parents and grandparents married
- the baptismal font where generations of the client's family were baptized
- the grade school the client's parents attended
- the houses, as they stand today, where the client's grandparents and great-grandparents lived
- a turf bank, photographed at a folk museum in Ireland, to help readers understand what this was
- an open hearth in a rural Irish cottage, photographed at an Irish folk museum
- ancestors' tombstones

Figure 16-3
Teapot owned by Angelina (Vallarelli) Ebetino, which she brought to America from Italy in 1910. Currently owned by Isabel Vallarelli. Don't forget to include photographs of family artifacts, so everyone can enjoy them.

Figure 16-4
Baptismal font, Church of the Resurrection, Rye, New York. Be creative when you include illustrations in your family history. A photograph of a church your ancestors attended or the font where they were baptised would make an interesting illustration.

Here are other items to consider photographing for use as illustrations in your book:

- family artifacts, such as pottery, china, jewelry, and silver
- heirloom furniture or musical instruments
- quilts or other needlework
- antique clothing
- family Bible pages

Museums as Photographic Resources

Don't limit your search for photographs to just your family's collections, or include photographs of only your ancestors. In the *Ebetino and Vallarelli Family History*, I included photographs of the ships my ancestors immigrated on. These came from a maritime museum. One of the ancestors of my client was a policeman in the early 1900s, and another was a fireman in the same time period. While there are no known surviving photographs of these two men in their uniforms, I was able to obtain photographs through a museum of other men who served during this time to illustrate what the uniforms would have looked like. Flip through some of the family histories listed in the bibliography and see what these authors used for illustrations. Keep in mind that when you find photographs in a museum, library, or archive collection that you might like to use, you will probably have to pay a reprint fee. (See the case study on page 174 and also STEP 18, the sections on copyright, fair use, and permissions.)

MAPS

Genealogists love to look at maps, so consider having some as illustrations in your family history book. If you are talented enough to sketch your own maps, this would be ideal; but if you're art disabled like I am, you'll need to find your maps elsewhere. Check the Internet first. Go to a search engine, such as Google.com or Altavista.com, and type in the country or locality followed by *map*, and see what comes up. Local libraries, museums, and archives, as well as the Library of Congress, are also good sources for maps. No matter where you find them, however, most maps are protected by copyright, so you will need permission to reproduce them in your book, and you might have to pay a reprint fee.

HISTORICAL DOCUMENTS

Do you have a really good, clear copy of your ancestor's will, a passenger list, or land record? Consider using those as illustrations as well. Even though these documents may be old hat to us, nongenealogists like looking at them. Nearly all of the historical documents you would want to use as illustrations in your book are in the public domain and free from copyright restrictions.

Go through all the copies of documents you've collected as you researched the family you're writing about, and look at them with the eyes of an illustrator. Look for clear copies, but also think about how this copy will look once

169

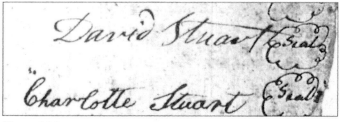

Figure 16-5
Signatures of David and Charlotte Stuart, 1808. While a whole document may not reproduce well, family members will enjoy seeing portions of it, such as signatures of ancestors.

it's reduced to an appropriate size for your book. If you have a computer scanner, try scanning the document and then reducing it to see if you're happy with the quality. If not, you might not want to include it.

Sometimes, the entire document may not be clear enough to scan or reproduce as an illustration, but perhaps just a part of it would be. **If you have a copy of a document with an ancestor's signature or mark, you can crop it to include only that detail.** A page or two reproduced from an ancestor's diary or a letter always makes an interesting illustration. Just make sure you don't choose an example that begins or ends in mid-sentence.

Idea Generator

ILLUSTRATIONS IN THE PUBLIC DOMAIN

Whether you seek art (drawings, engravings, woodcuts), maps, photographs, documents, or advertisements as illustrations for your family history, there are thousands available to you in the public domain that do not require anyone's permission to use. But how do you determine if the material you want to use is in the public domain?

All creative works are protected by copyright law for a given number of years, regardless of whether the author or creator is living (see STEP 18). But this protection doesn't last forever, and when the copyright expires, the work becomes part of the public domain. When that happens, a public-domain work may be used without anyone's permission and often without paying a fee. Some works, such as those produced by the U.S. government, are never eligible for copyright, so they are always in the public domain. Determining whether material you want to use has passed into the public domain is *your* responsibility, and it's not always an easy task. There is a handy table of "When Works Pass into the Public Domain" online at <www.unc.edu/~unclng/public-d.htm>, but here is a brief overview of works that are in the public domain:

- all works published before 1923; these cannot be retroactively protected
- about 85% of works published between 1922 and 1963
- U.S. government works created entirely by federal employees as part of their duties
- certain works commissioned by the U.S. government as works for hire

Lloyd J. Jassin, Esq., author of "New Rules for Using Public Domain Materials," available at <www.copylaw.com/new_articles/PublicDomain.html>, writes that you should know the answers to these questions before assuming a work is in the public domain:

- When was the work created?
- Who created the work? (An individual, two or more individuals, or an employee?)
- Is the author still alive? If not, when did he or she die?
- When was the work registered or published?

Jassin, who also wrote *The Copyright Permission and Libel Handbook* (with Steven C. Schechter), cautions that just because you find something on the Internet does not mean that it is in the public domain. There is much infringement on the Internet, and a work could have been posted without the owner's knowledge or consent.

Because copyright laws have changed and different rules apply to different publication dates, you should research the topic beyond what can be covered here, or seek the advice of an intellectual property attorney. Perhaps the best and easiest-to-understand guide is *The Public Domain:*

PHOTOGRAPHS IN THE PUBLIC DOMAIN

Using public domain photographs is a complicated issue. There are public domain images you can use for free, but in some cases they are in private collections, and the owner will charge you a royalty fee for usage. So when is a photograph in the public domain? It depends on several factors, including whether the photograph is unique, if it has been published, and the creation date. Keep in mind that a photograph does not require a copyright symbol to be protected under the law.

According to copyright law, a photographer is considered the "author" or creator of photographic works and as such the legal copyright holder. If you want to make copies of a photograph, alter it, or publish it, you need the photographer's permission to do so. You need to proceed carefully when using old images and other illustrations rather than assuming they are in the public domain.

If you want to use a photograph taken or published after 1978, obtaining permission can be a simple procedure as long as you can contact the current copyright holder. Send the photographer a letter requesting permission and outlining how the image will be used. In most cases, you will have to pay a royalty (usage fee) for the right to publish the image.

Historical Images

While historical photographs published prior to 1923 are in the public domain, the situation is a little more complex. Before you use any historical images, determine if they were ever published, i.e. made available for general distribution to the public, and when the photographer died. Under the 1978 law, unpublished materials created prior to 1923, including photographs, are covered by special rules. If the images were published after 1978, then they are under copyright for an additional 45 years or at least until December 31, 2047. Suppose you purchase an original image at an antique store. It was never published, the photographer is dead, and it is unidentified. Can you use it? Stephen Fishman in *The Public Domain* advises evaluating the risk in using unpublished images in terms of their economic value and the risk of being discovered. In many cases where the copyright status is uncertain, you may be able to safely use the picture. When in doubt, contact an attorney for reassurance.

There are also ethical concerns with historical images found in museum collections. Even though the museum may not be able to claim copyright to these images and many are in the public domain, they can license you to use them and charge a

continued

fee. If it is a unique item, then you should pay the fee; however, if the photograph was published prior to 1923 and unaltered copies are available in other institutions, then they are in the public domain.

Family Photographs

If you want to use a family photograph, the copyright issues remain the same. Photographers hold the copyright for images; therefore, you cannot use any professional studio photographs of relatives without permission. In order for professional photographers to use your image in advertising or publications they also need a release from you beforehand. Reprints of releases and an explanation of rights appear in the *ASMP Guide to Professional Practices in Photography*.

Several professional organizations including the Professional Photographers of America have agreed to adhere to a set of copyright guidelines outlined by the Photo Marketing Association International. A complete set of the responsibilities of the consumer and professional photographers is on the Kodak Web site <www.kodak.com/global/en/consumer/doingMore/copyright.shtml> or in the *ASMP Guide to Professional Practices in Photography*.

—Maureen Taylor, author of *Preserving Your Family Photographs* and *Uncovering Your Ancestry Through Family Photographs*. Originally published as part of Taylor and Carmack's article, "Free Art? Not So Fast." *Writer's Digest* (September 2001): 31–33 and reprinted with permission.

How to Find Copyright-Free Writings, Music, Art & More, by Stephen Fishman. He offers this advice about determining if a work is in the public domain:

If you do not intend to use the work to compete with someone's business, it might be relatively safe for you to treat it as being in the public domain. However, you should carefully consider the following two factors before deciding what to do:

- the likelihood your use will be discovered, and
- the economic value of the material.

The smaller the chance of discovery, the more willing you should be to use materials whose public domain status is uncertain. Likewise, the lower the economic value of the materials, the safer it is for you to treat them as being in the public domain.

He further states: "The chances of discovery are virtually nil if you use a work for your personal use or make it available only to a restricted group of people." Most published family histories are printed in small quantities and are available to only a "restricted group of people." The same would *not* hold true if you were publishing your family history on the Web, however. There, access is worldwide and the chance of discovery rises tremendously.

Case Study

Illustration Case Study

In an 1869 city directory, I found an advertisement I wanted to use as an illustration in one of my books. The city directory was on microfilm, and at the lead of the microfilm was a statement that no reproduction could be made without the permission of the "publisher." The pub-

Figure 16-6
Even if you don't have a drawing or photograph of the vessel that brought your ancestors to America, you can use a copyright-free illustration of a representative ship. This sailing ship is from *Ready-to-Use Old Fashioned Transportation Cuts*, edited by Carol Belanger Grafton (New York: Dover Publications, 1987). Dover Publications, 31 East 2nd Street, Mineola, New York 11501-3852, <http://store.dover publications.com/>, produces many copyright-free clip-art books with historical illustrations.

lisher of the microfilm was identified as an antiquarian society. Although a city directory published in 1869 is in the public domain (it was published before 1923), I nevertheless wrote for permission, thinking it a mere formality and that I would be supplied with an appropriate credit line. I was granted permission, but I was informed that there would be a seventy-five dollar reprint fee.

I wondered whether the reprint fee was truly necessary, because the directory itself was clearly in the public domain. Ownership of a physical volume does not entitle one to charge a fee, unless that item is unquestionably one of a kind. This city directory was not. I found both original and microfilm copies of the same directory by other "publishers" in other repositories. Moreover, because a microfilm copy is no different from a photocopy, it is not considered copyrightable because no creativity was involved or additional material added to make it a derivative work. A copyright attorney, whose opinion I sought through the Authors Guild, agreed that the work was in the public domain and that I did not need permission to use the ad, nor should I have to pay a reprint fee. So I felt comfortable using the illustration without paying the fee.

ILLUSTRATIONS THAT YOU OR A FAMILY MEMBER CREATE

If you or someone in your family is an artist, why not make an artist's rendition of the ship your ancestor came to America on? If you can't find a photograph or drawing of the ship to refer to in creating your own sketch, research how other ships of the time period looked and sketch one. Make sure, however, that you include in the caption that this is a drawing of a *typical* steamship or sailing ship from the era when Grandpa Michael arrived. Here are other sketches to consider:

- houses and buildings
- floor plans of houses
- tombstones
- maps of neighborhoods
- furniture

- landscape and scenery during your ancestor's day
- land plats showing property boundaries
- cars
- representations of how people looked in your ancestor's day

You hold the copyright in any sketches you create, but if a relative creates artwork for your book, you will need his or her permission to use it.

CAPTIONS

Important

Remember that every illustration needs a caption. Readers need to know what they are looking at. Like endnote citations, the captions need to be as complete as possible. For a photograph, try to include the names of the individuals in the photo, and when and where it was taken. For historical documents, you can use your endnote citation as the full caption, or add whatever else you'd like to bring to the reader's attention. When you wrote to ask permission to use an illustration from a museum, library, or archive, the response should have included a credit line to use as part of the caption. If not, you still should name the repository.

ILLUSTRATION PLACEMENT

Where you place illustrations depends on your personal preference, your skill at using software programs, and how you plan to publish the book. The best place for an illustration is near the text that discusses or relates to that art. Some authors and publishers prefer inserting a set of pages devoted to illustrations halfway through the book. Look at commercially produced family histories and see how each publisher handles art, then decide which method you like best for your book.

Hooray! Your book is almost finished! Now let's wrap up what goes at the end.

The End Matters

Quality research is not accessible unless the book has a quality index.—PATRICIA LAW HATCHER,

PRODUCING A QUALITY FAMILY HISTORY

G enealogists are backward people. Have you ever noticed that while they, too, will flip through a book looking for illustrations, the first part of a book a genealogist typically looks at is the back. That's where the index is. And, if you are writing the book using the two-part format I suggested in STEP 2, the back of the book, or part two, will contain the family summaries. So let's look at how to format those summaries using a standard numbering system; what types of charts you should include; what types of appendixes you may want to include; and how to create an index.

GENEALOGICAL FAMILY SUMMARIES

Remember back in STEP 3 where I suggested you convert all of your family group sheets into the family summary format? If you did that before you began writing, then half of the work for the second part of your book is done. Now all you have to do is insert a numbering system so the reader can easily follow through the generations, and edit out any duplicate material that you covered fully in the narrative section.

Numbering Systems

If you are writing a family history for a single line of descent (see page 15 in STEP 2), you won't need to use any numbering system. Although your summaries will include siblings of your ancestors, all you need to do to help the reader follow the line of descent is to use bold-face type for your ancestors, like this:

Samuel^1 **Ashton**
   i. **Samuel**^{2} **Ashton**
  ii. Francis Ashton
 iii. Elizabeth Ashton

Samuel^2 **Ashton** (Samuel^1)
   i. **William**^{3} **Ashton**
  ii. Robert Ashton
 iii. Mary Ashton
 iv. Catlett Ashton

William^3 **Ashton** (Samuel^2, Samuel^1)
   and so on . . .

Use lowercase Roman numerals to indicate number and birth order of children, and italicized superscript numbers to indicate the generation. (These numbers are italicized so your readers don't confuse them with end-note numbers.)

Assuming that your family summaries start with the earliest known ancestor and then come forward in time, you'll need to use one of the two accepted genealogical numbering systems for your other projects. **There are other numbering systems (and authors sometimes think they can create better ones of their own), but the two described below are considered standard, and have been used successfully for more than a century.**

Important

Register System

So named because it's used by the *New England Historical and Genealogical Register*, the *Register* System is one of the oldest genealogical numbering systems. It works like this:

1. Samuel[1] Ashton
   2.   i.   Samuel[2] Ashton
   3.   ii.   Francis Ashton
       iii. Elizabeth Ashton

2. Samuel[2] Ashton (Samuel[1])
   4.   i.   William[3] Ashton
       ii. Robert Ashton
   5.   iii. Mary Ashton
   6.   iv. Catlett Ashton

3. Francis[2] Ashton (Samuel[1])
   7.   i.   Samuel[3] Ashton
   8.   ii. George Ashton
   9.   iii. Edward Ashton

4. William[3] Ashton (Samuel[2], Samuel[1])

- The superscript numbers after the first names of individuals are the generation numbers. The *Register* System does not set these in italics. Samuel is generation one; Samuel Jr. and Francis are generation two; William and Samuel III are generation three.
- The Arabic numerals are the identifying numbers. These are assigned to only those individuals who will be carried forward in the genealogy; in other words, the people assigned identifying numbers eventually married and had children. In the example above, 2. Samuel, 3. Francis, 4. William, 5. Mary, 6. Catlett, 7. Samuel, 8. George, and 9. Edward are all going to appear later in the genealogy as heads of households with families of their own. There will not be any further information written about Elizabeth and Robert Ashton.
- Lowercase Roman numerals indicate birth order and total number of children for a parent or couple.

The problem with the *Register* System is that if you discover information later about Elizabeth or Robert Ashton, you will have to renumber the entire genealogy.

However, if you are using a computer genealogy software program that uses the *Register* System, the program will automatically renumber for you.

NGSQ System

This system is used by the *National Genealogical Society Quarterly*. You might also see it referred to as the Modified *Register* System, because it works on the same principles as the *Register* System but with slight variations.

1. Samuel^1 Ashton
+ 2.   i.   Samuel^2 Ashton
+ 3.   ii.   Francis Ashton
   4.   iii.   Elizabeth Ashton

2. Samuel^2 Ashton (Samuel^1)
+ 5.   i.   William^3 Ashton
   6.   ii.   Robert Ashton
+ 7.   iii.   Mary Ashton
+ 8.   iv.   Catlett Ashton

3. Francis^2 Ashton (Samuel^1)
+ 9.   i.   Samuel^3 Ashton
+ 10.   ii.   George Ashton
+ 11.   iii.   Edward Ashton

5. William^3 Ashton (Samuel^2, Samuel^1)

- The superscript numbers after the first names of individuals are the generation numbers. They are set in italics, however, to avoid confusion with footnote numbers.
- The Arabic numerals are the identifying numbers. Whereas the *Register* System assigns a number only to those individuals who will be carried forward in the genealogy, the *NGSQ* System gives everyone a number. To indicate that a person is carried forward in the genealogy, a plus sign is placed before the number. This way, if you discover more about Elizabeth or Robert, you will

not have to renumber. You would have to renumber, however, if you discover another child and need to add that person to a family. Here again, a genealogy software program that uses the *NGSQ* System will automatically renumber for you.

- Lowercase Roman numerals indicate birth order and total number of children of a parent or couple.

In part two of your book, it is probably best to arrange the family summaries alphabetically by surname. So, for example, the information and family summaries for three generations of the Brown surname would come first, followed by the information and summaries for four generations of Hagues, then three generations of McCashlands, and the five generations of the Spooners. Thus your table of contents might look like this:

Introduction
Part I: Family Narrative
Part II: Family Summaries
    Brown
    Hague
    McCashland
    Spooner

CHARTS

Pedigree charts and family group sheets are your worksheets. The type of chart that goes into a published family history is the descedancy or drop-line chart, which looks like this:

For More Info

Consult Joan F. Curran's "Numbering Your Genealogy: Sound and Simple Systems," in the September 1991 *National Genealogical Society Quarterly* (see bibliography) for a thorough explanation. It's also available for purchase as a special publication through the NGS Web site: <www.ngsgenealogy.org>. Also see "Numbering Systems in Genealogy," by Richard A. Pence at <www.saintclair.org/numbers/>.

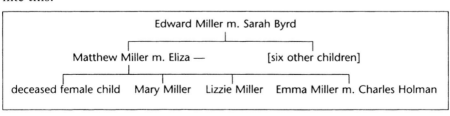

Many genealogical software programs will print out descendancy charts for you to use as illustrations in your book. These charts can be placed in the book wherever the reader may need help visualizing the line of descent. Some authors place the chart at the front of the book so that the reader encounters it immediately, but can easily flip back to it to keep relationships straight while reading the narrative.

APPENDIX

The appendix is where you put items that don't logically fit anywhere else in the book. These might include, but are certainly not limited to

- a list of people you encountered in your research who have the same surnames as the ones covered in your book, but who you have determined are not related to your family.
- full transcriptions of wills, inventories, deeds, letters, or other documents.
- all abstracted entries from a cemetery, parish register, deed book, etc. for the families covered in your book.
- family summaries on an allied branch of your family.

INDEX

An index is not optional when you are producing a family history. Unfortunately, most genealogists index only names and maybe places. Since you are writing a family history narrative, it's important that you also include a subject index so your book is more useful to other researchers.

Several good resources are available to instruct you on the finer points of indexing. I suggest you consult these before you begin:

- *The Chicago Manual of Style*, chapter 17: Indexing
- Patricia Law Hatcher and John V. Wylie's *Indexing Family Histories*
- Katherine Scott Sturdevant's *Organizing and Preserving Your Heirloom Documents*, pages 183-189

Some word processors or genealogy software programs are sophisticated enough to allow you to highlight words or names to be placed in the index automatically. The problem comes when you want to create a subject index. For example, let's say you want a subject category of *Death, causes of*, under which you'll put entries like *tuberculosis, drowning,* and *childbirth*. You may have to index these manually under the proper subject heading.

For a major project like a family history book, I suggest you use a computer indexing program, such as Sky Index <www.sky-software.com>, which will automatically sort and alphabetize the entries. You will still need to manually highlight your manuscript, type in the entries (names, places, subjects) and page numbers, then edit the index once you transfer it into your word processor. Even though an indexing program is wonderful, remember that there are usually glitches—often operator errors. For instance, if you don't enter something exactly the same way each time, you'll end up with multiple entries.

Before you use the software program, go through your final printout page by page (after all the editing and proofreading is finished; see STEP 18), and highlight the items to include in the index: names, places, and subjects. Once this is finished, you can enter the data into your computer program.

The other, old-fashioned method is to record entries on 3 × 5 cards. Make a card for each entry, then as you encounter it on a page, record the page number on the appropriate card. Put the cards in alphabetical order, then enter them into the computer. Obviously, this method is much more time-consuming.

Here is an example of some index entries in *My Wild Irish Rose*:

Adirondack Cottage
   Sanatorium, 33
Albrecht, David J., 71
Alcoholism, 6–7, 16, 36, 41,
   66

Allcorn, Luther H., 55
Armstrong, Harold T., 74
Catholic religion, 6, 15,
   22, 27, 31
Cemeteries

Your book is nearing the finishing line. But before you head to the printer, there are just a few more things you need to do to make it ready to publish.

Getting Ready to Publish

I can't stress enough the importance of revision. That first draft is wonderful and exciting—that's when you fall in love. The revision is more like the marriage. You take what you love and come to terms with the practical, domestic life.—JILL McCORKLE

B efore you publish, you will want to make your manuscript pages as "clean" as they can be, that is, free from typographical errors and problems with grammar, punctuation, and sentence structure. You also need to double-check that you haven't infringed anyone else's copyright, and that you have all the parts that make a book. After all, think of all the time you've already invested in this project. You don't want typos and other mechanical problems detracting from your research and prose. You want this book to be the best it can be, and these final steps are what will give your book the professional polish it deserves.

COPYEDITING AND PROOFREADING

When a book is published by a commercial publisher, it goes through many pairs of eyes before it's bound and distributed. Your book should be no different just because you are self-publishing it. After all, this is your baby. You worked hard on it, and spent years researching and writing it. Rare is the book that escapes some type of error after publishing, but you want to do all you can to make it as close to perfect as possible.

After you have completed the draft of your book but

before you do the index, have someone with good English skills copyedit your book. A copy editor should correct grammar, punctuation, and spelling errors; and check content, sentence structure, flow, paragraph arrangement, logical paragraph transitions, and continuity. If you don't know someone with these skills, then you may need to hire a freelance copy editor. Check the Editorial Services listings in the *Literary Market Place* <www.literarymarketplace.com/lmp/us/services OrgList.asp?ID = 5>, as well as the listings for editors in the *Association of Professional Genealogists Directory* <www.apgen.org>. Try to catch as many errors at this stage as you possibly can. Along with the copy editor, you, too, should read the entire manuscript all the way through.

After the manuscript has been copyedited and you have made all the corrections, you will no doubt need to prepare camera-ready pages or electronic text to take to a printer or small-print-run publisher. Patricia Law Hatcher's *Producing a Quality Family History* and Henry B. Hoff's *Genealogical Writing in the 21st Century* are valuable references for this stage of your book. These give page-layout guidelines and suggestions for creating a page template in your word processor.

Once you have the camera-ready pages, engage the services of a proofreader. A proofreader looks for typographical errors and checks the page layout and design for consistency. Even though you will be proofreading the pages, too, it helps to have at least one other pair of eyes look them over. After you've made corrections from the proofreading stage, create the index (see pages 182–184). The reason you don't want to start indexing until you've made all the corrections is that some changes may affect the pagination, which in turn will throw off your index entries. Shifting even one line of text can cause problems.

Here is a checklist of things to watch for when proofing a family history narrative and family summaries, in addition to spelling, grammar, and punctuation:

Notes

☑ Titles, heads, and subheads. (This is frequently where there is a glaring typo.)

☑ The last line of a page and the top line of a new page. (Make sure the text flows properly from one page to the next.)

☑ Page numbers. (Are the even numbers on the left page and odd numbers on the right page? Do the page numbers follow sequentially for each new chapter, appendix, etc.?)

☑ Consistency in the use of numbers in the text. (Depending on which style you've decided to use, have you spelled out all numbers that should be and used numerals where appropriate?)

☑ Consistency in the spelling of names and places. (Your ancestor's legal name may be Jay Roscoe Rhoads, but friends and family called him Roscoe. Which are you using, and are you consistent?)

☑ Proper punctuation. (For example, are all commas and periods inside quotation marks? Are colons and semi-colons used properly?)

☑ Photo and illustration captions. (Do all illustrations have captions? Did you properly identify who, what, where, and when for each? Double-check for typos and consistency.)

☑ Genealogical numbering system. (Double-check that generations and children are numbered properly.)

☑ Ages and dates. (Are there at least nine months between births of children? Are mom and dad of the right age to be married and having children? Did wife number 1 die before dad married wife number 2? Is mom too old to be having children? Is mom still alive for the births of all her children?)

☑ Notes. (Have you used a consistent format for source citations?)

PARTS OF A BOOK

A book is composed of several standard parts, but not every part must be included in every book. I'll be discussing those commonly used in family histories, but for full details on the parts of a book, see *The Chicago Manual of Style.*

Front Matter

The front matter consists of the following, in the order listed:

- Half-title page (only the title, not the subtitle or author, appears)
- Title page (full title, subtitle, author, publisher, and publisher's place appears)
- Copyright page (see more on this on pages 189-195)
- Dedication
- Table of Contents
- List of illustrations
- Foreword (Please watch how you spell this word! It's not *forward*.)
- Acknowledgments
- Introduction (how the project came about, research repositories used, explanation of records, how you decided whom to include, etc.)
- List of abbreviations

Some of these items may be combined or omitted. For example, you may not need both a foreword and an introduction, and you can include in the introduction acknowledgment of people who helped with the project. Not all books have half-title pages, but they all have full title pages. If you can't think of anyone you want to dedicate the book to, then leave out the dedication, too.

Front matter items are numbered consecutively with lowercase Roman numerals. The first page the reader encounters, either the half-title or full-title page, is considered page *i*—although it is not a printed number.

Text

Your text might consist of two parts: the family narrative and the family summaries. The narrative may be divided into chapters; the summaries, into surname headings. You should also include a separate, short introduction before the summaries to explain the numbering system you used. It's better to include this just before the summaries rather than in the introduction in the front matter, because the reader may forget it was there after reading the narrative.

Text pages begin with number 1 and are numbered consecutively, of course. The page on the left (verso) carries the even page numbers, and the page on the right (recto) carries the odd page numbers. These can be placed at the top of the page or at the bottom, in the outer margins or in the center—although page numbers are easier to see if they are on the outside of the page.

Important

Back or End Matter

Here is where you put any appendixes, the endnotes, bibliography, and index, in that order. (See STEPS 15 and 17 for details on these items.)

WHAT YOU NEED TO KNOW ABOUT COPYRIGHT

You should understand the basics of copyright law, not only to protect what you have written, but to ensure that you have not infringed upon the rights of others. So let's begin with an overview of what copyright is all about.

According to Stephen Fishman in *The Copyright Handbook* (2/2), copyright is a "legal device that provides the creator of a work of art or literature, or a work that conveys information or ideas, the right to control how the work is used." Copyright is needed to promote the progress of the arts and sciences. After all, how many people would bother creating something if, as soon as they put it out to the public, another person could claim it as his or her own? Therefore, Fishman continues, "Copyright encourages authors in their creative efforts by giving them a mini-monopoly over their works."

Copyright consists of a bundle of rights, such as the right to make and distribute copies of a work, the right to create adaptations or derivative works, and the right to perform or display the work. Only the copyright

I'm not an attorney. The information in this section and the one on public domain in STEP 16 came from my own experiences, my extensive research on the subject of copyright, and numerous conversations with my copyright attorney. Therefore, this section is not intended as legal advice, and I assume no responsibility for any actions taken based on information contained here. When in doubt, seek legal advice from an intellectual property attorney.

holder—the author or creator—may exercise these rights, unless the author has transferred them to another party. If someone wrongfully uses the material, the copyright owner can sue and obtain compensation for any losses.

Definitions

Copyright applies to what is called *intellectual property*. As with any property you own, you can do whatever you want with your own intellectual property. Let's liken it to a piece of real estate. If you own your house and the property on which it stands, you can do whatever you want with it. You can keep everything as is. You can rent it. You can sell pieces of it. You can sell the entire thing—in which case, you have no further claim on that property. The same is true of copyright. Once you write your family history, you automatically become the copyright holder the minute you put it in fixed form. A fixed form can be a typed manuscript, a Web publication, a book printed on paper, an audio- or videotape, or a CD.

As the copyright holder of your family history, you can grant individual rights from your bundle to different people. For example, you can grant to Publisher A the right to publish your work as a print book. You can grant the right to publish it as a CD-ROM to Publisher B. You can grant the right to publish an excerpt of your book in a magazine to Publisher C. And you can grant the right to publish it in a foreign language to Publisher D. As long as you have not relinquished all your rights to any one else, you are free to do with the material whatever you wish with the rights you still hold.

Here are the types of works that are protected by copyright:

- literary works: books, magazines, newspapers, diaries, manuscripts, poetry, catalogs, brochures, ads, directories, encyclopedias, electronic databases, computer programs
- pictorial, graphic, and sculptural works: photographs, prints, art reproductions, maps, charts, cartoon characters, paintings, drawings, diagrams, statues, dolls

- motion pictures and other audiovisual works, including interactive multimedia works
- musical works
- dramatic works
- pantomime and choreographic works
- sound recordings
- architectural works

Copyright does not protect these items:
- works in the public domain (see STEP 16)
- ideas, concepts, procedures, principles
- facts
- names, titles, slogans
- blank forms designed solely to record information but which do not convey information (blank family group sheets and pedigree charts would not be protected by copyright)
- recipe ingredients (the instructions, however, are protected)
- extemporaneous speeches
- federal government works

Let's talk about facts, since genealogists deal with facts all the time: births, marriages, and death dates and places, for example. You've spent years researching a branch of your family history. You've compiled the facts—names, dates, places—using one of the standard genealogical formats, such as the *Register* or *NGSQ* system. To this, you've added some analysis, biographical information, and some historical context. On the eve of publishing your book, you happen to be on a genealogy Web site and find many of your facts—names, dates, and places—in a database. Apparently, some family member with whom you shared family group sheets over the years of gathering, took your data and submitted it to the database. Is that a violation of your copyright? Unfortunately, no. Facts you've gathered from public domain sources, such as vital records—almost all of the records genealogists use are public domain records—are not protected by copyright. What is protected is your creative selection and arrangement of the facts in your book.

Does a work have to be registered with the Copyright Office for it to be protected under the law? No. From the moment of creation in a fixed or tangible form, your work is protected. But by registering your work, you make it a matter of public record; and if you ever have to go to court, registration also provides you with certain advantages.

Copyright does not last forever. If the work was created on or after 1 January 1978, copyright protection lasts for the life of the author plus seventy years. If a work was *created* before 1 January 1978, but *published* between then and the end of 2002, it's protected for the life of the author plus seventy years, or until the end of 2047, whichever is greater. Any work published or created before 1923 is now in the public domain. If a work was published between 1923 and 1978, different rules apply, and I suggest you consult the chart at <www.unc.edu/~unclng/public-d.htm>.

Avoiding Copyright Infringement

How do you know if a work is protected by copyright? Ideally, there should be a notice, and this is the same notice that you should put on the copyright page of your own book. According to Copyright Law §401:

> If a notice appears on the copies, it shall consist of the following three elements:
> 1. the symbol ©
> 2. the year of first publication of the work
> 3. the name of the owner[s] of copyright in the work

But what if you are quoting from something and the copyright notice isn't there? Does that mean it's not protected and you're free to use it? No. A good rule of thumb is to assume that anything published less than seventy-five years ago is protected, and that includes anything you find on the Internet.

Fair Use of Another Author's Work

In *The Copyright Permission and Libel Handbook* (page 26), Lloyd J. Jassin and Steven C. Schechter remind us that "fair use is a privilege. It permits authors, scholars, researchers, and educators to borrow small portions of a copyrighted work for socially productive purposes without asking permission or paying a fee." But how much can you quote and still be within the boundaries of fair use? One hundred words? Two hundred words? Much less? Unfortunately, there's no magic number, although it's generally accepted in publishing that using one hundred words from a short work and three hundred from a long work might be okay, if you take strict care not to use critical information from the work. Fair use depends on these and other factors:

- the purpose of the use (commercial vs. noncommercial use; most family histories are for noncommercial use)
- the nature of the work being quoted (the amount you could quote from a poem or song lyrics would be much less than from a book-length work)
- the amount and importance of the quoted passage
- the effect of the use on the market; that is, its economic value

Here are two more rules of thumb to follow when you want to quote someone:

- Would you have a problem with someone quoting that much of your work without asking permission?
- Quote only as much as is necessary to make your point.

Is a source citation sufficient under fair use? Sometimes, sometimes not. It's really up to the courts to decide, but use the above as guidelines. What about when you paraphrase? Is a source citation enough to classify that as fair use? Again, it depends on how much paraphrasing you do and how close your paraphrasing is to the original. (I'm sorry to be so wishy-washy about this, but it *is* the law we're talking about, and it's rarely black and white.)

Case Study

Real-life Scenario

You find a family history published in 1896, and you would like to reprint several paragraphs from it in your own book. There are also some cool illustrations, photographs of some of your ancestors, and a map that would be perfect for your book. You're sure the author must be dead by now, so do you need to track down the author's heirs to get permission? No. You don't need anyone's permission to reprint information or illustrations from a family history that was published in 1896. In fact, you could reprint the entire book if you wanted to without permission. Why? It's in the public domain. It was published prior to 1923, and therefore, the copyright has expired. Anyone can reprint it.

Obtaining Permission

When in doubt, it's always best to ask permission to reprint something in your book or on the Web. But whose permission do you need? The author's? The publisher's? Here's a breakdown:

- Books, commercially published: Write to the publisher for permission. Even though the author may still retain the copyright, in the book contract the author assigns many rights to the publisher.
- Books, self-published: Write to the author.
- Periodicals: Write to the editor; however, absent any publishing agreement to the contrary, freelance writers own the copyright to their articles, so you may need to write directly to the writer. When a journal places the copyright notice on their publication, it protects the journal as a whole, not the individual contributions.
- Photographs: Track down the photographer, especially for studio portraits taken since 1 January 1978.
- Song lyrics: Contact the music publisher(s).
- News items: Write to the newspaper publisher.

Don't wait until the last minute to secure permissions. Some commercial publishers may require four to six weeks to process your request.

REGISTERING YOUR WORK

Be sure to register your family history book with the Copyright Office. It's not at all difficult, and you can find complete instructions and forms online at the Library of Congress Web site <www.loc.gov/copyright>. A software package that makes the process even easier, called Official Copyright, is available for purchase at <www.officialcopyright.com>. You will need to send the Copyright Office two copies of your book, the required form, and the current fee (as of this writing, it was thirty dollars).

While few books go to press with no errors, if you've done all these steps—copyediting, proofreading, double checking for copyright infringement—then you've taken all reasonable precautions to ensure your book is as error-free as possible. Good job! Now you're ready to take it to the printer.

Publishing and Marketing

Success is a finished book, a stack of pages each of which is filled with words. If you reach that point, you have won a victory over yourself no less impressive than sailing single-handed around the world.—TOM CLANCY

Y ou have two options when it comes time to publish your family history: you can do it yourself or you can find a commercial publisher who will publish and distribute the book for you. Both have their pros and cons, which we'll explore, but the vast majority of family histories are self-published. Why? Because the vast majority lack a wide audience appeal. If you've written your family history as a narrative as this book suggests, however, you increase your chances of finding a commercial publisher. I said, "increase your chances"; I didn't say it was a sure thing. It takes a lot to entice a publisher, so let's look at what's involved in self-publication first, as that will be the route you more than likely will take.

BE YOUR OWN PUBLISHER

Doing it yourself—that is, preparing the camera-ready copy and taking it to a print shop or contracting with a small-print-run publisher—has the benefit that you retain complete control over the project. You'll make all the decisions about how the book will look, what title it gets, how much to sell it for, whether it will be hardcover or paperback, and so on. The disadvantage is not only do you do all the work, you also pay all the costs for publication, marketing, and distribution of your book.

There are economical ways to self-publish your family history, however, and still have it look professionally done. First, decide the following:

Money Saver

• *Number of copies.* The greater the number, the less the cost per copy. But do you want five hundred copies of a family history sitting in your garage if you can't sell them all? Some small-print-run publishers, however, have a minimum that you must print. It may be as few as twenty-five or as many as one hundred.

• *Paper quality.* Many genealogists like to have their family histories printed on archival-quality paper. This is quite costly, but it will last much longer than regular bond paper. But do you really need archival-quality paper? Most commercially published books aren't printed on paper like this, and a number of them have been around for more than a century. Besides, if you donate a copy of your family history to the Family History Library in Salt Lake City, Utah, and give permission for it to be microfilmed (at no cost to you), you're ensuring the book will be around as long as the library is.

• *Hardcover or paperback.* Again, while hardcover does survive longer than paperback, paperback is usually less expensive to print and also within the budget of your relatives who will be buying the book. Libraries, of course, prefer hardcover, but often they will rebind (at their cost) a paperback such as a family history in a hardcover library binding. If you choose hardcover for your family history, and the price per book is over, say, twenty-five dollars, will your relatives buy it? Paperback keeps it more affordable.

• *Size of the book.* Large books are generally more awkward to hold and read than smaller ones. For that reason, I'd avoid an 8.5″ × 11″ trim size and go for a trim size of 6″ × 9″. If the book at that size is too voluminous— more than five or six hundred pages—you may have to consider publishing two volumes.

• *Number of illustrations.* The more illustrations the printer has to deal with, the higher the cost, unless you have a high-quality scanner and place the photographs in the camera-ready copy yourself. But this brings up another point: what type of printing do you want? Reproducing your camera-ready pages on a photocopier won't produce pages and illustrations with the high quality that you may have expected. Having the printer make photographic plates is more expensive, but the quality is better. (That's why the pages are called "camera-ready," by the way.) Check with the printer about the best way to submit electronic photographs.

• *Lead time.* A publisher who specializes in family histories has two busiest times: late spring (before summer family reunions), and a couple of months before Christmas. (See, you aren't the only one who wants a book published in time for the family reunion or to give as gifts). If your goal is to have a book for either of those two events, you should submit your camera-ready manuscript to the printer several months in advance. And if you plan to have the publisher provide the camera-ready copy from your computer disk, add several months to the printing time in case the printer has a backlog.

Contact several small-print-run publishers (see page 199). They will send you forms to complete—or they may have forms available online—asking for specific information about your book, such as the number of pages and illustrations. The printer will give you a price quote on the entire print run, which you can divide by the number of copies to get the cost per copy. While it's doubtful that you'll make a profit on sales, you don't want to lose money on this book, either. To determine a selling price for each book, be sure to figure in additional expenses such as shipping and the cost of the copies you plan to donate to libraries, as well as that of the two or three copies you will keep for yourself. After all, *you* did all the work; you should get a few free copies. Most small-print-run publishers will require the full payment up front.

So far, I've been explaining the standard method of publishing a book: that is, printing copies on an offset press from a camera-ready copy. There is another method, however.

FAMILY HISTORY PUBLISHERS

Anundsen Publishing Co.
108 Washington St., P.O. Box 230, Decorah, IA 52101 Phone: (563) 382-4295
E-mail: mail@anundsenpubl.com Web: www.anundsenpubl.com

Closson Press
1935 Sampson Dr., Apollo, PA 15613-9208 Phone: (724) 337-4482
E-mail: rclosson@nb.net Web: www.clossonpress.com

Family History Publishers, Inc.
845 S. Main St., Bountiful, UT 84010 Phone: (801) 295-7490
E-mail: Jayl@familyhistorypublisher.com Web: www.familyhistorypublisher.com

Gateway Press, Inc.
1001 N. Calvert St., Baltimore, MD 21202 Phone: (800) 296-6687
E-mail: ahughes@gatewaypress.com Web: www.gatewaypress.com

Heritage Books, Inc.
1540 Pointer Ridge Place, #E, Bowie, MD 20716 Phone: (800) 398-7709
E-mail: info@heritagebooks.com Web: www.heritagebooks.com

Newbury Street Press
101 Newbury St., Boston, MA 02116-3007 Phone: (617) 536-5740
Web: www.newenglandancestors.org/articles/newbury_press/

Picton Press
P.O. Box 250, Rockport, ME 04856-0250 Phone: (207) 236-6565
E-mail: sales@pictonpress.com Web: www.pictonpress.com

PRINT-ON-DEMAND PUBLISHING

Today, you have another option for publishing your family history besides the small-print-run publisher. It's called print-on-demand publishing or POD, which means **the POD publisher stores copies of your family history electronically, printing a copy only when someone orders one. With POD, you can order only as few copies at a time as you want to sell.** Some POD publishers have a lengthy turnaround time (about four to six weeks) to publish a book because they subcontract the printing

\di'fin\ *vb*

Definitions

199

to another firm; others, like InfinityPublishing.com, have their own printing equipment and can turn books out in less than forty-eight hours. This can be important if you've decided at the last minute to have copies of your family history ready for the family reunion or to use as Christmas gifts.

POD PUBLISHERS

Infinity Publishing
www.infinitypublishing.com

1stBooksLibrary
www.1stbooks.com

Xlibris
www.xlibris.com

Booklocker
www.booklocker.com

iUniverse
www.iuniverse.com

Creative Imaging, Inc.
www.creativeimaginginc.com

Advantages of POD

The advantages of publishing your family history through POD are many:

- You won't have to subsidize publishing more books than you need.
- You won't have to find a place to store a multitude of copies that you haven't been able to sell or distribute yet.
- You won't have to handle the sales or the shipping.
- It's less expensive than traditional small-print-run publishing.
- Some POD publishers pay authors a royalty.
- POD publishers usually offer as part of their services step-by-step instructions on how to prepare your book for publication.
- Some provide a list of freelance editors and typists.
- Authors typically get a discount on copies they purchase.
- Many POD publishers let you keep all rights to your book.

- Some offer marketing packages to help sell your book.

Do your homework before choosing a POD publisher, however. Find out about rights, costs, when royalties will be paid, author's discounts, and what happens if the publisher goes out of business. Get a written agreement that covers these items and that offers you the option to terminate your agreement should you decide to no longer publish your family history.

Costs of POD

According to John F. Harnish in *Everything You Always Wanted to Know About POD But Didn't Know Who to Ask*, setup prices vary greatly depending on the publisher. For example, in 2001, Infinity Publishing charged a $400 setup fee, while Xlibris offered packages ranging from $200 to $1,600; iUniverse had setup packages from $99 to $299, with additional services available for an additional fee; and 1stBooks Library charged $399 for setup plus $199 for the distribution of a POD paperback. Obviously, you'll want to shop around and compare what each publisher offers in their setup package. These packages can include

- assigning an ISBN [International Standard Book Number], which helps booksellers find your book.
- providing you with proof copies.
- providing copies and forms so you can register your book with the Copyright Office.
- adding your book to the publisher's online catalog.
- listing your book in *Books in Print* and with online booksellers.
- supporting your marketing and promotional efforts.

Many POD publishers offer free publishing guides and information, so gather them all and compare.

DISTRIBUTING YOUR FAMILY HISTORY

If you go the route of using a traditional small-print-run publisher, how do you know how many copies to have printed? **While your manuscript is with the copy editor and after you've gotten a price quote from the printer for the number of copies you think you can sell, send a prepublication notice to every relative and descendant you know of, and to libraries that may want to purchase the book.** Here's a sample letter:

Tip

> Dear _____,
>
> After many years of research, I have completed *Italians in Transition.* Thanks to everyone who contributed stories and information.
>
> The book will be available the beginning of August. It will be a hardcover volume containing approximately 125 pages, including photographs, maps, and documents. The book is a narrative account of our Vallarelli and DeBartolo ancestors and their lives in Italy and America. It also includes a genealogy of all their known descendants.
>
> Since there will be a limited number of copies printed, please return the enclosed order form by 28 April if you would like to reserve a copy. The cost is $25 plus $4 for postage and handling.

Once you receive these prepaid orders, then add to that number a couple of copies for you, the number of copies you think you'll donate to repositories or send out for book reviews (see page 203), and two copies for the Copyright Office. Then add at least another one to two dozen. Trust me, once one relative shows your book to another or your book gets good reviews, you'll get more orders. It is better to have a few too many than to be out of stock within a few months.

Recently, as an experiment, I suppose, in psychic survival, I reread every horrific review I've ever received to see what I would learn. This is what I learned: I'm right. They're wrong.—DAVID SHIELDS

Donation and Review Copies

You'll want your family history to have as wide a distribution as you can give it. After all of the work you put into it, you want to make it available to other researchers. While you can certainly donate as many or as few copies as you want, here are some places you should consider sending them:

- Family History Library, 35 North West Temple, Salt Lake City, UT 84150
- Allen County Public Library, Genealogy Department, 900 Webster St., P.O. Box 2270, Ft. Wayne, IN 46802
- Libraries, archives, historical societies, or other repositories in the localities where your ancestors were from, and where they settled
- Copies you provide to the Copyright Office if you register your work will automatically go to the Library of Congress

Sending your book out for review will give it some free publicity and generate orders from people and repositories you may not have considered. Many periodicals in the genealogy field review family histories or publish book notices.

Marketing

Jack Canfield, one of the authors of the *Chicken Soup for the Soul* series, advises: "Realize that for six months to a year after your book is published 90% of your time should be spent on marketing your book and self-promotion." While that may be unrealistic for a family history book, **here are some ways you can promote your book:**

- Send book notices to genealogical publications, libraries, and historical societies in the areas where the family lived. Consider placing ads in selected publications.

Idea Generator

- Do you know someone associated with the media? Think of all the people in your life, past and present. Did you attend school with someone who is now in journalism or broadcasting? Have you notified all organizations—not just genealogical ones—to which you belong that you are the author of a book or book(s)? This is not a time to be shy.
- Do you have your own Web site? If so, use it to promote your book on it. If not, you may want to consider creating a Web site for this purpose.
- Consider having post cards printed showing the cover of your book. You can mail these to family, friends, or clients when you need to send a quick note. Or consider handing out bookmarks showing the cover of your book and explaining how to order copies.
- Add a signature file (*sig*) to all of your e-mails that includes the title of your book. Show the title on your personalized stationery.

For more promotion ideas, see *Guerrilla Marketing for Writers* by Levinson, Frishman, and Larsen.

COMMERCIAL PUBLICATION

With commercial publishing, you lose some control over your work. You will have little or no say over the book's title, cover design, citation styles (footnotes, endnotes, blind notes, no notes), indexing, and the layout of interior pages. But, a commercial publisher pays to produce, market, and distribute your book, and you might get an advance against royalties. Commercial publishers do pay royalties, usually 10 percent of the net receipts, meaning that you get 10 percent of whatever the publisher earns from the book. So if the publisher sells your work to a bookseller like Amazon.com at 50 percent off the cover price, you get 10 percent of that 50 percent.

Commercial Publishers of Family Histories

Turn to the bibliography, and look over the sections with examples of family history books. Notice who the publishers are. There are quite a few of them, aren't there? Some are commercial presses; others are university presses. These are the publishers who may be interested in publishing your family history. To find out how to contact them, see the current issue of *Writer's Market*, which is available at most bookstores and libraries, and online for a subscriber fee at <www.writersmarket.com>.

Using an Agent vs. Doing It Yourself

An agent typically works on a commission basis and takes 15 percent of everything you ever make on the book. The advantage of having an agent is that he or she will query publishers for you, and when it comes time to negotiate the contract, the agent consults with you and then handles this task. To find an agent, see the current edition of *Guide to Literary Agents*.

For a nonfiction book, however, you may be able to get by without an agent, and it's certainly worth the effort to try a few publishers on your own first. If you aren't getting anywhere, then look for an agent. Some publishers will not read manuscripts unless they are submitted by the author's agent. *Writer's Market* will tell you if a publisher works with unagented authors.

If you plan to approach publishers yourself, you will need to send a one-page query letter. On letterhead, the query letter should

- address the editor by name. *To Whom It May Concern* is acceptable, but do not use *Dear Sir* because many editors are women.
- grab the editor's attention in the opening paragraph as you would in the first paragraph of your family history.
- clearly state your book's focus, what your slant is, why this is a hot topic, and how many words your book contains.
- give your qualifications and publishing history (articles or books).

Writer's Market offers further guidelines and sample

query letters. With your query letter, you'll include a book proposal and a self-addressed, stamped envelope. Here are the items that go into the proposal:

- Title of proposed book. Don't wed yourself to a title; the publisher will likely change it.
- Overview. What is this book about? How have you written and structured it?
- Audience and competition. Who is this book intended for and who will buy it? What are its key selling points? Are similar books available? Although this book is unique to your family, how does the style compare to best-sellers such as *Angela's Ashes* or *Slaves in the Family*, which have a universal appeal? (Check the Internet bookstores. List titles, publishers, dates of publication, prices, and whether hard- or softcover.) How is your book different and better than these? If your book is totally unique, how do you know it will sell?
- Chapter outline. For each chapter, give a one- to two-paragraph summary of its contents.
- Sample chapter. Include a sample chapter, usually the first one.
- Author biography. What are your credentials? How can you help the publisher market your book (e.g., through speaking engagements, a Web site, etc.)? This is the place to brag!

Don't send your query and book proposal by e-mail or fax unless the *Writer's Market* tells you the publisher accepts queries and proposals this way. Typically, it will take about two months to receive a response. If you haven't received a response within two months, follow up with a *letter*, not a phone call or e-mail.

The Book Contract

If you are lucky enough to attract a publisher who wants to publish your family history, you will receive a boiler-plate publishing contract. Never sign the boilerplate. Seek the advice of an intellectual property attorney, who will review and negotiate the contract for you, if you wish; or consult one of the many books on publishing contracts in the bibliography; or join the National Writers Union (113 University Place, Sixth Floor, New York, New York 10003; <www.nwu.org>) or the Author's Guild (31 East 28th Street, Tenth Floor, New York, New York 10016-7923; <www.authorsguild.org>), both of which offer free contract advice to its members. Keep in mind that contracts are negotiable, so don't be afraid to ask and negotiate. Above all, never sign anything that you don't fully understand.

YOU DID IT!

Congratulations! You have researched, written, and published your family history. That's quite an accomplishment. You have every reason to feel proud of yourself. You have left a legacy for future generations. Do something special for yourself—but don't rest on your laurels too long. Remember, it's never too soon to start thinking about your next book project.

Bibliography

Writing Guides

Barrington, Judith. *Writing the Memoir: From Truth to Art*. Portland, Ore.: Eighth Mountain Press, 1997.

Bickham, Jack M. *Setting*. Cincinnati: Writer's Digest Books, 1994.

Brohaugh, William. *Write Tight: How to Keep Your Prose Sharp, Focused and Concise*. Cincinnati: Writer's Digest Books, 1993; 2d edition, Wilmington, Del.: ISI Books, 2002.

Cheney, Theodore A. Rees. *Writing Creative Nonfiction*. Cincinnati: Writer's Digest Books, 1987; revised edition, Berkeley, Calif.: Ten Speed Press, 2001.

Earnest, Russell and Corrine. *Skeletons in Your Closet: Deciding the Fate of Family Secrets*. East Berlin, Pa.: Russell D. Earnest Associates, 1998.

Files, Meg. *Write From Life: Turning Your Personal Experiences Into Compelling Stories*. Cincinnati: Writer's Digest Books, 2002.

Franklin, Jon. *Writing for Story: Craft Secrets of Dramatic Nonfiction*. New York: Atheneum, 1986.

Fryxell, David A. *How to Write Fast (While Writing Well)*. Cincinnati: Writer's Digest Books, 1992.

———. *Structure & Flow: How to focus, organize and unify all types of magazine articles to hold your reader from the lead to the end*. Cincinnati: Writer's Digest Books, 1996.

Gerard, Philip. *Creative Nonfiction: Researching and Crafting Stories of Real Life*. Cincinnati: Story Press, 1996.

Gouldrup, Lawrence P. *Writing the Family Narrative*. Salt Lake City: Ancestry Publishing, 1987.

Gutkind, Lee. *The Art of Creative Nonfiction: Writing*

and Selling the Literature of Reality. New York: John Wiley and Sons, 1997.

Hatcher, Patricia Law. *Producing a Quality Family History.* Salt Lake City: Ancestry, 1996.

———. "Do We Share the Blame?" *Association of Professional Genealogists Quarterly* 15 (December 2000): 146-150.

Hauser, Susan Carol. *You Can Write a Memoir.* Cincinnati: Writer's Digest Books, 2001.

Heilbrun, Carolyn G. *Writing a Woman's Life.* New York: W.W. Norton & Co., 1988; reissue by New York: Ballantine Books, 2002.

Hemley, Robin. *Turning Life into Fiction.* Cincinnati: Story Press, 1994.

Hoff, Henry B., ed. *Genealogical Writing in the 21st Century: A Guide to* Register *Style and More.* Boston: New England Historic Genealogical Society, 2002.

Kempthorne, Charley. *For All Time: A Complete Guide to Writing Your Family History.* Portsmouth, N.H.: Boynton/Cook Publishers, 1996.

Marius, Richard. *A Short Guide to Writing About History.* New York: HarperCollins College Publishers, 1995; 4th edition (written by Melvin Page), New York: Longman, 2001.

Martin, Rhona. *Writing Historical Fiction.* New York: St. Martin's Press, 1988.

Noble, William. *Writing Dramatic Nonfiction.* Forest Dale, Vt.: Paul S. Eriksson, 2000.

Polking, Kirk. *Writing Family Histories and Memoirs.* Cincinnati: Betterway Books, 1995.

Schwarz, Ted. *The Complete Guide to Writing Biographies.* Cincinnati: Writer's Digest Books, 1990.

Sturdevant, Katherine Scott. *Bringing Your Family History to Life Through Social History.* Cincinnati: Betterway Books, 2000.

———. *Organizing and Preserving Family Heirloom Documents.* Cincinnati: Betterway Books, 2002.

Tobias, Ronald B. *20 Master Plots (and How to Build Them).* Cincinnati: Writer's Digest Books, 1993.

Wagner-Martin, Linda. *Telling Women's Lives: The New Biography*. New Brunswick, N.J.: Rutgers University Press, 1994.

Woolley, Persia. *How to Write and Sell Historical Fiction*. Cincinnati: Writer's Digest Books, 1997.

Zinsser, William, ed. *Extraordinary Lives: The Art and Craft of American Biography*. Boston: Houghton Mifflin, 1988.

Examples of . . .
Genealogical Narratives

Carmack, Sharon DeBartolo. *David and Charlotte Hawes (Buckner) Stuart of King George County, Virginia, Including Three Generations of Their Descendants*. Simla, Colo.: the author, 2000.

Dorman, Franklin A. *Twenty Families of Color in Massachusetts, 1742–1998*. Boston: New England Historic Genealogical Society, 1998.

Hatcher, Patricia Law. *Rhoads Family History: The Family and Ancestry of Jay Roscoe Rhoads*. Boston: Newbury Street Press, 2001.

Simons, D. Brenton. *The Langhornes of Langhorne Park*. Boston: Newbury Street Press, 1997.

Life Stories (Historical Biographies of Ordinary People)

Bundles, A'Lelia. *On Her Own Ground: The Life and Times of Madam C.J. Walker*. New York: Scribner, 2001.

Cohen, Patricia Cline. *The Murder of Helen Jewett: The Life and Death of a Prostitute in Nineteenth-Century New York*. New York: Alfred A. Knopf, 1998.

McLaurin, Melton A. *Celia, A Slave*. New York: Avon Books, 1991.

Navas, Deborah. *Murdered by His Wife: A History With Documentation of the Joshua Spooner Murder*. Amherst: University of Massachusetts Press, 1999.

Pettem, Silvia. *Separate Lives: The Story of Mary Rippon*. Longmont, Colo.: The Book Lode, 1999.

Pucci, Idanna. *The Trials of Maria Barbella: The True*

Story of a 19th Century Crime of Passion. New York: Vintage Books, 1997.

Srebnick, Amy Gilman. *The Mysterious Death of Mary Rogers: Sex and Culture in Nineteenth-Century New York.* New York: Oxford University Press, 1995.

Family History Narratives

Bonfield, Lynn A. and Mary C. Morrison. *Roxanna's Children: The Biography of a Nineteenth-Century Vermont Family.* Boston: University of Massachusetts, 1995.

Buel, Joy Day and Richard Buel Jr. *The Way of Duty: A Woman and Her Family in Revolutionary America.* New York: W.W. Norton, 1984.

Bushman, Claudia L. *"A Good Poor Man's Wife": Being a Chronicle of Harriet Hanson Robinson and Her Family in Nineteenth-Century New England.* Hanover, N.H.: University Press of New England, 1998.

Carmack, Sharon DeBartolo. *My Wild Irish Rose: The Life of Rose (Norris) (O'Connor) Fitzhugh and her mother Delia (Gordon) Norris.* Boston: Newbury Street Press, 2001.

———. *The Ebetino and Vallarelli Family History: Italian Immigrants to Westchester County, New York.* Decorah, Iowa: Anundsen Publishing Co., 1990.

———. *Italians in Transition: The Vallarelli Family of Terlizzi, Italy, and Westchester County, New York and The DeBartolo Family of Terlizzi, Italy, New York, and San Francisco, California.* Boston: Newbury Street Press, 2003.

Colletta, John Philip. *Only a Few Bones: A True Account of the Rolling Fork Tragedy and Its Aftermath.* Washington, D.C.: Direct Descent, 2000.

Fox, James. *Five Sisters: The Langhornes of Virginia.* New York: Simon & Schuster, 2000.

Frazier, Ian. *Family.* New York: Farrar, Straus and Giroux, 1994.

Harrell, Carolyn L. *Kith and Kin: A Portrait of a*

Southern Family (1630–1934). Macon, Ga.: Mercer University Press, 1984.

Judd, Peter Haring. *The Hatch and Brood of Time: Five Phelps Families in the Atlantic World, 1720–1880*. Boston: Newbury Street Press, 1999.

Keneally, Thomas. *The Great Shame: And the Triumph of the Irish in the English-Speaking World*. New York: Nan A. Talese (Doubleday), 1999.

McFarland, Gerald. *A Scattered People: An American Family Moves West*. Chicago: Ivan R. Dee, 2000.

Mills, Donna Rachal. *Some Southern Balls: From Valentine to Ferdinand and Beyond*. Orlando, Florida: Mills Historical Press, 1993.

Talese, Gay. *Unto the Sons*. New York: Alfred Knopf Publisher, 1992.

Wiencek, Henry. *The Hairstons: An American Family in Black and White*. New York: St. Martin's Press, 1999.

Personal and Family History Memoirs

Ball, Edward. *Slaves in the Family*. New York: Farrar, Straus and Giroux, 1998.

———. *The Sweet Hell Inside: A Family History*. New York: William Morrow, 2001.

Connelly, Bridget. *Forgetting Ireland*. St. Paul, Minn.: Borealis Books, 2003.

Epstein, Helen. *Where She Came From: A Daughter's Search for Her Mother's History*. New York: Penguin Group, 1997.

Logue, Mary. *Halfway Home: A Granddaughter's Biography*. St. Paul: Minnesota Historical Press, 1996.

Luther, Kem. *Cottonwood Roots*. Lincoln: University of Nebraska Press, 1993.

Madden, T.O. Jr. with Ann L. Miller. *We Were Always Free: The Maddens of Culpeper County, Virginia: A 200-Year Family History*. New York: Vintage Books, 1993.

McCourt, Frank. *Angela's Ashes: A Memoir*. New York: Scribner, 1996.

Miner, Valerie. *The Low Road: A Scottish Family Memoir*. East Lansing: Michigan State University Press, 2001.

Murray, Pauli. *Proud Shoes: The Story of an American Family*. New York: Harper and Row, 1956, 1978.

Paolicelli, Paul. *Dances with Luigi: A Grandson's Search for His Italian Roots*. New York: St. Martin's Press, 2001.

Redford, Dorothy Spruill with Michael D'Orso. *Somerset Homecoming: Recovering a Lost Heritage*. New York: Anchor Books, 1988.

Viviano, Frank. *Blood Washes Blood: A True Story of Love, Murder, and Redemption Under the Sicilian Sun*. New York: Pocket Books, 2001.

Edited Letters and Diaries

Blakey, Arch Fredric, Ann Smith Lainhart, and Winston Bryant Stephens Jr. *Rose Cottage Chronicles: Civil War Letters of the Bryant-Stephens Families of North Florida*. Gainsville, Fla.: University Press of Florida, 1998.

Brumgardt, John R. *Civil War Nurse: The Diary and Letters of Hannah Ropes*. Knoxville: University of Tennessee Press, 1980, 1993.

Carmack, Sharon DeBartolo. *A Sense of Duty: The Life and Times of Jay Roscoe Rhoads and His Wife, Mary Grace Rudolph*. Boston: Newbury Street Press, 2002.

Schwartz, Gerald, ed. *A Woman Doctor's Civil War: Esther Hill Hawks' Diary*. Columbia: University of South Carolina Press, 1984.

Stabler, Lois K., ed. *Very Poor and of a Lo Make: The Journal of Abner Sanger*. Portsmouth, N.H.: Peter E. Randall Publisher, 1987.

Ulrich, Laurel Thatcher. *A Midwife's Tale: The Life of Martha Ballard, Based on Her Diary, 1785–1812*. New York: Vintage Books, 1991.

Woodward, C. Vann, ed. *Mary Chesnut's Civil War*. New Haven: Yale University Press, 1981.

Fictional Family Sagas Based on Truth

Haley, Alex. *Roots: The Saga of an American Family.* New York: Doubleday, 1976; reissue by New York: Gramercy Books, 2000.

Tademy, Lalilta. *Cane River.* New York: Warner Books, 2001.

A Sampling of Social Histories

Demos, John. *Past, Present, and Personal: The Family and the Life Course in American History.* New York: Oxford University Press, 1986.

Earle, Alice Morse. *Home Life in Colonial Days.* Reprint of 1898 ed. Stockbridge, Mass.: Berkshire House, 1992.

Fischer, David Hackett. *Albion's Seed: Four British Folkways in America.* New York: Oxford University Press, 1989.

Green, Harvey. *The Uncertainty of Everyday Life, 1915–1945.* New York: HarperCollins, 1992.

Hawke, David Freeman. *Everyday Life in Early America.* New York: Harper and Row, 1988.

Hiner, N. Ray and Joseph M. Hawes, eds. *Growing Up in America: Children in Historical Perspective.* Urbana: University of Illinois Press, 1985.

Hooker, Richard J. *A History of Food and Drink in America.* Indianapolis: Bobbs-Merrill Co., 1981.

Larkin, Jack. *The Reshaping of Everyday Life, 1790–1840.* New York: Harper and Row, 1988.

McCutcheon, Marc. *The Writer's Guide to Everyday Life from Prohibition Through World War II.* Cincinnati: Writer's Digest Books, 1995.

————. *The Writer's Guide to Everyday Life in the 1800s.* Cincinnati: Writer's Digest Books, 2001.

Mintz, Steven and Susan Kellogg. *Domestic Revolutions: A Social History of American Family Life.* New York: Free Press, 1988.

Moulton, Candy. *Everyday Life Among the American Indians.* Cincinnati: Writer's Digest Books, 2001.

The Peoples of North America Series published by

Chelsea House Publishers in New York deals with fifty ethnic groups, discussing the history, culture, and religion of each group.

Rothman, Ellen K. *Hands and Hearts: A History of Courtship in America*. New York: Basic Books, 1984.

Schlereth, Thomas. *Victorian America: Transformations in Everyday Life, 1876–1915*. New York: HarperCollins, 1991.

Sutherland, Donald M. *The Expansion of Everyday Life, 1860–1876*. New York: Harper and Row, 1989.

Taylor, Dale. *The Writer's Guide to Everyday Life in Colonial America*. Cincinnati: Writer's Digest Books, 1997.

Ulrich, Laurel Thacher. *Good Wives: Image and Reality in the Lives of Women in Northern New England, 1650–1750*. New York: Vintage Books, 1982, 1991.

Varhola, Michael J. *Everyday Life During the Civil War*. Cincinnati: Writer's Digest Books, 1999.

Wolf, Stephanie Grauman. *As Various as Their Land: The Everyday Lives of Eighteenth-Century Americans*. New York: HarperPerrennial, 1993.

Reference Guides

America: History and Life—A Guide to Periodical Literature. Santa Barbara: ABC-Clio, Inc., annual.

Curran, Joan Ferris. "Numbering Your Genealogy: Sound and Simple Systems." *National Genealogical Society Quarterly* 79 (September 1991): 183-93.

Hatcher, Patricia Law, and John V. Wylie. *Indexing Family Histories*. Arlington, Va.: National Genealogical Society Special Publication, 1994.

Taylor, Maureen A. *Preserving Your Family Photographs*. Cincinnati: Betterway Books, 2001.

———. *Uncovering Your Ancestry Through Family Photographs*. Cincinnati: Betterway Books, 2000.

Copyright

Carmack, Sharon DeBartolo and Roger D. Joslyn. "Who Owns the Client Report? What We Learned from

Being Sued in Federal Court." *Association of Professional Genealogists Quarterly* 16 (June 2001): 137-140.

Copyright Law of the United States of America and Related Laws Contained in Title 17 of the United States Code. Circular 92. Washington, D.C.: U.S. Copyright Office, Library of Congress, April 2000.

"Copyright, Photography and the Web," <www.chimwa smp.org/photoweb/copyrite.htm>.

Fishman, Stephen. *The Copyright Handbook: How to Protect & Use Written Works,* 5th edition. Berkeley, Calif.: Nolo Press, 2000.

———. *The Public Domain: How to Find and Use Copyright-Free Writings, Music, Art and More.* Berkeley, Calif.: Nolo Press, 1999.

Gasaway, Lolly. "When Works Pass Into the Public Domain," <owww.unc.edu/~unclng/public-d.htm>.

Jassin, Lloyd J. "New Rules for Using Public Domain Materials," <www.copylaw.com/new_articles/Public Domain.html>.

———. and Steven C. Schechter. *The Copyright Permission and Libel Handbook: A Step-by-Step Guide for Writers, Editors, and Publishers.* New York: John Wiley and Sons, 1998.

Stim, Richard. *Getting Permission: How to License and Clear Copyrighted Materials Online & Off.* Berkeley, Calif.: Nolo Press, 2000.

Taylor, Maureen A. and Sharon DeBartolo Carmack. "Free Art? Not So Fast." *Writer's Digest* (September 2001): 31-33.

Publishing and Marketing

Bunnin, Brad, and Peter Beren. *The Writer's Legal Companion.* Reading, Mass.: Perseus Books, 1998.

Camenson, Blythe. *How to Sell, Then Write Your Nonfiction Book.* Chicago: Contemporary Books, 2002.

Curtis, Richard, and William Thomas Quick. *How to*

Get Your E-Book Published. Cincinnati: Writer's Digest Books, 2002.

Guide to Literary Agents. Current edition. Cincinnati: Writer's Digest Books, annual.

Harnish, John F. *Everything You Always Wanted to Know About POD Publishing But Didn't Know Who To Ask*. InfinityPublishing.com, 2002.

Herman, Jeff and Deborah M. Adams. *Write the Perfect Book Proposal: 10 Proposals That Sold and Why*. New York: John Wiley and Sons, 1993.

Kirsch, Jonathan. *Kirsch's Guide to the Book Contract*. Los Angeles: Acrobat Books, 1999.

Levinson, Jay Conrad, Rick Frishman, and Michael Larsen. *Guerrilla Marketing for Writers*. Cincinnati: Writer's Digest Books, 2001.

Perkins, Lori. *The Insider's Guide to Getting an Agent*. Cincinnati: Writer's Digest Books, 1999.

Polking, Kirk, ed. *Writer's Friendly Legal Guide*. Cincinnati: Writer's Digest Books, 1989.

Ross, Marilyn, and Tom Ross. *The Complete Guide to Self Publishing*, 4th ed. Cincinnati: Writer's Digest Books, 2002.

Writer's Market. Current edition. Cincinnati: Writer's Digest, annual.

The Charles Fearn Family Narrative

Note on Appendixes A-B: I cannot take full credit for all the data in these narratives: Roger D. Joslyn, CG, FASG, did the extensive genealogical research on these families. From his findings, I then researched the historical context and turned the bare-bones information into family history narratives. I've chosen to use footnotes, so you can easily determine the source of each piece of information.

Frontier Military Life[1]

Lizards, snakes, tarantulas, scorpions, and black ants likely became dreaded creatures to the Charles Fearn family during their stay at Fort Grant, in the southern part of Arizona, in the early 1880s. The Fearns would find living conditions in the desert of Arizona challenging and quite unlike what they were used to back home in Ohio. Summer temperatures rose to more than 110° in the shade. In the evenings, the heat would dissipate only about twenty degrees, making it stifling to sleep indoors. Families moved their beds—iron cots with bedsacks filled with straw and a mattress laid atop—outside in the summer months for sleeping. To keep the ants from crawling on the bed, they set cot legs inside tin cans full of water, making it impossible for the ants to find their way onto the bed.[2] Desert night sounds frightened many women and children unaccustomed to such noises. The Fearns would attempt to sleep through the howls of

---

[1]Roger D. Joslyn and Sharon DeBartolo Carmack, *American Lives and Lines* (Privately published, 2000).
[2]Martha Summerhayes, *Vanished Arizona: Recollections of the Army Life of a New England Woman* (Lincoln: University of Nebraska Press, 1979; reprint of second edition originally published in 1911), 77-78, 204.

coyotes, the calls of wild cats, and the chirping of crickets and toads.

Charles had enlisted in the United States Army in 1874 at the age of twenty-two when he lived in Columbus, Ohio. He was stationed at the Columbus Arsenal for three years before the military began moving him. While still in Columbus, he married Martha "Mattie" Jane Bainter on 26 March 1878.[3] In a photograph that may have been taken either on their wedding day or shortly after, Martha was wearing a high-collared blouse and a suit made from faille, a soft-ribbed fabric. As was so common in portraits taken during this time, Mattie stood with her right hand resting on Charles's shoulder as he sat in a chair. His hair was neatly groomed and cut short; thin mutton chops adorned his cheeks. Later in life, he would wear round spectacles.

Eighteen months after their wedding, their first child, Charles Elliott, was born. In a fort-life photograph of the Fearn family taken about six to eight months after Charles Elliott was born, the family had gathered their household possessions outside to display for the photographer. Charles, who served as a hospital steward during his military career, was in dress uniform and stood just behind his wife with his left arm resting on the awning of their tent house. Mattie was seated and held baby Elliott; the infant appeared in what looks like a christening gown. Mattie was wearing one of her best dresses for the occasion: a white blouse with bow at the neck, a dark, solid-colored jacket, and a plaid skirt. She also wore a hat. A birdcage and bird (perhaps a canary?) were hung on the horizontal post that held up the tent's canvas roof. Two wooden chairs were placed outside, one containing Charles's gun, with his sword leaning against the

---

[3]Franklin Co., Ohio, Marriages, 14:337; military pension file of Charles H. Fearn, #186125, National Archives (NARA), Washington, D.C., Record Group 94: Records of the Adjutant General's Office, Entry 91: Regular Army Enlistment Papers, 1st Series, 1798-14 July 1894; enlistment papers of Charles H. Fearn; Record Group 112: Records of the Surgeon General's Office; Entry 113: Registers of Military Service of Hospital Stewards, 1856–87, Volume 7 and Volume 8, NARA, Washington, D.C.

chair. Other household items displayed in the picture were an oil-burning lamp and a washbowl and pitcher. The trees and grass were in full bloom, so the photograph was taken sometime in the spring or summer.[4]

Charles's first far-western assignment, between September and December of 1880, was at Fort D.A. Russell near Cheyenne, Wyoming.[5] Fort David A. Russell dated back to 1867, when its construction was necessary to protect the crews and settlements along the Transcontinental Railroad. The cavalrymen's participation in Indian campaigns ended before Charles and his little family arrived, but only just before. In 1876 and 1877, troops from Fort D.A. Russell had fought in the Sioux wars that involved Sitting Bull and Crazy Horse. In late 1879, the troops traveled to western Colorado to suppress the uprising of White River Utes known as the Meeker Massacre. The Fearns arrived after these last Indian campaigns. Indeed, the fort would switch from cavalry to infantry in 1883. Yet the Indian wars would have been fresh in the recollections and expectations of the men at the fort in the fall of 1880.

Fort D.A. Russell sat at about 6,000 feet elevation at the point where the Rocky Mountain foothills meet the Great Plains. For the fall and early winter of Charles's stay, he would have experienced both mild and extreme climates. Always, whether or not it carried a severe blizzard, the wind blew strong from the northwest.[6] The terrain was dry and flat. There were still traces of the

[4]Photograph in the possession of the client. The photograph has no identifying remarks to indicate where and when it was taken; however, judging from the approximate age of the child (presumably Charles Elliott at about six to nine months), it had to have been taken ca. spring/summer 1880. The foliage and grass are not likely Arizona landscape to which the Fearns were not sent until 1883. The picture was probably taken at Little Rock Arsenal, although it could have been taken in early fall when the Fearns arrived at Fort D.A. Russell. Clipping of newspaper death notice of Warren Foss Fearn, "younger son of Chas. H. and Mattie B. Fearn," in possession of the client.

[5]Military pension file of Charles H. Fearn, enlistment papers of Charles H. Fearn.

[6]Jane R. Kendall, "History of Fort Francis E. Warren," *Annals of Wyoming* 18 (January 1946): 4; Peggy Dickey Kirkus, "Fort David A. Russell: A Study of Its History from 1867 to 1890," Part I, *Annals of Wyoming* 40 (October 1968): 166.

huge herds of buffalo that the army had helped extermi-
nate in the 1870s. Prairie dog towns abounded. Water
came from wells that dried up every year and daily water
wagons from Crow Creek. The shortage of water meant
that vegetation was scarce, the diamond-shaped wooded
fort was dusty, and devastating fire was a constant
threat.[7] "A tree in the vicinity of the post was indeed a
rare sight," so soldiers had transplanted cottonwood and
pine trees around the fort. Charles and Mattie may have
lived near the creek if she, like many wives, worked as a
laundress.[8]

In some ways, Fort D.A. Russell would have been an
easier place to live than those to which Charles was later
assigned. There were no Indian reservations nearby; no
danger of Indian conflict after 1879; and it was near a
bustling settlement, Cheyenne, whose population in
1880 was 5,047. Thus, there was no stockade surround-
ing the fort, and people traveled freely to town. Wives
such as Mattie could purchase fruits and vegetables in
Cheyenne if they could afford it.[9] There was entertainment available on post. For the soldiers, this consisted
of drinking and horse racing; drunkenness was a major
problem. There were wholesome activities, too, of which
Charles and Mattie might have partaken: Masonic
lodges, theatricals, musicales [sic], dances, a library, and
a chapel. These indoor events made winter, when the
Fearns lived there, the happiest time of the year at the
fort. Charles might even have taught school, which was
held in the hospital building in the winter months. An
enlisted man could receive thirty-five cents a day as ex-
tra-duty pay for teaching.[10]

The soldiers' furniture included chairs made by prisoners at Leavenworth and iron bunks with wood slats

[7]Kirkus, "Fort David A. Russell," Part II, *Annals of Wyoming* 41 (April 1969): 35-
45; Kirkus, "Fort David A. Russell," Part I, 166.
[8]Kirkus, "Fort David A. Russell," Part I, quote 167, 170; Kirkus, "Fort David A.
Russell," Part II, 86, Kendall; "History of Fort Francis E. Warren," 16.
[9]Kirkus, "Fort David A. Russell," Part I, 184, 167, 187; census figure from Kendall,
"History of Fort Francis E. Warren," 62.
[10]Kirkus, "Fort David A. Russell," Part II, 83-91.

to hold straw-tick mattresses. The stoves used Wyoming coal by 1880, and for lighting there were candles, candle lanterns, and small brass lamps fueled with mineral oil.[11] Diets were army rations augmented by commissary goods (such as molasses, raisins, and dried vegetables); by hunting (antelope, deer, elk, rabbits, and pheasants) and fishing; and by women keeping cows and chickens or gathering berries and greens. Whether the Fearns had time to establish themselves so well in two months is doubtful. Charles would have been allowed to eat meals with his family, although they would have had only tin and iron for "dishes," unless they carted china around with them. The army discouraged even officers from doing that.[12]

Health at the fort was poor because of overcrowding and unsanitary conditions. The surgeon wanted men to bathe weekly but complained that the walk between the bathhouse and barracks exposed damp men to greater chance of illness. Medical care was primitive, relying heavily on purgatives, quinine, and whiskey. Common ailments at the fort included chronic rheumatism (of which Charles was a sufferer), dysentery and diarrhea, and all varieties of respiratory infections and inflammations.[13]

Life at the fort may have been hardest for women like Mattie. The low pay was such a "sore spot" that wives usually did laundry in the creek or housekeeping for officers. Although Mattie may have taken solace in her baby, stitchery, writing, socializing, or riding, she would have suffered fear for her child's safety and for any future experience with childbirth. Army regulations "did not even recognize the presence of military dependents. They were looked upon officially only as camp followers, and as such could claim no privileges or rights." If Mattie dreaded having a baby on the frontier, she might have

[11]Kendall, "History of Fort Francis E. Warren," 14-15.
[12]Kirkus, "Fort David A. Russell," Part I, 186-87; Kirkus, "Fort David A. Russell," Part II, 89.
[13]Kirkus, "Fort David A. Russell," Part II, 83-86.

feared being a widow there all the more. Had Charles died, she would have become "a pitiful victim of circumstance," losing all claim to her husband's benefits and facing eviction.[14] For the Fearns, "life on the frontier was a mixture of excitement, boredom, fresh air, poor pay, and hard work," as well as ill health, danger, and worry. Little did they know that assignments two years later would take them to the even more rugged frontier of Arizona in the days of Geronimo.[15]

After Fort D.A. Russell, the Fearns were sent for two years to the arsenal in Little Rock, Arkansas, where their second son, Warren, died when he was ten months old. When the orders came in August 1882 to move to Fort Grant, Arizona, it must have been difficult for Charles and Mattie to leave this child buried in Little Rock, knowing that they may never return to the area again.[16]

Charles, Mattie, and their first son, Charles Elliott, would have probably traveled part of the way by rail from Arkansas to Arizona. One means of travel to the Southwest was to take the railroad to San Francisco, followed by a steamer down the Pacific Coast, up the Gulf of California to Fort Yuma, then by rivers or overland to the Arizona forts.[17]

Fort Grant, located on a mesa at the head of Grant Creek Valley, was built in 1872. Its purpose was to control the Apaches, making it safe for settlers to move into the area. Fort Lowell, seven miles northeast of Tucson, was established in 1873, and served as a supply depot and full-company post for southern Arizona. Charles and his family were stationed there from 1885 through 1886. This base was expanded to include operations against Apaches as

[14]Kirkus, "Fort David A. Russell," Part I, pay quote from 185, 170; Kirkus, "Fort David A. Russell," Part II, women quotes from 89-90.

[15]Kirkus, "Fort David A. Russell," Part I, quote from 184.

[16]Death notice of Warren Foss Fearn; military pension file of Charles H. Fearn; enlistment papers of Charles H. Fearn.

[17]Telephone conversation between Roger D. Joslyn and David Faust, curator, Ft. Lowell, Arizona, Museum, 21 Nov. 1998; Ray Allen Billington, *Westward Expansion*, 5th ed. (New York: Macmillan Publishing Co., 1982), 587; Summerhayes, *Vanished Arizona*, 20, 238.

well as to supply military escorts. Soldiers stationed at these forts "guarded depot supplies, escorted wagon trains to other posts, and made expeditions clear to the Mexican border chasing the elusive Apaches."[18]

Fort Lowell was under constant repair during the time the Fearns resided there. "Roofs leaked and the dirt floors became mud puddles during the rainy season." One of the fort's biggest problems was maintaining an adequate water supply. While the Fearns were stationed there, the Rillito Creek supplied water that was undependable in quantity. Not until 1887, a year after the Fearns had left the area, was there a steam pump to solve the problem.[19]

Nearby Tucson offered stores and plenty of social activities, including dances, concerts, picnics, parades, and even baseball games. Gambling, dance halls, and saloons offered entertainment for men without families. The soldiers as well as the townspeople participated in these amusements.[20]

Charles, who stood five-feet seven-inches tall and had gray eyes, light-colored hair, and a fair complexion, was an enlisted private, who worked as a hospital steward.[21] Although there were definite distinctions between officers and enlisted men, hospital stewards belonged to an in-between group, "enlisted men of a certain status." As a hospital steward in most of his known assignments, Charles could have some authority for running the hospital, perhaps including provisions, purchasing, cooking, the dispensary, hygiene, and even assisting the surgeon. He would answer to roll call at least two or three times a day and would wear a dress uniform for the commanding officers' inspections, often on Sunday mornings. On those occasions, even patients were to sit or lie at atten-

[18]Telephone conversation between Roger D. Joslyn and David Faust; Robert B. Roberts, *Encyclopedia of Historic Forts* (New York: Macmillan Publishing Co., 1988), 38, 42; brochure from Fort Lowell Museum.
[19]Typed history of Fort Lowell, Arizona, 4 pages, unnumbered, undated, The National Archives, Records of the War Department, Office of the Quartermaster General.
[20]Roberts, *Encyclopedia of Historic Forts*; brochure from Fort Lowell Museum.
[21]Military pension file of Charles H. Fearn.

tion and in uniform, if possible. The steward would have to concern himself with ridding the hospital of bed bugs and lice; preventing smoking, swearing, "spirituous liquors," and loud noise; making sure floors were swept and air ventilated; warming the hospital (even a tent) by wood or coal stoves; burning contaminated hair mattresses; and monitoring rations of pork or beef, beans, peas, rice, hominy, or potatoes. An 1867 steward's manual recommended chicken soup, although beef or mutton soup were just as good. The steward might also prepare medications and dress wounds. He could participate in dentistry, mostly tooth extraction. A hospital steward on a remote post definitely played a vital role and was a jack-of-all-trades. He was to be "industrious, temperate, patient, and good-tempered."[22]

There was also a caste system among the military wives. In fact, "there [was] more caste distinction among the ladies of the Army than among the officers."[23] This would have been an aspect of military life to which Mattie would have had to grow accustomed. In the military, it did not matter how much education, position, or money a person had in civilian life; "rank seemed to be the one and only thing in the army."[24]

Even among officers, the Arizona housing was assigned according to rank: a lieutenant lived in one-room quarters with a kitchen, a captain was housed in a structure with two rooms and a kitchen, a major lived in quarters with three rooms, and a colonel in a four-room dwelling. Fort Lowell's quarters were constructed from adobe, and generally, the lower ranking men's quarters were located north of the post. Housekeeping would have been almost fruitless for Mattie. Dust and sand

[22]Joseph Janvier Woodward, M.D., *The Hospital Steward's Manual: For the Instruction of Hospital Stewards, Ward-masters, and Attendants, in Their Several Duties* (Philadelphia, Penn.: J.B. Lippincott and Co., 1862), passim, quote from p. 21. Copy in the possession of Paula B. Taylor, Director, Warren ICBM and Heritage Museum, R.E. Warren AFB, Wyoming (formerly Ft. D.A. Russell).

[23]Oliver Knight, *Life and Manners in the Frontier Army* (Norman: University of Oklahoma Press, 1978), 6-7, 43.

[24]Summerhayes, *Vanished Arizona*, 80.

coated everything inside and outside of their living quarters. Sand clung to hair and clothing. With water in great demand, Mattie was no doubt frustrated, trying to keep her family and house clean. At the fort, there were seven officers' quarters, a hospital, four enlisted men's quarters, a quartermaster's warehouse, a guardhouse, a bakery, and the adjutant's office.[25]

In Arizona, the Fearns would have mixed with two cultures new to them during their stay: Mexicans and Indians. While most women feared the Apaches, there were a few Indians who were friendly and engaged as servants on the posts. Mattie may have been one of the many white military wives who envied the way the Mexican women dressed for the summer's heat. Custom dictated that military wives wear high-necked, long-sleeved dresses, although they did wear lighter colors than their sisters back east, particularly white. The Mexican women, however, wore short-sleeved white linen blouses with calico skirts. If Mattie had not brought an adequate supply of dresses for her three-year stay in the desert, she would have had to make her own or purchase new ones during an excursion to Tucson seven miles away, a one-hour trip by horse and buggy.[26]

Life on the fort was dictated by bugle calls. Reveille meant sunrise and time to start the day. In the evenings, "tattoo" called company officers to check on the garrison and to report whether all were present and accounted for. Lights out was signaled by the playing of taps.[27] Sundays were not much different from any other day of the week at the forts, except there was a formal inspection on Sunday mornings. There was a post chaplain, who catered to the garrison, baptizing babies and marrying couples, and in Tucson, there were two Protestant churches and one Catholic church.[28]

---

[25]Telephone conversation between Roger D. Joslyn and David Faust; Summerhayes, *Vanished Arizona*, 12-13; Knight, *Life and Manners in the Frontier Army*, 40, 70.
[26]Summerhayes, *Vanished Arizona*, 146.
[27]Summerhayes, *Vanished Arizona*, 208.
[28]Telephone conversation between Roger D. Joslyn and David Faust.

Mattie gave birth to two sons while stationed in Arizona with her husband. Otto was born in September 1883 at Fort Grant. Guy was born two years later at Fort Lowell. With few women around to assist her, Mattie was no doubt apprehensive about giving birth in the middle of the desert, not to mention raising small children in this barren, dusty, and vermin-rich atmosphere.

After leaving Arizona, the Fearns returned to Columbus where they purchased a home at 1074 Michigan Avenue.[29] After spending three years in Arizona, the family must have acclimated to the hot, dry climate. The first snow and winter in Columbus after they arrived home probably felt especially cold to them.

Charles opened the Fearn Drug Company in Columbus and later secured a job as a postal clerk. The Fearn Drug Company was a manufacturing business that sold a product called "Hairline." It was advertised as a cure for scalp diseases and "restores gray hair to original color, removes dandruff, prevents falling hair, cures eczema."[30]

Suffering from chronic heart disease, rheumatism, and rectal problems, Charles worked as long as he could to support his family. He quit working 2 December 1915. Mattie said, "Much of the time he sat in his chair all night being so short of breath he could not lie down. And in the last weeks he was out of his mind a great part of the time. He imagined someone was pressing charges against him for something he didn't seem to know what. Other times he was looking out of the window for someone that was coming to take him home. When I asked him where he was, he said in California."[31]

Charles, in pain and having difficulty breathing, suffered mentally, too. His mind had become weakened from his "long suffering from heart lesion[s] which caused him to

---

[29]1900 census, Ohio, Franklin Co., Columbus, Ward 18, Pct. D, ED 126, p. 11, #236-246, NARA T623, roll 1270.

[30]1900 census, Ohio, Franklin Co., Columbus, Ward 18, Pct. D, ED 126, p. 11, #236-246, NARA T623, roll 1270; stationery letterhead of Fearn Drug Co., in possession of the client.

[31]Affidavit of Mattie Fearn, 27 Jan. 1917, in support of requesting a widow's pension, found in Charles Fearn's pension file.

almost gasp for his breath at times."[32] Friends who visited with Charles a day or so before he died said he had undergone a "decided change," scarcely speaking or noticing people in the room.[33] A close friend of Charles, C. N. Bernhardt, the president of the Ohio State Branch of the United National Association of Post Office Clerks, said, "I saw [Charles] about three days prior to his death. He was in a very emaciated physical condition and did not seem his former self mentally. He recognized me but kept out of conversation altogether except to answr [sic] questions, which was a very strange and unusual attitude for him to assume toward me since I had been one of his most intimate friends and his counselor on numerous occasions."[34] Mattie agreed: "When several of his friends were in to see him, he acted very strange and did not seem to know them and ask[ed] me what all those people were doing here. All of this was brought on by his long suffering."[35] Charles died on 15 March 1916. Family and friends mourned Charles's death at the age of sixty-three and met at the graveside of Greenlawn Cemetery in Columbus.

After Charles's death, Mattie continued to live at the Vermont Place home with her son Otto and his wife. When Otto took a position in Washington, D.C., Mattie moved with them. After a while, she moved in with her son, Elliott, in South Bend, Indiana, where she joined the King Avenue Methodist Episcopal Church. Mattie was also a member of the Loraine Chapter, Order of the Eastern Star and of the McCoy Post of the Women's Relief Corps. She died on 26 March 1928.[36]

[32]Affidavit signed by John M. Thomas, M.D., 24 Jan. 1917, contained in Charles Fearn's pension file.

[33]Affidavits of D.T. O'Brien and B.K. Black, Columbus, Ohio, 29 Jan. 1917, in Charles Fearn's pension file.

[34]Letter to Hon. C.L. Brunbaugh from C.N. Bernhardt, 27 Jan. 1917, Columbus, Ohio, in Charles Fearn's pension file.

[35]Affidavit of Mattie Fearn, 27 Jan. 1917, in support of requesting a widow's pension, found in Charles Fearn's pension file.

[36]Indiana death certificate of Mrs. Mattie B. Fearn, 1928, #340; obituary of Mrs. Mattie B. Fearn, *The South Bend* (Indiana) *Tribune*, 23 March 1928, Sec. 1, p. 6; Record of Family Lots, Greenlawn Cemetery, Columbus, Ohio, FHL 1402482, arranged alphabetically.

Charles and Mattie Fearn experienced a way of life different from most families during the late 1800s. Because of Charles's military career, they saw and lived in Arkansas, Wyoming, and Arizona, but it was the desert of Arizona that brought the most challenges to the family. Perhaps more frustrating than the lizards, snakes, tarantulas, scorpions, and black ants were the wind and the dust. But despite the obstacles of desert military camp life, they endured and walked away with fascinating stories to tell their grandchildren.

Example of Reverse Chronology Structure

"A Place Among Nations"[1]

The war for American independence had been raging for seven years when Philip's third great-grandfather, Thomas McQueen, enlisted in 1782. Thomas's brother, Joshua, joined the cause the year before. Joshua served his country as a spy with the Pennsylvania troops and partook in the battles of Brandywine, Germantown, Trenton, and others, yet his experience could not compare with his brother's. Tom saw killing and savagery of a different nature; his battle began against the Redcoats but ended with a fight for survival as a captive among the Indians and the British.[2]

Like most men who fought in the American Revolution, Tom had several terms of enlistment, which were voluntary and short. There was a widespread belief that an army would no longer be needed after the war, so there was no need for a "professional standing army." Americans believed a standing army was a threat to liberty. Consequently, men left the ranks just as they learned their duties, only to return home or re-enlist in another unit. Tom first served for about thirty days in Captain Hoglan's Company as a ranger on the banks of the Ohio River. A short time later, Tom volunteered in the Virginia State Line under Colonel Williamson's command, serving just sixteen days before his life would take a drastic turn.[3]

---

[1]Roger D. Joslyn and Sharon DeBartolo Carmack, *American Lives and Lines* (Privately published, 2000).

[2]Revolutionary War pension file of Joshua McQueen, S36102, National Archives (NARA), Washington, D.C.; Revolutionary War pension file of Thomas McQueen, S33080, NARA Microfilm M804, roll 1700; Rev. John D. Shane's interview with Joshua McQueen, n.d., Draper Mss., 33 CC 13: 115-29 (Madison, Wisc.: State Historical Society of Wisconsin, microfilm edition 1980).

[3]Quote from Daniel J. Boorstin, *The Americans: The Colonial Experience* (New York: Vintage Books, 1958), 368; Revolutionary War pension file of Thomas McQueen.

Even while the war was underway, land-hungry Americans were fighting over property lines and ownership. Three hundred Pennsylvanians found themselves removed from their homes stemming from a dispute over the Virginia-Pennsylvania border. They crossed the Ohio River to seize land. Living peacefully in the area were Delaware Indians and Moravian missionaries. Within a few days, the displaced Pennsylvanians attacked the missionaries and Indians during one of their church services at Gnadenhütten, "slaughtering all of them—men, women, and children—'in a most cool and deliberate manner.' " Not only the Delawares, but also the Shawnee and Wyandot Indians retaliated, raiding the northwestern frontier settlement. An expedition led by Colonel William Crawford from Ft. Pitt headed for the Ohio country in May 1782, burning the Sandusky Indian villages along the Muskingum River. Tom McQueen was part of this unit. The unit continued to march up the Sandusky River, but stopped after a few days, contemplating whether to return home since they had not encountered "the enemy." The officers decided to continue their march one more day.[4]

"About the time the [officers] broke up," said Tom, "a horseman rode up and gave information that the enemy was close by. We men immediately formed in order of battle and pressed forward to meet the enemy. About 12 o'clock, we came in contact with the enemy." A bitter battle ensued, lasting until dusk. On the next morning, the battle resumed and continued throughout the day and that evening. Tom reported that there were continual reinforcements of the enemy, so the officers in his unit decided to retreat. At least fifty Americans were killed and many others were missing. Col. Crawford "died by

[4]Ray Allen Billington, *Westward Expansion: A History of the American Frontier*, 5th ed. (New York: Macmillan Publishing Co., 1982), 196; Revolutionary War pension file of Thomas McQueen. For other accounts of Crawford's expedition, see J. Lewis Peyton, *History of Augusta County, Virginia* (Harrisonburg, Va.: C.J. Carrier Co., 1972), 189-92, and Allan W. Eckert, *That Dark and Bloody River* (New York: Bantam Books, 1995), 360-63, 376-77.

slow roasting—the sign of supreme Indian contempt" and "nine [were] carried away to the Delaware villages to be tortured to death." Tom was one of the nine.[5]

"My brother Tom was taken in Crawford's campaign," recalled Joshua McQueen. "They burned the Leftenant, and made Tom run the gauntlet," which was a form of torture, in which the prisoner is made to run between two rows of braves who strike at him. "There was not a sound place [on his] head when he got through. But a squaw gave, I forget how many, buckskins for him."[6] Tom was fortunate to survive when many prisoners were killed. He was enslaved for about a year and ultimately taken to Detroit, where he finally was able to make his escape, only to fall into the hands of British troops. Two soldiers nearly beat Tom to death, then he was held captive for about six months.[7]

Tom's will to survive was strong. When the opportunity presented itself, Tom and a fellow officer escaped again and found refuge with a trading company. One trader "said he could land them on the main shore," recalled Joshua. "They went down a steep bank—three negroes and two white men—and landed on an island, then let the boat go, thinking it was the main land. They got way down on the Ohio, and being nearly starved, the leftenant shot a raccoon in the tree. The Indians heard them and took them, carrying them back to Detroit." The Indians then sold Tom back to the British. He was offered his freedom if he would enlist with the British Army. Tom refused and was kept in irons until the

---

[5]Quotes taken from the Revolutionary War pension file of Thomas McQueen, which have been edited here for readability. A summary of this battle may also be found in Billington, *Westward Expansion*, 196. Quotes "nine carried away" and "died by slow roasting" from Billington, 196. According to Tom McQueen's account, 147 were killed and missing. According to Peyton, *History of Augusta County, Virginia*, 191-92, Crawford was stripped naked and tortured with hot embers and burning brands for two hours before he died. Also see Colin G. Calloway, *The American Revolution in Indian Country: Crisis and Diversity in Native American Communities* (Cambridge: Cambridge University Press, 1995), 63, 273, 294.

[6]Rev. Shane's interview with Joshua McQueen.

[7]Boorstin, *The Americans*, 347; Revolutionary War pension file of Thomas McQueen.

end of the war three months later in April 1783. Although Tom survived, in later years when applying for a pension, he was nearly blind and believed it was a result of the beating he received from the Indians in running the gauntlet.[8]

Two years after his service, Tom married Sarah Wilson Vaughn, probably in Ohio County, Virginia (now Brooke County, West Virginia), where Tom returned following his release from the Redcoats. He fathered twelve children between 1785 and 1809, six sons and six daughters. Two sons, Uriah and Joseph, became Separate Baptist ministers, representing a more "rough-and-ready, 'enthusiastic' approach" to traditional Baptists, although they were united in theology; and one son, Benjamin, served in the War of 1812. But it would be one of Tom and Sarah's daughters, Sarah Vaughn McQueen, who would marry James Neely Love, also a minister, and become Philip's second great-grandparents. Like all of Philip's ancestors, the McQueens were a migratory family. Tom was "a man of roving tendencies, and after rambling over various parts of the country [Kentucky and Ohio], came to [Bartholomew County] Indiana, and died" there in 1838 when he was seventy-five.[9]

Tom's brother, Joshua, lived to be 106, dying in 1853. Both brothers were revered during their lifetimes

---

[8]Quotes taken from Rev. Shane's interview with Joshua McQueen, which have been edited here for readability. Also see Revolutionary War pension file of Thomas McQueen. The exact chronology and events of Tom's captivity are difficult to ascertain accurately from Joshua's interview, which, not uncommonly, skips around in time; however, this narrative, which includes quotes from Joshua, takes into consideration Tom's own declaration in his pension application.

[9]Photographs of grave markers of Sarah and Thomas McQueen, in Thomas McQueen Data File, National Society, Daughters of the American Revolution Library Office, Washington, DC; Liberty Cemetery, 10, typed list in Bartholomew County Clerk's Office, genealogy section, Columbus, Ind.; Nettie Beth Cosgrove, *I Had a Thousand Relatives: McQueen, Rawlins, Everett and Related Families, And a Supplemental Genealogy: Glazier, Blagrave, Taylor, Hardisty, Davis, Cosgrove*, by Lee D. Cosgrove (n.p., 1978), n.p.; sketch of Uriah McQueen, in Morgan Scott, *History of the Separate Baptist Church* (Indianapolis: The Hollenbeck Press, 1901), 264-65; Peter W. Williams, *America's Religions: Traditions and Cultures* (New York: Macmillan Publishing Co., 1990), "rough-and- ready" quote from p. 134; Bartholomew Historical Society, *History of Bartholomew County, Indiana-1888* (Columbus, Ind.: the Society, 1976), 485, 791.

as Revolutionary War soldiers who rendered services in the "great struggle which gave our country a place among nations."[10]

Tom and Joshua, sons of Thomas McQueen, had served valiantly in the Revolutionary War. Son Tom had been captured during the war by Indians, made to run the gauntlet, and escaped only to be captured by British. But this was not the first time the McQueen family had dealings with native tribesmen. Supposedly, the elder Thomas McQueen was the Thomas "Query" who was killed by Indians in "the Great Cove," in Frederick County, Maryland, on 8 November 1763.[11]

"I was seven or nine years old when I lost my father," reported Joshua McQueen, the eldest child of Thomas and Elizabeth (Berry) McQueen. Elizabeth became a widow with six small children to raise alone. After Thomas's death, she may have married William West, an Ohio River trader closely associated with the same families as the McQueens and with whom son Joshua McQueen was living on that river in 1774.[12]

After her children had grown, she eventually headed west, doubtless with her children. For a while, she may have lived in Washington County in southwestern Pennsylvania, where her brother-in-law, William McQueen, had settled. In 1782 her sons James and Benjamin McQueen were privates in the company of George Brown, probably their brother-in-law, that was part of the ill-fated Sandusky Expedition commanded by Colonel William Crawford.[13]

It appeared the McQueen men had a history of vio-

[10]Obituary of Joshua McQueen, *The Frankfort Commonwealth*, Frankfort, Ky., 2 May 1853.

[11]Robert Barnes, comp. *Marriages and Deaths from the Maryland Gazette, 1727–1839* (Baltimore: Genealogical Publishing Co., 1973), 148.

[12]Rev. Shane's interview with Joshua McQueen; Donna Hechler, *Metes & Bounds I: Dugal McQueen and Some Descendants* (Wyandotte, Okla.: The Gregath Publishing Company, 1997), 46-47.

[13]*Pennsylvania Archives*, Sixth Series, 2:228.

lence and rebellion, starting at least with Philip's fifth great-grandfather, Dugal McQueen, in Scotland.

The impetus forcing Dugal McQueen, one of Philip's fifth great-grandfathers, to come to America in 1716 was beyond Dugal's control. In November 1715, Dugal was among the rebel supporters of the exiled Scottish King of England James II. These supporters, known as Jacobites, adhered to the house of Stuart after the Glorious Revolution of 1688. Taking their name from the Latin form of the name James (Jacobus), the Jacobites sought to restore James II to the throne. In an uprising which attempted to crown the Old Pretender, James Edward Stuart, the Jacobites were defeated in the bloody battles of Preston and Sheriffmuir. Dugal was an ensign in Colonel McIntosh's Regiment and was among the 1,103 Scotsmen captured in Preston in Lancashire, England. Some prisoners were put to death; others, like Dugal, "were left to the merchants of Liverpool, to be transported to the plantations of America."[14]

Sailing aboard the *Friendship*, Dugal embarked from Liverpool on 24 May 1716. Three other McQueens, Alexander, David, and Hector, who may have been Dugal's relatives, were among the eighty prisoners on the ship. Other McQueen prisoners were transported to South Carolina. The *Friendship*'s destination was Maryland, where Dugal would be auctioned as an indentured servant.[15]

Like the colony of Virginia, Maryland throve under wealthy landowners who cultivated tobacco and acquired hundreds of acres of land through the headright system. Each male who willingly came to settle in the colony received fifty acres, along with more acreage for transporting his wife, children, and servants. Landown-

---

[14]Clifford Neal Smith, "Transported Jacobite Rebels, 1716," *National Genealogical Society Quarterly* 64 (1976): 27, 31; Samuel Hibbert-Ware, *Lancashire Memorials of the Rebellion, MDCCXV* (Bishops Stortford, England: Chadwyck-Healey, 1974), 160-62, 238-39, quote from p. 239.

[15]The relationship of the other McQueens to Dugal has not been determined for this study. Smith, "Transported Jacobite Rebels, 1716," 27, 31.

ers paid the passage of those who could not afford it on their own, acquiring an additional fifty acres per head and creating a system of temporary servitude. Although the headright system of acquiring land was abandoned in Maryland in 1680,[16] planters still needed servants to work the fields. Dugal McQueen was one of a large population of indentured servants who arrived in colonial Maryland and Virginia. Most came voluntarily, but others, like Dugal, fell victim to the English government's method for dealing with military prisoners and convicts. As the ship neared its destination in the colonies, "convicts were handed wigs, fictitious trades were invented, and arrangements were made. After [the ship] landed, the planters came aboard and walked the prospects up and down, chatting them up and feeling their biceps."[17]

William Holland of Maryland purchased Dugal's services for seven years. "The term of service, when not fixed by a contract was limited by the act of 1715 [the year before Dugal arrived] to five years for those persons over twenty-five, and longer periods for those who were younger." Upon completion of servitude, male indentured servants were supposed to receive clothing, tools, and occasionally a small parcel of land. In reality, many left with nothing but the clothes on their backs. Nothing is known of Dugal's servitude, and after the end of his indenture (about 1723), he apparently remained landless until the fall of 1739, when as a resident of Prince George's County, he was warranted by the Province of Maryland seventy-two acres near what is today Westminster, Carroll County, but was then a part of Baltimore County.[18]

---

[16]Peter Wilson Coldham, *Settlers of Maryland, 1679–1783*, 5 vols. (Baltimore: Genealogical Publishing Co., 1995–96), 1:vii.

[17]Ted Morgan, *Wilderness at Dawn: The Settling of the North American Continent* (New York: Simon and Schuster, 1993), 126.

[18]Robert W. Barnes, *Baltimore County Families, 1659–1759* (Baltimore: Genealogical Publishing Co., 1989), 441; "term of service . . ." from J. Thomas Scharf, *History of Baltimore City and County From the Earliest Period to the Present Day, Including Biographical Sketches of Their Representative Men* (Philadelphia: Louis H. Everts, 1881), 765; Maryland Patent Certificates and Warrants #60, 1734-1741, Liber E1, No. 5, p. 506; #62, 1739–1743, Liber LG No. B, pp. 183-84.

Whether Dugal had a wife and children in Scotland before his exile to America is not known, but he had at least three children in America who survived to adulthood: Thomas (Philip's fourth great-grandfather), William, and Francis. At the time of Dugal's death, Dugal was married to a woman named Grace, but it is uncertain whether she was the mother of Dugal's three sons.[19]

Dugal did not live long to enjoy being a landowner. In his will dated 26 March 1746 and proved March 1746/47, "Dugal Macquain . . . being very sick and weak," named his "beloved wife Grace Macquaine" executrix and bequeathed "my Land which I now live on" to be "equally divided between my two Sons William and Francis," and son William "shall have my fear nothing Coat[20] & my new Jacket." Son Thomas was to have "all the rest of my wearing Cloths except my white Coat which I give unto my son in Law [stepson?] John Brown."[21]

Dugal's will is telling of the time period in which he lived. Phonetic spellings in original documents, such as in his will, are good indicators of how colonial Marylanders spoke and pronounced words. Dugal's surname, although spelled in Scottish records as "McQueen," was recorded as "Macquain," and "Macquaine" in America, suggesting its pronunciation in the colonies.[22] Additionally, Dugal carefully selected the recipients of his clothing. Clothing was made to last several generations, being altered and mended to ensure longevity, so it was common to bequeath such items in a will. . . .

[19]Maryland Wills, Vol. 25, DD:4:10-11; Barnes, *Baltimore County Families, 1659–1759*, 441; Hechler, *Metes & Bounds I*, 3, 5.

[20]A fearnothing, or fearnought, was a "stout kind of woolen cloth, used chiefly on board ship in the form of outside clothing in the most inclement weather." *The Compact Edition of the Oxford English Dictionary*, 2 vols. (Oxford University Press, 1971), 1:973.

[21]Maryland Prerogative Wills, Vol. 25, DD:4:10-11. In colonial times the term "son in law" was often used to denote what today would be a stepson.

[22]David Hackett Fischer, *Albion's Seed: Four British Folkways in America* (New York: Oxford University Press, 1989), 258 at note 5. In Smith, "Transported Jacobite Rebels, 1716," 31, and Samuel Hibbert-Ware, *Lancashire Memorials of the Rebellion, MDCCXV* (Bishops Stortford, England: Chadwyck-Healey, 1974), 160-62, the name is spelled "McQueen."

Writing Courses, Contests, Organizations, and Conferences

Online Writing Courses
WritingClasses.com
www.writingclasses.com
> Includes courses on memoir and nonfiction writing.

Writer's Online Workshops
www.WritersOnlineWorkshops.com
> Includes courses on personal and family memoir writing.

Genealogical Institutes Offering Writing Courses
Note: The writing courses at these institutes are not offered every year. Please check the course offerings on their Web sites.

Institute of Genealogy and Historical Research
Samford University Library
Birmingham, Alabama 35229
E-mail: mbthomas@samford.edu
Web site: www.samford.edu/schools/ighr/ighr.html

Salt Lake Institute of Genealogy
Utah Genealogical Association
P.O. Box 1144 Salt Lake City, UT 84110
E-mail: info@infouga.org
Web site: www.infouga.org/slig2003.htm

Writing Contests
American Society of Genealogists Scholar Award
www.fasg.org/asg_scholar_award.html
> Among other items, applicants should submit three copies of a manuscript or published work of at least 5,000 words, demonstrating an ability to conduct quality genealogical research, analyze results, and report findings in an appropriately documented fashion.

International Society of Family History Writers and Editors
www.rootsweb.com/~cgc/#ANNUALWRITINGCONTEST
> The ISFHWE sponsors an annual competition for published and unpublished writers. You must be a member of ISFHWE in order to participate in the contest.

The contest is judged by professionals in the field of journalism and genealogy. Three categories: newspaper columns, articles, and genealogy research story.

National Genealogical Society's Genealogical Writing Competitions

www.ngsgenealogy.org/comgenwriting.htm
NGS offers three Awards for Excellence:

Genealogy and Family History: An award for a specific, significant, single contribution in the form of a family genealogy or family history book published during the past five years that serves to foster scholarship and/or advances or promotes excellence in genealogy.

Genealogical Methods and Sources: An award for a specific, significant, single contribution in the form of a book, an article, or a series of articles published during the past five years that discusses genealogical methods and sources that serves to foster scholarship and/or advances or promotes excellence in genealogy.

National Genealogical Society Quarterly: An award for a specific, significant, single contribution in the form of an article or series of articles published in the *NGS Quarterly* during the past year that serves to foster scholarship and/or advances or promotes excellence in genealogy.

Writer's Digest Self-Published

www.writersdigest.com/contests/self_published.asp

Writer's Digest offers awards in nine categories, including Life Stories (biographies, autobiographies, family histories, memoirs).

The competition is open to self-published books for which the authors have paid the full cost of publication. Entrants must send a printed and bound book. Entries will be judged primarily by content and writing quality. No photocopied or handwritten books are accepted. Production quality will determine the winner in the event of a tie.

Professional Organizations
Association of Personal Historians
%Rebecca Beegle, APH Membership Chair
601 W. Eleventh Street, Apt. 122
Austin, TX 78701
E-mail: info@personalhistoryproject.com
Web site: www.personalhistorians.org

Association of Professional Genealogists
P.O. Box 350998
Westminster, CO 80035-0998
E-mail: admin@apgen.org
Web site: www.apgen.org

Board for Certification of Genealogists
P.O. Box 14291
Washington, DC 20044
Web site: www.bcgcertification.org

International Commission for the Accreditation of Professional Genealogists
P.O. Box 970204
Orem, UT 84097-0204
Phone: (866) 813-6729 (toll free)
E-mail: information@icapgen.org
Web site: www.icapgen.org

International Society of Family History Writers and Editors
(formerly Council of Genealogical Columnists)
%Martha Everman Jones
506 W. Larkspur St.
Victoria, TX 77904-1341
Web site: www.rootsweb.com/~cgc/

National Genealogical Conferences
There are usually sessions about writing and copyright at these conferences.

Federation of Genealogical Societies
P.O. Box 200940
Austin, TX 78720-0940
Phone: (512) 336-2731
Fax: (512) 336-2731
E-mail: fgs-office@fgs.org
Web site: www.fgs.org

Gentech
A division of the National Genealogical Society (see below)

National Genealogical Society
4527 Seventeenth Street, North
Arlington, VA 22207-2399
Phone: (800) 473-0060
Fax: (703) 525-0052
Web site: http://ngsgenealogy.org

Index

Also by Sharon Carmack

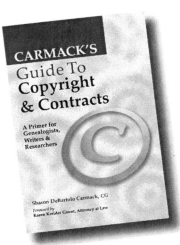

CARMACK'S
Guide To Copyright & Contracts
A Primer for Genealogists, Writers & Researchers

As a genealogist, you may have struggled with certain questions:

- Do I need permission to use something off the Internet?
- Can I reproduce a newspaper obituary on my ancestor without permission?
- How do I know whether something is in the public domain?
- Does copyright protect my Web site?
- Who owns the client report?
- Can I publish my ancestor's diary without anyone's permission?
- Is my lecture or lesson protected by copyright?
- If I write something for my genealogical society as a volunteer, who owns the copyright?
- Do I need permission to download GEDCOM files?

Now there is an easy-to-understand guide written for genealogists that answers these questions and more. In *Carmack's Guide to Copyright & Contracts: A Primer for Genealogists, Writers & Researchers*, Sharon DeBartolo Carmack uses her popular, conversational writing style to answer your questions. In simple language, she explains copyright, rights, and publishing agreements and how these apply to genealogists, writers, and researchers.

134 pp., indexed, paperback. (2005), repr. 2007.
ISBN 978-0-8063-1758-8. $15.95